KINGDOMS OF EXPERIENCE
EVEREST, THE UNCLIMBED RIDGE

KINGDOMS OF EXPERIENCE

Everest, the Unclimbed Ridge

Andrew Greig

CANONGATE

First published in paperback in Great Britain in 1999 by
Canongate Books Ltd,
14 High Street, Edinburgh EH1 1TE

First published in hardback in 1986 by Century Hutchinson Ltd

Copyright © Andrew Greig, 1986, 1999
Introduction copyright © Chris Bonington 1999

10 9 8 7 6 5 4 3 2 1

British Library Cataloguing-in-Publication Data
A catalogue record for this book is available
on request from the British Library

ISBN 0 86241 881 X

Printed and bound by WSOY, Finland

For my mother, partners and travelling companions – semper tibi pendeat hamus.

I thank the following for their assistance, advice and support during the writing of this book: Marsali Baxter, Ingrid von Essen, Peter and Eileen at the Clachaig Inn, Deborah Simmons, Isobel Wylie and above all the members of the 1985 Pilkington Everest Expedition.

In memory of Malcolm Roy Duff, who made it happen.

Author's note: passages accredited to members of the Expedition are taken from their personal diaries or occasionally from transcribed conversation, as are thoughts and feelings ascribed to them.
In this book, as in *Summit Fever*, I have followed the option of using the plural 'their' after a singular, impersonal subject e.g. 'each', 'anyone', 'everyone'. To write 'each of us has his own opinion' would be both sexist and inaccurate, given the composition of the Expedition, while writing 'his or her' on every such occasion is laboured.

CONTENTS

A NOTE ON THE 1999 EDITION

It was a curious experience re-reading for this new edition, like coming across a camp that has been buried under snow for many years. So many little details the memory abandons once an experience is over came fresh to the surface again. I'd forgotten that for an hour or two we'd watched a man who never was, moving steadily up the north-east ridge. I'd forgotten the sheer pain and drudgery of altitude, along with the shafts of clarity, exhilaration and euphoria. I'd forgotten the particular atmosphere of that expedition, an odd mix of personal isolation and the deep affection of company and shared endeavour.

It reads now like a time of innocence. Our expedition had the great good fortune to enter Tibet during a brief window of comparative tolerance from the Chinese authorities. We saw it before both the crackdown and the growth of tourism. It seems incredible now that we spent a week in Lhasa and saw only one Western face. Equally incredible is that we had the north-east ridge to ourselves, and for two months shared the entire Tibet side of Everest only with the Basques' expedition.

The expedition was on some kind of historic cusp. It came just before the controversial growth of commercial Himalayan climbing where clients pay to be taken up big peaks. It came at the very end of the big scale assaults. Ours was an odd hybrid of the large, expensive, complex, sustained siege, and the Alpine Style solo dash. We had oxygen but used it only once; we had a vast payload but no Sherpas to help carry it; we had a film crew who filmed everything but our climbing.

Summit Fever was an easier book to write, with a small, intimate cast and a wonderful natural climax of summitting after many set-backs. *Kingdoms of Experience* is both harder and far more typical of the big mountain expedition: attrition, tension, exhaustion, frustration. In that sense it is more truthful – certainly more typical! – to our normal lives than the storyline of triumph of disaster.

In my memory lingers yet brutally cold nights on the hill, lungs soured with the bitter taste of altitude, watching the Sultans of Pain gear up for another pre-dawn start and wondering why we bother, why we are so separate. Also days of R & R at Base Camp, sitting in the sun singing the Kinks' 'Sunny Afternoon' while enjoying the miracles of fresh bread, cheese, companionship, and the knowledge we were not going to die that day.

I hope some of that duality is in here. It was good to spend time again with those friends and companions, the living and the dead. We never fought so hard for breath, nor laughed so long.

Andrew Greig
Orkney 1999

INTRODUCTION

The majority of Himalayan expeditions do not get to their chosen summits. In a good many unsuccessful attempts – through luck and skill – no one dies. This does not make such expeditions a failure or a non-event. No serious Himalayan expedition – and in 1985 the North-east Ridge of Everest was about as serious as it could get – is a non-event.

This is a very human book. It is about a group of first-class climbers under pressure, where they are very much revealed as human beings, not heroes or super-stars. It brings out, as few books do, the sheer hard work and drudgery of siege-style Himalayan assaults. As in our own first attempt on the North-east Ridge in 1982, the team members did all the load carrying themselves, an exhausting process at 8000 metres. Under different conditions each of these would bring a Himalayan summit with it.

Another feature of the book is the skilful use of diary entries, which gradually makes clear that on any trip there are as many expeditions as there are members of it. Through it we glimpse the different expedition each was having, the sense of solitude each climber bears, with moments of great closeness and solidarity. All in all, *Kingdom of Experience* is a deeply moving and evocative account of a compact siege-style expedition on one of the last great unclimbed ridges in the Himalaya.

I found it a deeply engrossing read, a portrait from beginning to end of an ambitious, difficult and frustrating expedition. It also creates an all-round portrait of the spirit of the Himalayan climber, and as such stands as a celebration of my friends Peter Boardman and Joe Tasker, who disappeared high on this very route in 1982, and of Mal Duff who died not long ago on the other side of Everest. All three had a deep love of the challenge of exploratory mountaineering, an understanding and acceptance of the risks involved, and they believed in living life to the full. At the same time they were prepared to risk that very life for the sake of the adventure that was so much part of their lives.

This book helps us understand some of these seeming contradictions and at the same time is a lively and fascinating read.

Chris Bonington
February 1999

PROLOGUE

Sandy Allan, Advance Base Camp, Everest:

'For some godforsaken reason we (I) front-point as good as some other people, for some reason I can jam my ice-axe in, torqued to the max, in cracks that other people have failed to, and so my body heaves exhausted over some rock or ice bulge and hence at First Ascent . . . And God or whatever – me, I'll go for God – set the sun a-shining just before I got frostbite, or slowed down the winds just before we got hypothermia, or set the correct abseil position in the rock just when we needed it, or opened a little window so we could see the direction when we were totally lost. Some people call it luck, me – luck and unknown but most welcome INTERVENTION.'

Here, we're here, I'm here, hoping that my ability and the rest of the lads' ability and the gods will see us OK. We're gamblers, we've got no cash; we have lives, we love them, that's the stake. The reward for me is to continue this life, on this planet, driving down the roads I know and walking through the doors of my friends' houses . . . and in between that, *Inshallah*, a summit or two.'

Mal Duff at 8000 metres on Everest's North-east Ridge:

'Tony crouched on a rock 40 yards away, a small spark of life where none should exist. The spindrift swirled and battered, whirling over the ridge, pluming up 200 feet before hurling itself upon us . . . Reaching the lee of the rock and contacting Tony, another human in this madness, becomes all-important. A shattering pain suddenly erupts in my lower chest – a muscle rip in my diaphragm, can't inflate my lungs! A moment of panic subdued by years of training. No matter what, I must try, try to live, to descend or even to die but I must try . . . I must try because this is the big one, the master problem that perhaps I've been seeking for years, unwittingly . . .'

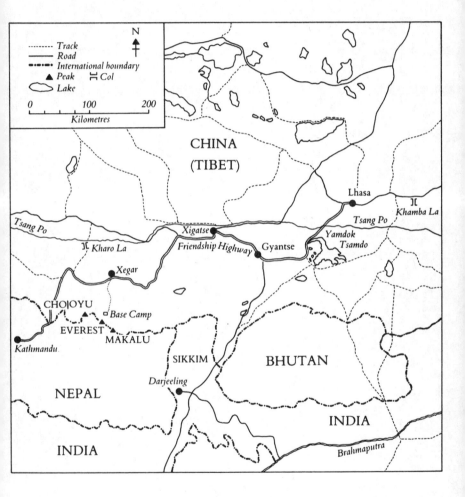

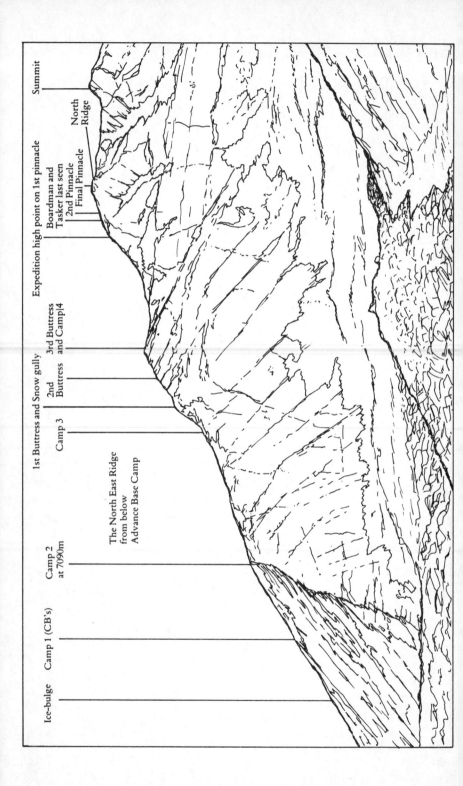

The North East Ridge from below Advance Base Camp

Ice-bulge Camp 1 (CB's) Camp 2 at 7090m 1st Buttress and Snow gully Camp 3 2nd Buttress 3rd Buttress and Camp 4 Expedition high point on 1st pinnacle Boardman and Tasker last seen 2nd Pinnacle Final Pinnacle North Ridge Summit

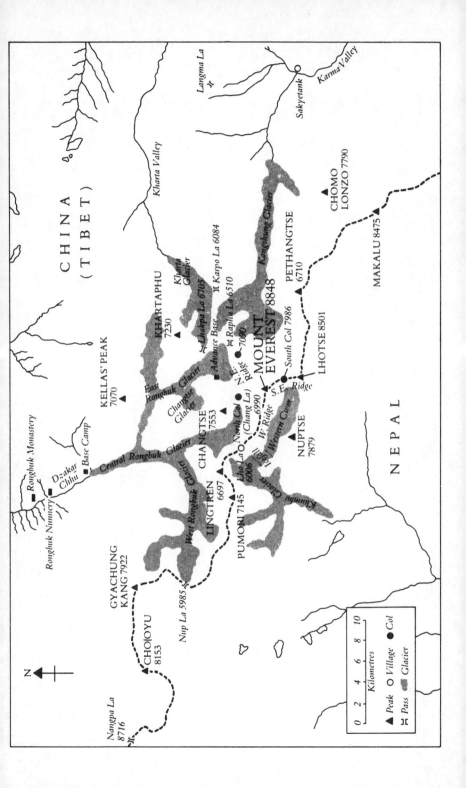

The Ploy

*'The Mustagh Tower was over, the ropes had all been
sold or coiled away. We were sitting in Mrs Davies'
while monsoon rain fell day by day . . .'*

The photograph is in front of me now: Mrs Davies' hotel, Rawalpindi, mid-August 1984. Mal Duff and I are lounging in old cane
chairs, smoking K2 cigarettes and laughing over some forgotten
joke. We're stripped to the waist but sweat still trickles from our
arm-pits, for the air is torrid with the monsoon season. I notice with
a shock how skinny we both are, how much weight we lost on the
Mustagh Tower expedition.

But that was all over, my first and only Himalayan trip, the one
that prompted me to take up climbing less than a year before, after
Mal's impulsive suggestion that I come along to support-climb and
write a book about it. It had been a deeply satisfying expedition:
I'd carried a load to Camp 2, and after many set-backs the four lead
climbers all made it to the top and safely back again. It was the
second ascent by the West Ridge, the third ascent in all of the
Mustagh Tower's 7,230 metres.

Now Mal and I were on our way home, thinking of bacon, beans
and beer and the women we wanted to see again. We drank coffee,
smoked and yarned while ineffectual fans whirred overhead, a flat-
footed old servant hobbled by, and ghekkos clung miraculously to
the wall as they stalked their supper. We were at peace, expecting
nothing and looking for nothing.

The renowned Polish climber Voytek joined us, his eyes pale blue
and direct, his air one of casual but absolute self-possession as we
exchange potted versions of our trips. Then a Norwegian from the
ill-fated Trango Peak expedition sat down. Two of his friends had
disappeared while abseiling down from the summit; they hadn't
been found and, barring miracles, they'd had it.

There was nothing much we could say about that, so the conversation passed to high-altitude traverses. The Norwegian mentioned
that he and his friends had an outside chance of pulling off one of
the great ones – a traverse of Everest from North to South, from

Tibet to Nepal. They had a permit for both sides of the mountain. But he added it was now unlikely that Norway had enough experienced climbers left to tackle both sides, and they would probably concentrate on the standard South Col route.

Mal seemed distant, only making conversation. I thought he was probably bored, or thinking of home and Liz. Voytek and the Norwegian left; I went to buy more cigarettes. When I returned Mal rocked back in his chair then said with elaborate casualness, 'How do you fancy raising twenty grand and coming to Everest, Andy?'

A pulse beat in my neck, even though I knew he was joking. 'Sure, why not?' I replied, equally casual. 'But I didn't know you were interested in Everest.'

'I'm *very* interested in the North-East Ridge, the *Unclimbed Ridge*. It's the last big route left on Everest. Maybe we could pick up that Norwegian permit for the Tibetan side of the hill. Are you on?'

At least Mal's jokes are big ones. I lit a K2 cigarette, tipped back my chair and considered for a moment. A ghekko pounced, its jaws closed on its prey with an audible snap. 'Yes,' I said.

'Shall I tell her now, Andy?'

I lean on the bar in an Edinburgh pub and wonder where to begin after three alcohol-free Muslim months.

'Tell me what?' Liz Duff asks.

'Oh, it doesn't matter,' Mal replies. I shake my head at his low cunning.

'You might as well tell me now.'

'Well, ah . . . We're planning to go to Everest in the spring.'

Liz lets go his arm for the first time since we landed in the UK. 'Oh no you're not,' she says firmly.

'I think I can get a permit for the North-East Ridge of Everest, but I'll only go if you lads think it's on and will come.'

Jon Tinker and Sandy Allan look at each other. They've just returned to London after the Mustagh Tower trip and found a message in Jon's parents' kitchen saying 'Phone Malcolm'. So they have, and this is what they get.

'Duff, you're . . . crazy!' Sandy says. A chuckle from the other end of the line. 'Jon and I will think about it and phone you back.'

They do. 'We're coming, but neither of us have any money.'

'That's alright. On this size of trip we either get complete sponsorship or else we can't go.'

Sandy puts the phone down. When he'd seen the message some

premonition had told him it would be Everest. But the 'Unclimbed Ridge' – ! – Jon shakes his head, laughs, 'Duff is mountaineering's answer to Malcolm MacLaren. Or Bonnie Prince Charlie . . .'

A fantasy, yes. The North-East Ridge, China, Tibet . . . Malcolm is dreaming and scheming again as he puts down the pints, his right knee jumping restlessly, pulling on another cigarette. He's a dietician's nightmare: fuelled on constant coffee, sugar, lager, cigarettes and fast-foods, he has the nerve to be healthy. He is the most dangerous kind of dreamer – one who acts with absolute commitment as though his dreams were already fact, and thus sometimes makes them so. The Mustagh Tower had been a dream ever since as a teenager he'd read Tom Patey's account of its classic first ascent; he'd planned it, froze and sweated and suffered and climbed till he finally stood on the top, one foot in Pakistan and the other in China. I have a very real chunk of summit rock in my desk drawer to remind me of the power of fantasy.

Mal, Jon and Sandy: they were the core of this latest ploy. They'd shared the Mustagh Tower experience and on the back of that felt ready for something bigger. Maybe one of the great 8,000 metre peaks . . . But Everest! Perhaps it had come too early, but they couldn't pass up on the chance. The three of them debated the feasibility and basic strategy of the expedition; their nominations of additional climbers reflected their very different natures, and were to determine the nature of the entire party.

'*There was smiling Sandy Allan, that amiable Hieland honeybear* . . .' Sandy with the pale, washed-out blue eyes, often obscured by thin reddish-blond hair falling over his forehead. Strongly built, solid with shoulder and arm muscles built up from rough-necking on North Sea oil rigs, which financed his climbing, he seems to be bigger than he actually is. A casual bear, giving the impression of great strength and stamina held in reserve.

He'd been brought up among the distilling glens of Scotland and as a child spent more and more time wandering among the Cairngorms, finding some kind of backdrop there for his restless thoughts. After doing one Scottish winter route, he'd briefly taken one of Mal's Alpine climbing courses. 'It was totally obvious that this youth could become a star,' Mal said. 'Immensely strong, persistent, the right sort of temperament, always in control – a natural.'

Sandy found his natural expression in snow/ice climbing. At 25 he finally gave up his job as a trainee distillery manager for the hand-to-mouth existence of the dedicated climber. There followed the customary apprenticeship: Scotland, the Alps in summer, the Alps in winter, some notable ascents, then Nuptse West Ridge with Mal, then the Mustagh Tower.

'Sandy just grins,' Mal had said to me before Mustagh, 'you'll find him easy to get on with.' Well, yes, but during the trip and in his diaries afterwards, I found a very different inner man behind that amiable exterior:

Sandy . . . One look into Jhaved's eyes and he knows what I want. One straight hit with my axe and I find a good ice placement. *C'est la vie*, Dominique would say. Don't worry, Sandy, she'd say. They'll never know you or what you've done.

I fade away to wash by the stream. It's good to wash the sweat of the hill away, and I watch the dirty soapy water. What right have I to pollute the water here? But it soon turns clear. What right have we to hold opinions? Every right, I say to myself, and then I say if we have the right to opinions, do we have a right to put them to other people to try and change their views? Do we have a right to build a small dam in the stream to make a convenient washing place, it's OK for us but by what RIGHT? And Jon says, every right. He's an opinion holder . . .

And climbing is not so important to me, it's more the way I feel, the way I react, the language I speak and the words I scribe, the mess that I leave behind, the way that I eat my food . . . These suit my feelings.

Smiling Sandy Allan indeed! I was astonished that Mal could have shared two expeditions with Sandy and know nothing of his inner nature. Yet the signs were there: his keeping a journal at all times, his inability to stay in one place for more than a few days, the way his glance focuses only briefly on the person he's talking to. In all our Mustagh photos he is always slightly blurred as if just about to move away, eyes averted or obscured by his hand or his hair.

'*We had to have Jon Tinker, that abrasive Cockney Rasta-man* . . .' Jon was Sandy's partner on the Mustagh Tower, but they are very different. He's a blue-eyed, fair-haired, compact Anglo-Saxon; edgy, alert, intelligent, one of life's stirrers. I picture him lounging back, exaggeratedly relaxed, hands stuffed in his pockets, obscure reggae dubs on his stereo, while he protests vigorously in his quasi-Cockney accent how lazy and uncompetitive he is. A master of giving stress, of sarcasm, of winding people up. We could never really understand why he tended to treat encounters as a form of verbal arm-wrestling, always looking for the upper hand – and at other times be disarmingly thoughtful, enthusiastic and open. When one has had enough of climbing talk, Jon is a good person for general conversation about music, books, politics, ideas. He is determined not to let climbing be his entire life, though it often seems to be. I came to like him a lot during and after the Mustagh trip. You can say this for Jon, he's a little fire-cracker; you have to be wide awake when he's around.

He'd taken a degree in politics and since then has lived largely as a 'shuffling dosser', working in climbing shops or guiding between expeditions, perpetually broke. At 24, he was to be the youngest of the Everest team's lead climbers, having made his name through a series of very bold Alpine winter ascents.

'I'm convinced I'm going to die on the hill before I'm 30,' he said once in Glencoe. Then he added, 'That's bullshit, of course . . . I know I'm immortal!' Pause. 'Everyone is till they die.' And when we first talked about Everest he suddenly confessed, 'My greatest fear is being left to die on the hill. I look at the people I'm climbing with and wonder if they'd stay with me . . .'

Mal and I drove down to the Lake District one wet day in October to see Chris Bonington. We needed his advice and his support before we could go any further. Bonington knew more about Everest and expedition organization than anyone in the country. Any potential sponsor would come to him to ask if we were worth backing. Most important, he knew the North-East Ridge, having led the only attempt ever made on it, three years before.

We'd quickly read his book[1] before driving down. The bare facts made grim reading. Of the four climbers, Joe Tasker and Pete Boardman had both disappeared forever somewhere on the Pinnacles that bar the way to the summit, Dick Renshaw had suffered two strokes, and Bonington himself had finally dropped out from sheer exhaustion. And these were four of the élite, among the finest mountaineers in the world.

I looked at Mal as he drove, his fingers drumming on the wheel. Born in Kenya but brought up in Scotland, I still thought of him as 'the wild colonial boy'. He has a grizzled, serious, sober air, yet loves high jinks and wild schemes. He once jokingly described his politics to me as 'crypto-liberal-fascist-anarchist-communist-conservative' and all those impulses are in his nature. He likes to play himself off against me as an unimaginative, down-to-earth realist, yet at the same time he's an impulsive romantic.

[1]*Everest: the Unclimbed Ridge*. Hodder & Stoughton, 1983

'Romantic? Malcolm?!' I can hear his wife Liz say. 'He can be romantic, but not about climbing. That makes him sound wet.'

True enough. Mal is about as wet as the Kalahari desert. Yet he is driven by dreams, as mountaineers are. There is nothing practical in climbing a mountain, and suffering and risking your neck for nothing. And certainly impulsive – who else would have asked someone like me with no climbing experience whatsoever on the Mustagh Tower expedition? 'Well, I'd never met one of you author types and I thought it would be interesting to see what you did when I put you on the spot!'

'Like a cigarette, youth?'

'Thanks.' His head bobbed as he whistled tunelessly, rehearsing the issues he wanted to bring up with Chris Bonington when we arrived. He's physically and mentally restless; the only time I see him entirely at peace is occasionally in the pub and always when he's climbing. 'It's a wonderful game,' he once said, 'only sometimes you look round and realise half your friends aren't there any more.' And I wondered what his life expectancy would be if he began getting involved in trips like this. Well over half the people who start climbing in the 'death zone' above 7,500 metres wind up dead, and half of the North-East Ridge is above that height . . .

I cut off this line of thought as Mal cut the ignition and we sat in the car outside Chris Bonington's house while the rain hammered down.

'Nice house.'

'Very.' Here was a survivor and a success. We picked up our notebooks and the bottle of whisky we'd brought by way of introduction, and dashed for the front door.

We shook hands with Chris and went into his office. While his secretary made coffee we looked around the filing cabinets, the ordered racks of slides, the word-processor, the signed photographs. I felt like a sixth-form schoolboy in the headmaster's study to discuss his career.

He was brisk and business-like, neither patronizing nor over-effusive. He congratulated Mal on the Mustagh Tower and asked some questions about it. He told us the modified Norwegian expedition was well in hand and he was going with them both as an advisor and climber, hoping to finally make the summit on this his yet-again last time on Everest. They were tackling the now standard South Col route, with sherpas and oxygen, so if the weather behaved they had a good chance.

But did we? Mal outlined the team and tactics he'd been considering, the few areas of improvement he felt could be made on the basis of Chris's experience on the North-East Ridge. Cut out one of the camps by making the first camp higher; take a slightly larger team; fix ropes across a couple of awkward sections where a lot of load-carrying would be necessary; use tents rather than try to dig a snow-hole below the Rock Buttresses.

Chris listened, letting his eyes flick over Malcolm, assessing him. Then he gave his opinion.

All of Mal's suggested changes were ones he'd have made. They would probably help. But he had to say he thought we hadn't a chance of making the summit by that route, 'And that's no slight on the team you've suggested.' He believed that the chances of anyone reaching the top of Everest via the North-East Ridge without using oxygen were virtually nil – for the first ascent, at least. We might just get through the Pinnacles. No modern mountaineer wants to use oxygen, which is regarded as a backward step and definitely uncool, but if one route in the world merited it, it was the North-East Ridge.

There was an emotional resonance behind his controlled voice, and we realized the depth of involvement Chris must have in the 'Unclimbed Ridge'. He'd lost two close friends in their oxygenless attempt – no wonder he was emphatic. Mal also thought he was right.

'But of course you can't use oxygen,' Chris added. Using oxygen would vastly increase the number of climbers needed to carry the cylinders (there being no Sherpas in Tibet to help with that donkey-work), which in turn would mean more tents, gear, food, clothing. We'd be talking about nearly 20 high-altitude climbers, and there simply weren't that many in Britain. Nor could we raise the inordinate amount of money involved, or organize an expedition on that scale in the time we had. A major expedition normally takes two years to set up; we had less than five months before the date set on the Everest permit we hadn't yet acquired.

Mal nodded, agreed. That was the heart of it: we couldn't do it without oxygen, but we couldn't take oxygen.

Even if we still wanted to have a go at it, Chris suggested we enlarge our proposed team from six to more like ten, to allow for the inevitable natural wastage arising from repeated load-carrying and nights sleeping above 7,000 metres. His experience had convinced him that a fast, lightweight, Alpine-style attempt on the Ridge was almost bound to fail, and fail dangerously. A serious attempt would mean a return to something like his 1975 Everest South-West Face expedition, the protracted leap-frog process of a siege-style assault, using many climbers, fixed ropes and camps slowly established up the mountain. But even at that, an attempt to go through the Pinnacles to the summit, leaving the unknown technical problems of the Pinnacles aside, would mean a minimum of three days and nights above 8,000 metres without oxygen – and nothing like that had ever been done.

'Frankly, I don't think you have a chance,' he concluded, 'but of course you should go for it if you want.' We shook hands and left.

Discouraged, we drove back north through the rain. Bonington's evaluation of our problems seemed realistic. Was it worth going any further? We knew the facts. At this point roughly a dozen people had reached the summit of Everest without oxygen; nearly half had died or had to be carried down on the descent. Other than the astonishing Messner and Habeler, they had all been helped by having companions with oxygen to break trail and help them down. Messner and Habeler had naturally taken the most straightforward routes up, a far cry from the North-East Ridge.

We could settle for having 'an outside chance' of climbing the Pinnacles only, without oxygen. That would still be a challenge from a mountaineering viewpoint, because above the Pinnacles the North-East Ridge joins the North Col route, so all the ground from there on up has been covered. The 'route', the unknown and unclimbed element, could be said to end above the Pinnacles. But that would mean kidding any potential sponsor that we intended to go for the summit; summits matter to sponsors and the public, whereas mountaineers tend to think in terms of 'the route' rather than 'the top'.

'Mal, it sounds like all we need is two cylinders of oxygen above the Pinnacles,' I said.

'Well, sure, but Chris explained why we can't get involved in a massive oxygen expedition, and I agree,' Mal replied impatiently.

'But can't we just use a minimum of oxygen?'

'To carry two bottles through the Pinnacles, you'd have to use oxygen to make up for the extra weight.'

'Well, why not? What I mean is, does oxygen have to be all or nothing? Could we not just use the minimum amount required to end up with two full bottles at the end of the Pinns, for giving you a real chance of going on to the summit?'

Mal drove on in silence, the calculations and permutations clicking through his head. Then he turned to me thoughtfully. 'You know, it could work if you didn't use oxygen before 8,000 metres. If two people each carried one cylinder through the Pinns . . . they'd need another cylinder each . . . Three days through the Pinns, that would mean . . .'

He glanced back at the road in time to avoid the oncoming truck that nearly ended the expedition right there and then. We pulled up at a café in Biggar, ordered coffees and began working out logistics on the back of an envelope. Starting from the desiderata of two full cylinders above the Pinnacles, Mal worked backwards using elaborate combinations of flow-rates, half-bottles, changeovers, support along fixed ropes without oxygen . . . More coffee and more cigarettes as the enthusiasm and excitement began to build and a solution began to appear. One of the most intoxicating moments of any adventure is this phase where you start mapping a dream on to reality and perceive it might just fit.

By the time we left the café, revving with caffeine, nicotine and adrenalin, Mal had concluded the outlines of a possible game-plan: with 13 oxygen cylinders, ten climbers, and some very complex and fragile logistics, we had a chance of making the summit.

When Mal wrote to him outlining the new game-plan, Chris Bonington seemed to agree, and said he would be happy to be our patron for the Expedition (which had now acquired a capital 'E' in our minds!). That was a step forward: Chris's backing gave us some credibility. All we had to do now was secure the permit, raise a team and some £80,000, plan and buy 5 tons of food, tentage, clothing, climbing gear, stoves and gas. There was not time to do things in that sensible order. Instead we had to go full-steam ahead, trying to raise money as though we had a permit, put together a team and start ordering gear as though we had the money, and immediately negotiate with the Chinese as though we had all these. Mal gave up his off-season casual labour and threw himself into organization full-time, and I got my head down over the Mustagh Tower book, which now had a possible early deadline: early March, when we would fly to Peking.

Developments fell into place thick and fast, overlapping and obscuring each other like cards being rapidly shuffled and dealt . . .

The Team. We were looking for another seven lead climbers. They had to have proven high-altitude abilities; just as important, they had to be able to get on and work together over three intense and stress-filled months. To have any chance of success, this had to be a team effort, demanding a great deal of selfless and possibly unrewarded load-carrying from everyone – so no stars, no prima donnas.

There was a limited field for Mal, Jon and Sandy to choose from. The grim truth was they could number on one hand the surviving British climbers who had been to 8,000 metres, and enquiries proved that all of them had other ploys for spring '85. There was a new generation of talented, thrusting young mountaineers, but they had concentrated on bold Alpine-style ascents, by very small teams, of hard routes on the 'smaller' Himalayan peaks. So any team we took to Everest would all be operating above their previous height records just in getting to the foot of the Pinnacles at 8,000 metres. 'It's not ideal,' Mal said, 'but we've all got to start sometime and it might as well be on Everest.'

'I just don't know if you're ready for it, Malcolm,' Liz said one evening.

'Look, Liz, what can you tell me about the North-East Ridge that I don't know already? That it's very long, very high, very hard, and it's a death route? I know that. There's only one way to find out if we're ready, and that's to go there. I've always jumped in at the deep end, it's the only way to learn . . .'

Sandy nominated Bob Barton – an exiled Yorkshireman and self-adopted Scot, working as an instructor at Glenmore Lodge outdoor centre. He had the requisite Scottish and Alpine background, expeditions to the Hindu Kush, Peru, Kenya, Alaska, and two notable Himalayan successes on Kalanka and Bhaghirathi II. Sandy had met him in Chamonix and the Cairngorms and been impressed by his steady, unflappable temperament and quiet determination. A natural team-member, he thought: friendly, selfless, easy-going.

'Want to come to Everest, Bob?' Sandy asked over the phone. Bob is a family man who, as he put it, at 37 is 'old enough not to want to die young'. He'd consider it if it was to be a non-Alpine style attempt with oxygen used above 8,000 metres. Assured that it was, the only remaining problem was that Bob realized his second child was due to be born just before our planned departure for China in early March. He was torn between two events he did not want to miss, but after talking it over with his wife Anna he said 'Yes' – and prayed that the baby would arrive on time.

Jon in turn suggested Nick Kekus, with whom he'd climbed on Annapurna III. Nick, like Jon, was known for being young and very bold. He'd made the usual transitions from hill-walking to scrambling to rock-climbing to snow and ice; progressed to the Alps, Kenya, Peru, then the challenge of altitude and sustained big mountains: Kalanka, Shiveling, Annapurna III. He'd just come back from another success on Ganesh II in Nepal and with his appetite for climbing undiminished said 'Yes, I'll come.' Tall, lean, forceful and temperamental, he was the antithesis of calm Bob Barton. He took on the responsibility of organizing food for some dozen people for three months – a massive piece of planning, involving endless letters and phone calls cajoling products from manufacturers and suppliers.

'*Meanwhile in Aberdeen a red beard is munching marzipan ...*' Sandy suggested to his friend Andy Nisbet that he get in touch with Mal about Everest. Mal confessed he felt somewhat put on the spot: Andy was a good friend whom he trusted, had a good expedition temperament, was a brilliant technical ice climber – but he had problems at altitude. He'd been with Mal on the West Ridge of Nuptse in 1981, and had beome seriously ill at 6,000 metres. Okay, so they'd rushed the acclimatization a bit, but the fact remained he'd got ill and the others hadn't. One is seldom given a second chance.

Mal talked it over with Andy, who admitted the problem but believed that given more time to acclimatize he'd be okay. Convinced of his sincerity and commitment, Mal decided to gamble on Andy.

Andy is an Aberdonian with wild red hair and a long pointed beard that some say make him look like a demented garden gnome. He's ill at ease in company, sits on his hands, fiddles and fidgets, finds it hard to look at people directly; he hides his inner nature and feelings almost completely. If he's interested in anything other than climbing, not many people know about it. He also has the sweetest tooth in Christendom, living mostly on fudge and whole blocks of marzipan. So he was nominated to work with Nick on food, with particular responsibility for planning hill-food and sweet goodies. He based his projection of our needs on his average daily consumption ... When we finally left Tibet we left behind enough chocolate to ruin an entire generation of Tibetan teeth, and my last sight of the ruined Rongbuk monastery was of a beaming old nun munching a Twix bar.

The Permit. Mal and I had arranged to go out for a formal Mustagh celebration meal with his wife Liz, my girlfriend Kathleen Jamie and Adrian Clifford, who had been our doctor on that trip. Just before we set out for the restaurant Mal answered the phone. He walked back in, trying to keep a straight face. He held out his hand. 'The Nords have given us their permit – we're on the way.' We shook on it and went to celebrate one trip by toasting the next.

Of course it wasn't as simple as that. The Chinese still had to agree to the transfer. The Norwegians wrote to Peking cancelling their permit and recommending us, while we wrote at the same time applying for the route. A long and nerve-wracking wait ensued. By this time we were heavily committed to the trip, without actually having secured the permit – an inadvisable way to proceed but we hadn't time to play it any other way.

Unfortunately Adrian was unable to come with us again as a support climber and doctor, having just started his obstetrics at Kirkaldy hospital. So we had to look again for a medic who was an experienced climber, had been to altitude, understood the ways of climbers and every aspect of mountain medicine – and was free to go.

Around this time Mal was interviewed in a climbing magazine and mentioned we were still looking for lead climbers and a climbing doctor for the trip. He was promptly smothered by an avalanche of letters:

'I am a 17 year old student . . . I've always been interested in climbing and go to the Fells most weekends. I'm sure I can carry a 5olb rucksack at 26,000 feet . . .'

'I have done some rock climbing and will be in Kathmandu next spring so I can join you on the way in . . .' (Overlooking the fact we would be in Tibet, not Nepal.)

'I have recently retired and have plenty of spare time on my hands . . .' The search went on.

The money. Raising £80,000 for a non-profit-making venture was always going to be difficult. Our public profile was so low only the tip of Mal's nose showed. And we needed the money fast. Only the magic word 'Everest', coupled with 'Unclimbed' gave us a chance. We drew up and Mal printed at his own expense a small brochure about the Expedition as though it actually existed, and we prepared to make a list of all the possible companies and individuals worth approaching, with an accent on the Scottish ones. It was going to be a big, time-consuming, expensive job. Then Liz Duff had an inspiration: one of their old climbing friends was now working for Saatchi & Saatchi as a strategic planner . . .

In his London office, Terry Dailey picks up the phone with his customary adrenalin rush. 'Mal here, Terry. How's things?' Terry feels guilty because he'd intended to call Mal to congratulate him on the Mustagh Tower ascent, but had never quite got round to it. 'Can we meet sometime today?' Mal continues. 'I've a proposition you might be interested in.'

Terry checks his diary, shuffles some appointments and makes space for lunchtime, sensing something is up. They meet, shake hands and go through the usual pleasantries, Terry dying to ask what it's all about but knowing Mal enjoys winding people up and will be direct enough when the time comes. Finally he grins at Terry and says simply 'Everest, North side.'

It is as though Mal has casually lobbed a grenade into Terry's world. When the dust clears, his heart and mind are racing. China . . . Tibet . . . *Everest*! The fantasies he'd been nursing in his imagination for years, never expecting them to come to anything. And now . . . He tries to attend to what Mal is saying. 'Powerful team . . . Jon Tinker . . . Sandy . . . oxygen for the Pinnacles, Bonington . . .'

Account executive realism re-asserts itself: 'Okay, that's the carrot – what do you want from me?'

'Fund raising. Help us find £80,000 and you come with us as Business Manager and a support climber.'

The possible approaches open up in Terry's mind: who to talk to, covering letters, the 'star' points to put in front of sponsors, a punchy selling brochure . . . He dimly hears Mal continue '. . . part funding from a book contract . . . Andy's agent . . .' That's good, we've got to be able to offer publicity. Try for a newspaper deal. TV is the important one. 'How long do we have?'

'Six weeks at the most.'

Strategy, credibility, deadlines and brinkmanship are Terry's meat and drink and daily bread. They give him the same adrenalin as climbing, the hit that makes him feel alive. He walks back to the office in a blur of excitement, and for once finds it difficult to discipline his mind to his next appointment. A rock and ice climber of reasonable standard in Britain and the Alps, keen but definitely a weekend and holiday climber, now to be offered Everest! . . . He'll have to find the right moment to talk it over with his wife Annie. How will she react? And she'd always wanted to go to Tibet . . .

Only a couple of miles away, Chris Watts was going through a very similar experience. Manager of the climbing section of Alpine Sports, where Jon sometimes worked, he'd been an early suggestion for the team. Chris knew very well that he'd been asked not just because of his climbing abilities and experience but also because he was in a perfect position to plan, organize and buy gear for the entire expedition at the best possible rates. He didn't resent that, just acknowledged it in his level-headed way; to get on a trip like this, everyone would be expected to do something in return. It was worth it. The problem was going to be his wife Sonja. She would be, to put it mildly, pissed off. She was a very talented rock climber who had been largely responsible for Chris taking up climbing after he'd given up competitive cycling and was looking for a new outlet for his energies. Now it was he who was being given all the expedition opportunities. And he'd promised her after the Pakistan trip that on the next expedition they'd go together. Oh dear.

He pushed aside the problem of how to tell her and began methodically drawing up lists of clothing, tentage, climbing gear. He looks like a Rolling Stone in the early phases of dissipation, but at 27 he was manager of the largest outdoor-sports shop in Britain thanks to his sheer drive, coupled with an ordered mind, attention to detail, and absolute absorption with the technical aspects of every kind of equipment. One of nature's technicians, he would be the Expedition's Mr Fix-it. He read Bonington's *Unclimbed Ridge* and considered the problems and requirements of the North-East Ridge. This gear is going to have to be state-of-the-art: the lightest and warmest and strongest that money can buy and contacts can secure . . .

I could see the doubt – are these lads serious or just jokers? – in my agent's eyes when Mal and I went to see her. I didn't blame her, I sometimes wondered myself. I had three chapters of a potential book about the Mustagh Tower expedition, but no contract for it; I hadn't yet proven I could write and sell a climbing book, and here we were asking her to find a publisher for another one. All she knew about Malcolm was from my Mustagh letters. Not surprisingly, she hadn't heard of any of the rest of the team. Mal pointed out why none of the few publicly known climbers were in the team; there was little of the 'first division' left, and someone had to come along and replace them. Okay, she'd do what she could, and that was the angle to take – a new generation of Himalayan climbers out to prove themselves. Make virtue out of necessity.

But she couldn't go far in securing a book or newspaper contract until we definitely had the money to make the Expedition happen. And as Terry was reflecting, one is not likely to attract a sponsor without being able to offer them media coverage. Sponsors want something back for their money, and what they want is good publicity and good public relations.

So where to start? It's a matter of confidence and credibility, of convincing certain people that you can do what you say you'll do, that you are serious. Once the first person is committed – be it sponsor, newspaper, patron, publisher – the rest tend to follow. The problem is breaking into that magic circle. At the moment the North-East Ridge expedition existed largely in Mal's imagination; he *believed*, he was absolutely convinced that we would make this Expedition happen, that we would go to Tibet in March and have a good chance of climbing the Unclimbed Ridge.

The offices of ITN News were round the corner from Terry's office. He went there with an outline of the Expedition and found enthusiastic interest from ITN, who have a history of covering and supporting a variety of British adventures. They agreed in principle to buy film reports of the trip. That was the first step into the magic circle of media and money; now we could offer coverage, it was time to make a pitch for major financial backing.

The Expedition brochure Terry produced was a remarkable one, and should be essential reference material for any expedition seeking sponsorship. Terry posed the potential sponsor's question 'What's in it for me?' and answered it so persuasively and exhaustively that it had us practically reaching for our own cheque-books. And so he sent out the brightly baited hooks and we waited for a bite . . .

Chris Bonington makes an accute comment on sponsorship in his book *Everest the Hard Way*. Financial considerations alone don't make a company decide to sponsor a project of this sort. The notion has to fire the imagination of a few key people – and then they sit down to try to justify it financially.

And so it was with David Wood, the Communications Manager of Pilkington Brothers, the world's largest glass and glass-related products company. The last major route on Everest, a new young British team, Tibet, China . . . And it just happened that the company was rethinking its sponsorship strategy. He picked up the phone and talked to Terry: 'We're interested, please send us more information for a Board Meeting this Friday.'

Terry's proposals went before the Board Meeting, and it happened that the Company Secretary was David Bricknell, a marathon-running outdoor enthusiast and armchair climber who noticed that Terry's sponsorship proposals included the option for a sponsor's representative going to Everest with the team . . .

'David Wood here, Terry. If we can call it the Pilkington Everest Expedition, we'll put up £80,000 and not a penny more.'

Putting it Together

*'You don't crack an egg because you want
to crack an egg . . .'*

Now that Pilkington had thrown their hat in the ring the rest
followed in swift succession. Hutchinson made an offer for the
Mustagh Tower book, then one for Everest. The *Sunday Express*
commissioned a series of reports. BBC radio wanted us to record
material for two 45-minute programmes. Now we needed a film of
the Expedition proper, in addition to the ITN reports.

*'These days it ain't enough to climb, you've got to get it down on
celluloid.'* Mal and I had bumped into Kurt Diemberger and Julie
Tullis on a warm, black night in Skardu, Baltistan. They had come
from four months of climbing and filming, first on K2 with an
expedition that eventually had to capitulate after sustained bad
weather. Kurt and Julie went on to Broad Peak, where they both
reached the summit and narrowly survived after being swept
tumbling in an avalanche down the mountain during the descent.
('It was very frightening,' Julie said simply, 'I thought, this is it.')

'Haven't you been on Broad Peak before?' I'd asked this balding,
tubby, bumbly looking man in his fifties. 'Yes,' he replied in heavily
accented English, 'I first climbed it in 1957 with Herman Buhl.'
Only then did I realize who I was talking to. This was the man who
made the first ascent of Broad Peak with Buhl, then went on to
Chogolisa with him. As they descended from near the summit in a
white-out, Buhl strayed over a cornice and disappeared forever.
Kurt's photo of the diverging lines of footprints, one weaving on
and the other ending in nothing, is one of the most famous and
haunting in all mountaineering.

Later Kurt climbed Dhaulagiri, making him the only man to make
the first ascents of two 8,000 metre peaks – and then Makalu,
Everest and Gasherbrum II. Latterly he'd become more involved in
filming and general exploration expeditions, though his astonishing
repeat of Broad Peak 27 years later showed that he was far from
being over the hill. Julie Tullis had become his regular partner and

sound-recordist on filming trips, and now she had just become the first British woman to do a 8,000 metre peak. She looked weathered, lean, calm and strong, giving an impression of great physical and psychological toughness – which she thinks derives in part from her training in karate and aikido; she has a black belt in both. We were considerably impressed by them, and spent more time with them at Mrs Davies's Rawalpindi.

Our chance meeting seemed fated in retrospect, one of those things that had to happen. Now we needed a TV film to raise more money for the Expedition. So Mal found Julie's card and phoned to ask if they'd like to come along as a film team. She in turn phoned Kurt in Italy, where he was happily putting on lost weight with pasta, and quarter of an hour later got back to Mal: 'We're coming.'

Like everyone else, they found the lure of Everest from the Tibet side irresistible, near-legendary to all of us who had grown up with stories of the exploits of Shipton, Tilman, Odell, Norton, Mallory and Irvine. After all the pre-war attempts on Everest, the Tibetan side had been closed for nearly 40 years. Pilks' Company Secretary, David Bricknell, could scarcely believe what was happening to him as he made arrangements with Malcolm to fit in an introduction to snow/ice climbing before he too went to Everest. There was little time for training now, as the company agreed to give him six weeks' leave to accompany the Expedition as Base Camp and Advance Base Camp Manager for the initial phase. From now on every minute of his spare time was spent co-ordinating between Pilkington's, Terry and Malcolm as, buoyed up by money, the Expedition rose like a sunken liner from the depths of Malcolm's dream to the unlikely light of day . . .

The Team. The climbing team was augmented. Rick Allen, a quiet, wiry, thin-faced Texaco chemical engineer based in Aberdeen, had heard about the Expedition when he was climbing in Nepal on Ganesh II with Nick Kekus. With the confidence of the first ascent of the South Face behind him ('the hardest climbing I've ever done'), Rick wrote to Mal saying if there was a place for him, he'd be interested. He went to ask if there was a chance of somehow getting three months' leave. Once again the magic word 'Everest' opened the door. 'If you've got a once in a lifetime chance, the company should support you,' he was told. That meant a lot, because while some of the climbers worked purely for cash between expeditions, Rick derived considerable satisfaction from his job. He was glad it hadn't come to a choice between Everest and Texaco. After Pilkington's made their offer, Mal phoned him up. 'You're in.'

'Everest', 'Tibet', the 'Unclimbed Ridge' – these proved to be the Open Sesame words that over and over made the unlikely possible and the possible actual. Liz Duff works for Scottish Life Assurance, and on impulse went to ask if she could add her various holiday periods past and future together to take six weeks off. Not only did they say yes, but they gave her extra unpaid holiday to cover the entire Expedition. She was very happy to be coming – partly for the adventure and partly because she was saved from the difficult position of staying at home waiting for news from the hill, which even when it comes is always out of date. 'I'm not a great worrier about Malcolm,' she said to me one evening in December, 'because I've great faith he'll be alright. Though this trip worries me a bit . . . It's more that my being there saves him worrying about me and whether I'm paying the bills!' It would be good having her there for her trenchant commonsense – and to keep up standards at Base and Advance Base. She'd done some rock and winter climbing in Britain, went with Mal to Nuptse, and hoped to do some load carrying on Everest if time and circumstance permitted.

We hadn't at first considered Tony Brindle for the trip. He'd been Mal's partner on the Mustagh Tower and they'd developed a good mocking father-and-son relationship there – but Tony was going into his final year in Outdoor Activities at Bangor College and didn't want to jeopardize that. But Mal wrote directly to the Principal saying that this diminutive youth was indispensable, a star, and could he possibly be granted the chance to defer the last of his courses? He could, so Tony was in.

Tony is a small, compact Lancastrian born with an innocent butter-wouldn't-melt face that belies his exceptional stamina. A few months older than Jon, because of his size, innocent appearance and open nature, he inevitably becomes the butt of much teasing – which as a rule he accepts with remarkable patience, though at the same time strengthening his resolve to prove himself as fast and fit as anybody. Unlike some of the climbers he never learned to hide his enthusiasm for climbing, hill-walking, fell-running, canoeing; he doesn't go in for the customary pose of self-mockery and diffidence – which throws him open to more teasing. He was openly jubilant at having the chance to go to Everest, and Mal now had the satisfaction of having reunited the successful Mustagh team.

Our search for a doctor was becoming pressing when Julie suggested Urs Wiget, the Swiss doctor on the 1984 K2 expedition. He had been to 7,500 metres, had a lot of Alpine climbing behind him, and was knowledgeable about all aspects of the theory and practice of mountain medicine. Conscientious without fussing, he inspired confidence and trust from climbers. He was the best they'd known.

And so one day in late November Urs opened Mal's letter in the surgery of an isolated village in Switzerland. '*Merde!*' He beamed, frowned, then with a loud 'Yahoo!' rushed next door to see his wife Madeleine to ask if she could possibly once again handle the practice and the children alone for three months . . .

Allen Fyffe I'm writing this in Peking but this is how it started. In September or October '84 Eileen and I were driving home from Inverness; at about Slocht a green car passed and in the back was this madly waving figure – Sandy Allan. Sandy got out and we chatted for a while about his last trip, routes, etc., and eventually he announced he was going to the North-East Ridge with Mal, etc., and Bob. He then asked me if I wanted to go. I prevaricated and said that I might see him in the Tavern for a pint that evening.

Eileen and I then talked about it and she said she wouldn't mind if I went, so later that night I saw Sandy, had a few pints and said yes, I was on for it if I could get off work and the money was found. Then nothing happened for a long time so I eventually phoned Malcolm to see if I was in or out – I apparently was 1st reserve depending on money. Then I asked for time off and was to my surprise told that it should be no problem. Then eventually I was told I was included, the money was found from Pilkington's and the trip was on.

I went to one team photocall in Glencoe which was good as for the first time I met the rest of the team and we had a chance to chat and discuss things. Only then did I get a vague feeling that it would happen . . .

In truth, Mal was uncertain whether to take Allen. At 39 he was a fair bit older than the rest of the team, and being mostly bald he was inevitably cast as the 'old man' of the team – but that was almost certainly an asset. Many Himalayan climbers seem to be at their peak in their forties, when experience, judgement and patience outweigh any decrease in pure power. Besides, a few older hands were needed to balance out the young revvers. And only Allen had had the experience of a large expedition, on Chris Bonington's classic 1975 South-West Face of Everest expedition. No, the problem was on that trip he'd acclimatized badly and eventually was recovered, exhausted and scarcely in his right mind, on the fixed ropes at 7,300 metres. Mal had already gambled on Andy Nisbet's acclimatization problem – could he afford to again? In the end he took him out of respect for his enormous mountaineering experience and good expedition character.

So that was the team completed: ten lead climbers plus a doctor who might well go high on the hill; Terry Dailey and myself to support as far as our abilities and other responsibilities would allow; Kurt and Julie to film; Dave Bricknell as Pilkington's representative, Base and Advance Base organizer; Liz Duff playing a floating role – paying much of her own way, she was free to do as little or as much as she wanted; knowing her she'd do whatever she possibly could. And Sarah Squibb, Nick Kekus's girlfriend, who was also paying her own way. She wanted to go to Tibet, to Everest, be with Nick, and hoped to learn something about Chinese music along the way.

By this time we had also acquired a large supporting cast. First an accountant to advise on and keep track of our finances, and then a lawyer. When a sponsor puts up £80,000 and the media put in additional cash, they naturally want clear contracts to ensure they have the exclusive rights and coverage they're paying for. Pilks also engaged a PR firm to help create the media coverage and public awareness that would justify their sponsorship.

For all of us, apart from Allen Fyffe, this world of contracts, promotions, logos, newsletters, interviews and press conferences was new and slightly alarming. At times it felt as though the original point of the Expedition – the desire of a handful of people to take on the private and personal challenge of climbing the North-East Ridge of Everest – was being obscured by the bewildering spindrift of publicity and business. But dreams have to be worked for in an imperfect world and most of us went along with it all.

But we were taken aback by the scale and professionalism of the first press conference, where Pilkington's announced the Expedition and their involvement in it. We drifted into the ballroom of a smart London hotel to find reporters and photographers waiting for us from all the national papers, in addition to radio and TV. Team jackets were laid out for us, each with the Pilks' logo – the precise maximum size permitted on BBC – sewn across the chest. Beside them, the Expedition sweaters. Then labels with our names and roles in the team. A session at the free buffet and bar did little to diminish our sense of unreality.

Then Dave Bricknell, Terry Dailey, Mal and Julie did their bit for the Media. They explained our objective, that the North-East Ridge was the last unclimbed pure route on Everest, and probably the hardest of the lot. They went into its short and tragic history, explained our intention to use limited oxygen above 8,000 metres if necessary, the frightening statistics of the 'Death Zone'. Then came the questions, most of them sensible and informed. 'I suppose you'll have to give up *that*,' said one journalist, pointing at Mal's cigarette. 'Not at all,' Mal replied, 'in fact I intend to smoke as high as possible!' He went on to explain the theory, which goes back as far as the doctor on the first 1921 Everest expedition and still has its adherents among climbers, that smoking aids acclimatization to altitude. It restores the lowered CO_2 level in the blood that controls involuntary breathing. (As a smoker, I naturally believe this.) 'Besides,' says Mal, lighting up another – 'it does your body good to be accustomed to a certain level of abuse.' This is the Mal Duff theory of Abuse Training, and he adheres to it rigorously.

'Will Julie Tullis be considered for a summit attempt?' The media had naturally centred a great deal of coverage on Julie. 'Anyone who is still on their feet can have a crack at the summit,' Mal replied. Then came the inevitable questions about the fate of Joe Tasker and Pete Boardman: where did we think they were? Had they fallen down the Kangshung Face, or were they still on the Ridge? What would we do if we found them? Mal's answers were models of tactful evasion, and I was struck by how much he'd changed, in terms of public persona at least, from the irreverent and casual enthusiast of a few months before. He now seemed the very model of a serious, responsible and business-like leader of a major expedition – at how much personal cost, I wondered. His preoccupation with the Expedition's overall planning and the demands made on him as our figurehead, had put a distance between him and the rest of us, and perhaps him and himself.

'I can't say I get any special thrill out of leading this trip,' he later said to me. 'It's more that I really wanted to go to Everest and no one else seemed keen to pick up the ball and run with it.'

Then one by one we were taken aside for photos and factual details, as if queuing for school medical examinations. Being processed. Name, age, role in Expedition. Then one of the photographers suggested we go onto the roof for team pictures. 'Be careful up there,' one of the hotel employees said nervously, 'there's ice on the roof.' We said we thought we could handle that, and trooped up.

'All I want to do is go climbing,' Jon complained, voicing a general feeling.

'So do I, Jon,' Mal replied. 'But it's not as simple as that, not on this one.'

No point in denying that elements of publicity and its attendant gravy-train are fun – particularly the free drinks and taxis and hotel rooms. And it's some recompense for parents and relatives after years of despairing of their off-springs' dangerous, erratic and unprofitable life-style, to have them enter the public realm.

I'd gone through the publicity process before in book promotions, and accepted it as a commitment made in return for someone else risking their money. Often it's silly, sometimes you're being asked to be false, mostly it's good fun. But the lads were uneasy. Their private pursuit had become public property. If anyone takes up serious mountaineering in order to become famous, I've never met them. What climbers do is deeply personal, between them and the rock and ice. They are reluctant to speak seriously about it because they fear they will be misunderstood or misrepresented – as heroes, perhaps, or people ruled by a death-wish, or seekers after enlightenment, or squaddies without nerves or imagination. At most they want the respect and recognition of their peers, and among peers there is little need to speak of the why and what of climbing.

'Still,' said Sandy as he opened *The Times* next morning, 'you don't crack an egg because you want to crack an egg, but because you want to eat an omelette, eh?'

Jon Tinker's Glencoe Notebook, Jan – Feb '85.
Duff climbing on Carn Dearg Buttress. A helmet pokes into view, Garfield-like sleepy eyes check the turf. Crank and clatter, huff and puff. 'You are definitely psychotic, Jon!' 'I blame it on Duff.' 'You always do.'

Half an hour later they're on their way back down to the Clachaig with a new Grade VI route under their belts. For these few weeks they'll be guiding six days a week and climbing on their own account on the seventh. 'Well, it's better than training,' says Mal, ordering another lager. Somewhat to their surprise they climb extremely well together in Scotland, swapping leads, silently urging each other on to the undiscovered limits of what's possible.

A semi-formalized relationship with Sandy. The bickering keeps the edge which lets us both perform at higher standards. Many's the quiet giggle we've had at outsiders' views on this ménage à deux.
Andy G. going up beside Clachaig Gully – the fluency is there now – next step is to find the rhythm out in front.
Liz too sensitive about her role. The Lizometer – check the age jokes. Does she know her role yet? At least she'll stop Malcolm pining for the fiords. Don't worry, kid.
Pre-route manoeuvring – who's going to make out on E., make it up and off. All a waste of time. Sandy and Bob the consensus so far. I'll keep quiet on this one. There must be no pairing off at the beginning though.
It'll be relaxing being on the hill again with my mates – Mal, Sandy, Tony, Nicko and Wattie. The rest will be by the end. Monk-cowled figures staring into the thin. That bitter taste of altitude. The sweet smell of sweat and the soured deflation of success.

Mal trains on beer and chips. Jon trains on fear and loathing. Tony trains on climbing and training. Sandy keeps quiet. Andy G. must learn to be stupid.

One-pint Wattie – flair and apeshit. Watch this man go! A dark horse by inclination. That youth will go far.

Dr Aido's PATENTED GO FASTER (GRADE V) PILL
½ oz garlic
⅛ oz snuff (Black Death brand)
2 slivers of red pepper
2 grains of cocaine
1 cut-down amphetamine suppository
MIX WELL AT BASE CAMP. ALLOW TO SET.
INSERT WHEN FACED WITH
    – Grade V
    – FAILURE, DEATH, PANIC
    – BORING PARTIES
EFFECTS UNCERTAIN BUT IT WILL MAKE YOU GO FASTER!!!

Chris Bonington lecturing at the Clachaig. 'I'll be sitting on the South Col with loads of Sherpas carrying up tons of food and oxygen; I'll look across at Mal Duff and his merry men and I'll think "You poor buggers, hee hee!" . . . I hope they reach the top but even more that I reach the top.'

Later, after the lecture, we had a quick talk. He thinks we've got a chance, and emphasized how bloody high, hard and long it is. I came away almost certain that I will not get above 8,000 metres and even that will take all I've got. It's quite nice to go without summit pressure or financial worries. Even load-carrying will be a privilege, so many people would sacrifice a lot to go on this sort of adventure.

The photo-call at the Clachaig. We play around on an ice-fall for the cameras. Kurt and Julie have seen it all before – they sit around – also they're outside their home ground. A trifle ruffled by the lads trying to pin down what they'd done the day before. 'We just went up the mountain.' It transpires they went up Summit Gully – a descent route off Bidean Nam Beith which Mal not unkindly calls 'a steep walk'. Later in the pub Kurt toasts Julie to a good day out 'even though Mal says it's just a steep walk'. I fall about. Legends can play this game better than most.

Andy said that he hadn't got the same excitement or sensed the same feeling about this trip. I think most of us feel the same. It's too big to comprehend, so many people are involved.

Andy playing guitar much later in the Lounge, Mal in babble-mode, Dave thumping his chair – it's great having him on our side. Meanwhile I'm reading Hornbein on thin cold air, Willi Unsoeld and the North Face traverse[1] in a back issue of *National Geographic* . . .

[1] Unsoeld and Hornbein climbed Everest via the West Ridge and North Face in the 1963 American expedition.

I needed to take the occasional weekend away from writing *Summit Fever* to go climbing in Glencoe and remind myself why I'd actually become involved in this game. There'd be little technical climbing for me on Everest, just the bottomless weariness of carrying loads at altitude, and from the point of view of training I'd have been as well just walking on the Scottish hills with a 40 lb rucksack. But I'd become addicted to the anxiety, adrenalin and purifying concentration of extending myself on a technical Scottish route.

My literary friends, surprised as I was at the way my life had been hi-jacked by climbing, asked if this was not a form of escape, its excitement being a distraction from more real problems. At the time I shrugged; they hadn't known what it was like. To climb is to know it's the real thing. I was going to Everest and I didn't care much why. What mattered now was a gradual physical and mental focusing – yes, a narrowing if you like – on the adventure ahead. Ask the big questions later when I had time to catch up with myself. Always later, sometime later . . .

Dave Bricknell, the Pilkington Company Secretary, who had now definitely obtained leave to come on the Expedition, came up to Glencoe for his initiation into climbing. On his first route he suffered the agonies of hot-aches through wearing inadequate gloves, and quietly passed out on a belay stance halfway up. Mal heard a rattle and looked down to see only Dave's feet resting on the ledge – the rest of him had slipped away and he was peacefully hanging upside down. Mal descended, put him on his feet again, and finished the route with an extremely embarrassed Dave struggling to make sense of it all through a confusion of axes, ropes, slings and gear.

The second day he went out with Mal and Liz. Halfway up, Liz heard 'Shit!' drift down from Dave who was seconding Mal up above her. 'What is it, Dave?' she shouted up, concerned. 'I think I'm beginning to enjoy this!' came the reply.

Dave was fitting in. 'The Right Stuff – not half bad for a Company Secretary' was Mal's verdict. 'Only trouble is he's too fit and doesn't drink enough. We'll have to handicap him. Going climbing with a hangover and four hours' sleep is the best rehearsal for altitude.' Dave, who was beginning to adjust to the style of these shuffling dossers he'd fallen among, promised to try to put this good advice into practise. He made no effort to conceal his excitement at the adventure he'd been caught up in. I could easily empathize with him; the first trip is like no other.

'The North-East Ridge is a typical modern mountaineering route –

very bold, very brave, very stupid,' Jon asserts in the Clachaig Bar.
'Great !'

'What's our chance of climbing it?' Dave asks.

'At the moment I'd give us an 80 per cent chance of doing the
Pinnacles, 30–35 per cent for the Summit,' Mal replies.

Jon, 'I'd say we've nil chance of doing it, and it's odds on someone
will croak.'

That's their natures. Mal's commitment and belief are absolute,
they have to be. Not a 'go out and see' but 'we *will* do it'. At the
same time, a detached part of him is quite objective and realistic –
he wouldn't still be alive otherwise. Whereas Jon says we'll go on
till we drop, expecting us to drop.

Mal stretches out his legs, relaxed for once. He and Jon have had
a good day. 'I don't expect to die young,' he observes into his pint.
Jon turns to me.

'How do you think you'll die, Andy?' This is not a question
demanding an answer, but Jon's characteristic testing-out. 'The statistics say 1.3 people should snuff it on this trip, and you've got as
good a chance of croaking as anybody else. More, I should say.'
And he leans back and laughs, eyes alight with mischief and something between malice and affection.

I'd thought about it. Everyone had in their own way weighed up
the risk and the hardship and the separations before reaffirming
their commitment to going to Everest. It had been something of a
shock when Pilkington's came in and I realized this was really going
to happen. This expedition was going to be much harder, more
demanding and probably more dangerous than Mustagh, making
that affair seem like a holiday jaunt. There I'd carried to 5,600 and
it had taken more out of me than I'd ever imagined was there in the
first place. This time Malcolm's sports plan was for me to carry to
7,000 metres if possible, on to the crest of the North-East Ridge.
I'd seen the photos in *The Unclimbed Ridge*, particularly the steep
exposed traverse above their first snow cave, and carried them in
the back of my mind ever since. From Bonington's account, the
weather at times would be desperate, light-years out with my experience. If anything at all went wrong up there, I'd be in serious trouble.

So you think it all through again, consider your life as it is, with its
problems and satisfactions and hopes and regrets, realize how very
much you want to live and yet discover deep down a certain fatalism
that verges on indifference. You weigh quality against quantity of
experience. And in the end, because that is the way you have become,

you decide yes it is worth it, yes of course you will go and give it
your best shot and accept the outcome.

Then your life becomes as simple as it's ever going to be.

'I suppose you do it for the money,' my dentist says hopefully as he
probes inside my mouth. In my choking laughter his pick digs into
my tongue and draws blood.

Walking back to the Clachaig after a day on the hill, Mal tells
me he has phases of nightmares when he wakes up soaking with
sweat but no memory of why. The only one he can remember is of
being trapped in an airliner falling out of the sky from 30,000 feet,
knowing it's going to deck out, that he is falling and going to die
and there's nothing he can do, looking over at Liz to say goodbye . . .

'Suppose it shows there must be a lot down there. Bit worrying
that.'

I nod and we talk about dreams and the anxieties one tries to
suppress. It's the first time he's opened up with me for a while, being
so preoccupied with the Expedition, and I know it's something he
does very rarely, except maybe with Liz. He's like most good climbers in that respect: emotions are to be rigorously controlled; fear,
anxiety and doubt are there to be overcome. That battle with oneself
is at the heart of climbing. It's appropriate in that situation, but
restrictive and unhealthy in everyday life, I suggest. 'I'm interested
more and more in uncontrolling,' I say.

'With the state of your private life, that's just as well!' Mal laughs.

'Yes, well . . . Better to ride wild horses than try to drag them to
the ground.'

This is definitely not a climbers' conversation, though it's only
possible because of the time we've spent together in the hills.

'When I was 14 I discovered I could will myself not to feel
anything I didn't want to,' he says casually.

'Was that when you took up climbing?'

'Soon after . . . It became a habit. Only recently I've come to think
it's maybe not such a good way to live. And living only for climbing
is like abseiling off one pin – if that pulls, you've got nothing left.
By the time you get to climbing in the Himalayas you've forgotten
why you started in the first place.'

We trudge down the road in silence through the gathering dark.
The air smells of snow and moor, a three-quarter moon is rising
yellow over Bidean. Ahead of us are lights where the world of
warmth, laughter and climbing talk awaits us. These moments linger
in the mind as significant pauses, as milestones in the Expedition
we're already on.

In Aberdeen Andy Nisbet gets a phone call from an insurance broker. 'I hear you're going to Everest soon – have you ever thought of taking out life insurance?' Andy laughs, declines politely, puts the phone down.

Jon presses me persistently to tell him how much my recent Scottish Arts Council Bursary is worth. Eventually I say, 'Look, I'm not telling you.'
    'Why not?'
    'Because it's private.'
    'I thought climbing was private,' he retorts. Must have been saving that one up for a while. I nod, concede the point. 'It used to be – though all those pre-war Everest trips had newspaper contracts. And books. If you can think of any other way of paying for this trip, let me know.'

We have another media session, this time in Glencoe.
    It's good for us to be together again, for most of us know only two or three others in the team and just dealing with the media gives us a kind of solidarity. We go to a nearby ice-fall for a photo-session; Kurt and Julie decline to participate, explaining they're not prepared to take the outside chance of even a minor injury which could put them out for Everest. The Press look slightly baffled as meanwhile the lads are casually swarming up and down the 750 ice, without bothering with ropes or helmets. I do it in more cautious style, but the ice is in good condition and the climb is very straightforward.
    'This "Ultimate Challenge" is bullshit,' said Sandy next morning, looking at a newspaper with that headline. 'The ultimate challenge has got to be having a normal life with kids and a job and doing that well. Maybe I should try that some day ... As long as I can still go off climbing once in a while!'

Our Expedition was inevitably attracting a degree of criticism in the climbing world because of our sponsorship commitments, media coverage and intention to use oxygen. 'If some of the people who slag us got off their backside and put together an expedition themselves they'd find out what it's all about,' Mal said, peeved. Jon delighted in spreading the rumour that all the lead climbers were being paid £5,000 each, and anyone who got to the top would be given a brand-new Porsche. 'Well, would *you* climb the North-East Ridge for free?' he'd reply with wide-eyed sincerity when asked if this was true.

The final weeks before departure were a desperate rush against the calendar. Chris Watts hassled, bullied, begged and cajoled for gear, some of it custom-made, to be delivered in time. Nick and Andy pressed on, assembling some four tons of food. Sandy finished on the oil-rigs and drove the Pilkington's van from Aberdeen to London to Liverpool to Edinburgh, frequently overnight and dozing off at the wheel. His driving is as terrifyingly approximate as his climbing is exact. An old man in Nepal had once looked into his eyes and told him he'd die in a van – but Sandy counted this vehicle as a truck, 'So that's alright, eh?'

British Airways came in to offer free flights to Peking for us and, crucially, to fly out much of our gear free. This prevented our escalating budget from getting completely out of hand.

Pilkington's were proving to be the ideal sponsor – supportive, involved but non-interfering. They seemed as excited by the project as we were. They didn't just give us money; they gave us secretarial services, a warehouse for the accumulating mountain of gear, the truck. They had a team of apprentices turning out snow-stakes and deadmen for us. From their diverse companies we received Reactolite sunglasses, an optical nightsight, and heat-reflecting foam mats like giant innersoles to go under our tents. These were a real find, making a tremendous difference in both warmth and comfort to tents pitched on rough moraine in Arctic conditions.

A crucial factor was Dave Bricknell's and Terry Dailey's flair for organization and co-ordination that among other things produced a 200-page computer print-out record of all our equipment down to the last tuna fish and toothbrush. Planning and providing food, clothing, shelter, cooking gear and climbing equipment for 19 people for three months is a military-scale undertaking. There is no room for mistakes or shortages – if you run out of lighters, pitons, gas, toilet rolls at Everest Base Camp, there's no popping round the corner for more.

It was only this combination of organization, facilities, and sheer hard work that made it possible to put together the Expedition in five months. Items still hadn't arrived a week before we were due to leave; the last odds and sods were picked up on the evening before departure.

The last pieces fell into place. Kurt and Julie concluded a contract to make a film for 'Pebble Mill At One' in addition to the ITN reports. The *Scottish Daily Record* printed that we were taking vast quantities of wine and whisky, and when we told them this was unfortunately no longer the case, they compensated in the best possible way – by arranging to have us given six crates of MacKinlay's blended whisky. Liz used her contacts to arrange for a precious crate of The Macallan malt. These were of limited medicinal use, but added greatly to morale and Base Camp relaxation.

On 2nd March I typed 'The End' to *Summit Fever* and went up to the attic to collect together all the gear accumulated there; I selected a few positive and high-spirited tapes and books, bought a lot of rolling tobacco and pencils and notebooks and a few personal treats like Drambuie and chicken breasts in jelly. Then the camera system, the Walkman, special fast- and slow-speed film, all the etceteras of contemporary expedition life. Across the country, 18 others were doing the same. Any anxiety was now replaced by a feverish impatience to be gone.

Then the final farewell drinks and meals, a party, all enjoyed and appreciated but in one's heart one has already left. The sudden poignancy of the last walk to the end of the harbour, gazing down into the water and wondering what lies ahead. The last handshake with a friend. The last night with a lover. Wake at dawn, clean the last dishes, close the doors, stroke the cats, lock the front door and walk away.

Isobel drives me to Turnhouse airport. It's a perfect Scottish morning of sun and dew, anticipating spring. There's little left for us to say as I sit and stare out the window at everything I'm leaving. We unload the car. Her silk shirt is cool on my palms, her red hair flares in the low, brilliant sunshine. It's a moment that will recur involuntarily over the next three months as I lie trying to sleep at altitude, or push myself one more time up the fixed ropes on the Ridge.

We look at each other.

'Bye.'

'Bye.'

A brief embrace and she walks away, drives to her office to do a day's work.

'Are you going to make it this time?' the check-in man asks cheerfully.

'It's uncertain enough to make it worthwhile,' I reply, glancing back to see her car turn on to the main road, 'I hope so.'

That afternoon we congregated at the London hotel Pilkington's had booked for our farewell Reception. Some of the faces are becoming familiar, hi Nick, hello Sarah, this is Bob Barton. I shake hands with the burly, bespectacled Yorkshireman, liking his warm and concerned air. Chris Watts handed out our remaining gear, and we packed it all in our individual blue barrels. Much bustle, commotion, everyone a little tense as we sorted out the final details. 'I've never felt so twitchy about any project as I do about this one,' Dave confessed. The ballroom was now crowded with media, family, friends, climbers, everyone who'd been involved with our Expedition. It was moving to feel all this support and we began to realize how many hopes were pinned on us.

A Pilkington director, Sol Kay, made a short speech; Mal replied, at once casual and formal, growing into the role as time went on. We were presented with a stained-glass picture to give to the Chinese Mountaineering Association – only Mal noticed that the Union Jack was upside down and wondered if that's a sign of bad luck. We decided to have it re-done and brought out by Terry Dailey five weeks later when his leave from Saatchi's began.

The media departed and it was time for some 'serious jollification' in Sandy's phrase. Allen Fyffe found himself in distinguished company with Lord Hunt and Sir Alastair and Lady Pilkington, but with a suitable amount of alcohol the situation was enjoyable, and he and Hunt discussed Everest at some length. Then we slipped away from the jollification for the Business Meeting.

It was the first time we'd all met together. Our doctor, Urs Wiget, was introduced, a small, broad, smiling, bearded man immediately dubbed 'the gnome'. We'd just started going over the contracts and finances when a tall lad with over-sized hands and feet stumbled in and slumped down. Eventually someone asked, 'Well, who are you?' Julie explained he was Danny Lewis, coming along as their film porter to help hump gear on the hill. 'How high have you been then, mate?' Jon enquired. Danny looked embarrassed, and I felt for him among this group of complete strangers. 'Twelve thousand' he replied awkwardly.

Eyebrows went up in silent incredulity. Kurt and Julie had picked a 19-year-old rock climber (climbing a very respectable 6b) with virtually no snow/ice experience and none whatsoever of altitude, to do heavy-duty carrying on an extreme route. We wondered if this was a very bright idea. 'Nothing against you personally, we don't even know you.' It was too late to do anything about it, and it wasn't his fault, so we just had to hope he wouldn't prove a liability to himself or anyone else. He sat quietly through the rest of the meeting, wide-eyed and attentive.

Our accountant set out our financial situation. Inevitably we'd considerably overspent our budget, but counting the newspaper, book, BBC and ITN money, we had a small surplus. Personal differences used to be the great unmentionable in climbing books, now it is often finance. One thing we learned from this trip was the importance of having financial details and contracts out in the open, to be candidly discussed and with luck agreed on. Jon made my position easier by asking outright if I got any of the *Sunday Express* money, and I was able to say no, that all went straight to the Expedition, as did the first part of the book advance.

And Nick was thinking to himself, Why are all these buggers making money out of us and we're not? The truth was, as Mal pointed out, these buggers (Kurt and Julie, myself, the PR firm, our accountant, lawyer, everyone down to the caterers) were being paid for doing a job, and that job was raising the publicity and money that gave us a three-month Everest expedition with a lot of valuable gear to keep, for the princely sum of £200 each. Without the climbers there'd be no film, no book, but without the media contracts there'd be no Expedition.

'So, can we sign the contracts, please?' We all signed, wrote out our nominal cheques, formally enlisting ourselves to the common venture. Then Dave Bricknell made a welcome and unexpected statement: Pilkington's were aware that we might feel a certain pressure to succeed because of all the money put behind us. They didn't want that. 'What we want to see,' Dave continued, 'is a successful expedition, and by that we mean going out and doing your best, which you will anyway, and coming back all in one piece and as a cohesive team.' Silent, appreciative nods. The ideal sponsor's ideal parting words.

Business over, we broke up the meeting and returned to pleasure. Though there was the usual laughter, drinking and carry-on, Jon noticed there was slightly less excitement and high spirits than customary before an expedition. It may have been the size of the team, and us not knowing each other well. There was also less of the death-and-destruction humour, precisely because this was a death route. There was a lurking seriousness behind the smiles. We were also very tired by the weeks and months of activity it had taken to get us to this point.

These factors, together with the prospect of a 5.0 am start next morning, kept most of us under control. We slipped away quietly upstairs with our partners by midnight, leaving only Jon and Sandy in full cry pursuit of a good time . . .

At 6.0 am on 6th March we stumble through our last Press conference in a basement room at Heathrow. We try to look suitably keen, fit and enthusiastic, but in reality we were grey and hungover. Allen Fyffe in particular is grim as Dundee in November. 'Can't you guys smile? Please!' We assume hideous rictus snarls.

In an alley on the way back to the departure lounge a ladder is propped against the wall. Bob Barton and Sandy hesitate then walk deliberately round it. Already we're becoming superstitious.

My Old China

'What's that about?' 'The future, I should think.'

Three hours gone, another nineteen before we arrive in Peking. The Expedition sleeps or slumps back blank-eyed. Jon and Chris have Thoroughly Modern Music on their headphones (New Order and Yellowman); Bob, as befits his age and temperament, listens to Dylan, thinking of his wife Anna and their new daughter. Andy Nisbet is white-faced and immobile, he travels very badly and this flight is a purgatory for him. He thinks of the two flights after this one, across China and on to Lhasa, then three days of journeying by truck, and groans inwardly. Nick and Sarah are talking quietly with each other, as they will for much of the trip. Others conscientiously sign their way through stacks of Expedition postcards for schoolkids.

Tony Brindle is missing his girlfriend Kathy to a degree he didn't know possible. They'd informally become engaged shortly before his departure; he's told only Liz about this to avoid teasing from the more cynically minded. I envy them their certainty, and the way Kathy had come to the airport with us to be with him till the last minute. I could use some of that certainty. For me the last three months have been an emotional soap-opera when everyone is in love with the wrong person, each wanting what we don't have. Once in a while we'd look at each other and laugh at our painful absurdity.

How are we to live? I'm not going back to the mountains just for more climbing and new scenery. We're all setting out with half-formulated questions to be resolved, even if it's just 'Can I go to 8,000 metres?' Each one of us on this plane has our own inner expedition, the secret expedition with its twists and turns, moving like an underground river below the surface of events.

Mal hands round blow-up photos of the Pinnacles, taken from the North Ridge. The lads pore over the problems that are going to dominate our thoughts for the next three months. The Pinnacles look chilling to my unpractised eye: hard climbing at any altitude, an unprecedented level of difficulty at over 8,000 metres. Falling away steeply on the West side, and the sheer drop of the Kangshung face on the other – there's no escape route off these Pinnacles till the far end of them when the North Col Ridge meets our one. 'See that little notch on the First Pinn, that's where Bonington turned back . . . Renshaw had his stroke a little higher . . . Looks like you turn the last Pinn on this side . . . See that tiny colour patch below the Second Pinnacle? It *might* be a bivvy tent . . . Or Pete and Joe . . .' A short silence, no one wants to think too much about that, though it's a mystery we all want solved.

'Looks real horrorshow,' Rick says quietly. No one disagrees.

Jon points out the base of the First Pinnacle. 'You see that? That's as far as I'm going. From then on you're on your own.'

But I am thinking of a last hug from Kathleen before boarding the bus to Heathrow, the softness of her pink sweater under my hands while over her shoulder the full moon was setting in the blue-black sky behind the hotel. I am thinking of our last night together, the things we said, and the hollow talismanic stone she hung on a thong round my neck. It'll stay there till I return. Then behind me Jon, who'd been up all night, his hair a devastated cornfield, enthuses 'I'm thoroughly rat-holed – great!'

Peking in March has the aethetic charm and oriental mystery of a fifties tower block; it is as stimulating as a wet January afternoon in Fort William. Or so it seemed to us as our coach nosed its way through Peking's 10 million rush hour cyclists. The city was utterly flat and utterly monochrome. Clouds of grey dust blew down the streets from endless building sites where hundreds of men and women laboured with picks and shovels and baskets. It seemed that the entire city was being rebuilt in grey concrete. The patient cyclists were swathed in dark, padded jackets, fur-lined hats, many wearing grey face-masks against the dust.

'These are new workers' apartments,' our interpreter Jack announced, pointing out another ten-storey concrete block. 'And this is the LARGEST GROCERY STORE IN BEIJING!' We try to look suitably impressed as we trundle by what looks like a particularly shabby and dimly-lit post-war Woolworth's.

Still, the Chinese arrangements had accorded with their reputation for efficiency. All our baggage was quickly retrieved at the airport, and we passed with almost indecent ease through the Diplomatic Channel of the Customs (two stages which can take several days at Delhi airport, many hours in Rawalpindi). Outside stood two coaches, one for us and one for our gear. We explained we'd only ordered one, but two was what we got and two is what we'd pay for. Which is also very Chinese. Rick, whose meticulous nature well suited him to being our money manager, noted it down as the first of our additional expenses. On the bus our interpreter introduced himself as Jack though he was in fact Yan – very slight, young, thin-faced with a long bony nose, bespectacled and given to blinking a lot; he did not look very Chinese and his English was easily the best we were to come across. In turn he introduced 'Mr Luo, your Liaison Officer.' A thick-set man with a broad Mongolian face, expressive mouth and a black crew-cut stood up and bowed. We chorused a ragged hello, feeling like Mystery Tour trippers introduced to our hosts. Which in a way we were. Jack and Luo would be with us right through the Expedition, as our troubleshooters and minders.

We arrived at the Bei Wei hotel, imposing with plate glass doors and plants and marble-floored lobby, though something in the Formica surfaces, carpets and black Bakelite telephones marked it out as 30 years behind the times. We picked up the room keys waiting for us and staggered upstairs with our blue barrels of personal gear.

'Basically, this trip is throwing together 14 people who desperately want to climb a mountain, and seeing if they want to enough.' That was Chris Watts's assessment as we sat chatting in our room. He was still feeling obscurely guilty about coming on the trip while Sonja stayed behind, 'though I know she'd do the same in my position. There's a lot of thinking climbers on this trip,' he continued. 'That's good and bad – you can expect to see a certain amount of tactical manoeuvring once we get on the mountain.' I nodded. I'd seen the forces of individual ambition and joint effort play off against each other on the Mustagh Tower, and between the lines of practically every climbing book. A big expedition is a choir composed of soloists.

Mal had suggested we all made a point of rooming with someone different at each stop on our journey through China and Tibet, so that by the time our trucks arrived at Base Camp we might feel more like a team. Thanks to the Chinese having created a 'road' to Everest, there'd be no long walk-in on this trip; and the walk-in is normally the phase an expedition uses to become fully fit and cohesive as a group. 'I see myself as the loner on this trip,' Chris said, 'I've climbed with no one on it, I'm not part of a pair.' From remarks the others had already made, I was beginning to wonder who did *not* regard themselves as outsiders. 'I suppose I associate myself with people like Bob and Allen, despite being younger. I like to see the sensible rewarded . . .' And with this remark he fell asleep, slumped over the jacket to which he was sewing a Pilkington's logo.

Peking looked less bleak the next day, probably because we were less grey with fatigue and jet-lag. People walked into the hotel with masks over their faces. In Britain this would be a cue to hit the floor, here it's a precaution against biting wind and swirling dust. On the streets we started noticing the occasional flash of colour in younger people's clothes; one or two girls had high heels, and the local wide-boys aspired to rolled-up jeans and wrap-around shades. Only the older people still wore the once-compulsory Mao tunic in dark blue, black or bottle-green. The many small stalls along the pavements, selling everything from Coke to combs to cabbages, were another sign of changing times in China.

The Chinese Mountaineering Association (CMA) had organized an excursion to the Great Wall. It was another chilling day. Clouds of grey dust blew through the city and across the utterly flat country-side; cyclists and workers on foot struggled head-down into the wind with their fur caps' ear-flaps streaming behind them, disciplined and determined, getting there.

The Wall itself is impressive enough, but to our minds it was slightly disappointing. The only section open to the public was entirely rebuilt 37 years ago. In effect, we were looking at a replica. There seemed to us something very Chinese about this wish to demonstrate what good condition everything is in, as if ruin would be a loss of national face. It's rather like rebuilding Hadrian's Wall, or those endless blocks of Workers' Apartments – an impressive but mis-aimed effort. Much more fascinating were the miles of out-of-bounds ruined Wall, snaking into the furthest distance along the wild crest of the hills.

For the first time we saw Kurt and Julie at work. They wanted a shot of someone climbing on the outside of a guard tower. Tony volunteered. The Arriflex camera was set up, Kurt crouched over it, Julie directed the bazooka-like microphone, Danny did the hand-clap that would enable later synchronization of sight and sound, and off Tony went. He climbed nimbly up the Wall, crawled through an arch, and ran round to the bottom again, his film career over. But Kurt coughed and said 'Vun more time please?' We would come to loathe and dread those words.

Tony climbed the Wall again and again under Kurt's direction while we huddled in the bitter wind, at once amused and apprehen-sive. When the climbing take was done to Kurt's satisfaction, 'And now, Tony, one more time for the close-up of the hands, yes?' The hands were turning blue, but Tony complied. Then the cameras were carried to the top of the wall for close-ups of Tony's face. We began to realize that this film would not be a hand-held camera cinéma vérité job. Instead Kurt had a very clear idea of what he wanted; he was manufacturing a reality, and directed his actors accordingly.

Someone remarked that if it was this cold here, imagine what it was going to be like on Everest. Kurt jumped on the remark, 'Good, that is good! Vill you say that again please . . . Yes, and then he say . . .' So Nick and I made our 'spontaneous' remarks half a dozen times while camera and sound were co-ordinated and we finally got it right.

Mixed reactions in the team. Jon admired Kurt and Julie's professionalism, Sandy was fascinated by the imaginative and technical aspects of filming. Some were amused (particularly those who weren't being filmed), while others felt unease and the first stirrings of resentment. Are we going to have to do this on the hill? Bugger that. Acting made us feel foolish because we were very bad at it, and that too generated irritation.

'When he gets behind a camera,' Jon noted, 'amiable Uncle Kurt suddenly becomes Joseph Goebbels.'

Signs of private enterprise at the Great Wall included women and boys selling *I CLIMBED THE GREAT WALL* T-shirts, Red Guard hats, postcards and paintings, at considerably cheaper prices than the official Tourist Shop. This was clearly permitted; our impression was that whatever happened in China was permitted. If it wasn't permitted, it didn't happen. Smiling was permitted, and the Chinese tourists at the Wall seemed to be having a marvellous time, taking pictures of the Wall, each other, and of the strange, jabbering foreigners climbing up the guard tower.

Then on to the Ming emperors' tombs, with lunch on the way, ready and waiting for us in a barn-like restaurant. The tombs are approached by a long, wide avenue lined with giant guardian warriors like 20-foot-high chess pieces, and a menagerie of stone elephants and camels. Inevitably some of the lads tried to climb these. The smooth, rounded backside of an elephant proved too hard, but Chris made his first ascent of a camel, leaping for its ear and mouth then pulling up from there ('Very necky'). He tried to repeat it for Kurt but found himself running out of strength – he'd been much too busy in the last two months to train at all – and had to be assisted by a leg-up from someone remaining out of the shot. 'Film is to snaps what the Himalaya is to Scotty,' Jon wrote that night. The tombs themselves are all underground and in the end only Rick, Nick and Sarah, who had managed to escape the filming, had time to see them. Jack checked his watch. 'And now we go back to hotel.'

Meanwhile Mal, Allen Fyffe and Dave Bricknell had gone to the CMA offices to check over our 'protocol' for the Expedition – part schedule, part financial agreement, detailed down to the last Yuan and yak for carrying gear from Base to Advance Base. Then they went shopping for the kind of common, heavy things there had been no point in bringing from the UK: pans, kitchen utensils, kettles and stoves. With a poor interpreter, this turned out to be a struggle.

They were taken to a store that sold electric toasters. Mal eventually explained that these would be of limited use at Base, and said we wanted the kind of stoves rural people used to cook with – thinking of the paraffin stoves used in Nepal and Pakistan. He was told that in that case we'd need to buy an awful lot of coal. It appeared there were no paraffin stoves in Peking, and precious little paraffin. This was baffling, because most of such stoves one finds in the Third World are marked 'Made in China'. We were assured we'd be able to buy them in Chengdu (our next stop in southern China) or in Lhasa.

The shopkeepers also appeared taken aback when they heard of the one huge and five medium-sized cattle we wanted to buy. Even when the cattle resolved into 'kettles' we had little satisfaction, so they too were put off till later.

Back at the hotel, a demonstration of Chinese punctuality. Jack announced, 'It is now one minute to seven. At seven o'clock we will eat dinner.' We sat in silence for some forty seconds. 'Now we go to dinner.' We descended the stairs and entered the enormous, empty dining room on the stroke of seven.

Dinner as always in China was a survival of the fastest; those who were slow with chopsticks tended to go hungry. Tony fantasized about chip butties as he tried yet again to pick up a slippery fungus. 'So where's the tomato ketchup?' the homesick Lancastrian complained. The food was never inspiring, but this was compensated for by the bottles of Green Leaf beer that came with every meal. 'Alcohol is very good for the high altitude,' Urs asserted enthusiastically.

'Is it really?' Danny asked innocently, eager to learn from these old-timers' experience.

'For sure,' Sandy replied, 'it stops you from ever getting there!'

That evening Jack took us through a recognizably 'downtown' area of Peking where there was a certain amount of night life, and turned into a theatre where we were to see a show of acrobats. The theatre was shabby and so was the audience; the sets were grubby, the costumes worn and tatty – holes in the tights and missing sequins – the music and lighting were hamfisted, the magicians were embarrassing with their transparent tricks . . . Against this shoddy and cut-rate backdrop shone an incomparable display of dance-juggling-contortion-tumbling-gymnastics.

We sat transfixed, hooked to every impossible development. Allen Fyffe reflected that if these near-children ever took up rock climbing, they'd be tackling 6b routes inside a week. The acrobats had that ideal combination of strength, balance, muscular control, nerve and absolute concentration. Like climbing at its most extreme, what we saw transcended the physical and became pure expression, devoid of practical value. In the finale, the whole troupe built a pyramid of themselves, an inverted pyramid resting on one person's headstand on a chair tilted back on two legs, each branching out higher on each other's legs, arms, shoulders, heads, backs . . . If we were to climb our mountain, that is the way it would be done.

Bob So far China has made a very good impression on me, and I found the fantastic, relaxed ability of the acrobats to be inspiring in its accomplishment. At first sight this does seem to be a much more equal society than Western or other Asian ones – there seems to be no grinding poverty, and if there are fat cats then the material signs of them are few. The people are obviously worked hard, but the cheerfulness and tranquillity that is seen in many faces, and the wonderful performances of tonight, make it hard to accept that they are really crushed under the iron heel of socialism!

Next morning we boarded a four-propellered Ilyushin to fly across China to Chengdu, the capital of Szechuan province in southern China. It was a bright, sunny morning and the Expedition was in high spirits. Mal as usual appeared immersed in a book, but was taking in the feel of the conversation round him: anecdotes, jokes, teasing, planning, discussion – yes, we were beginning to pull together. You can't force people to become a team, only let them. He'd keep a low profile as long as possible. What worried him more were the fragile logistics of the minimal oxygen plan . . .

Through much of the Expedition, Mal will be reading, lying in his tent, or sitting smoking with his headphones on. And though he will seldom show it except by a now habitual crease across his forehead, there is scarcely a minute when he is not thinking, anticipating, calculating, worrying. He is ageing several years in the course of a few months.

The Szechuan countryside round Chengdu was a mild, green world of order and fertility. Flat fields of rice, rape, beans, lettuce, divided

by irrigation channels, hedges and trees. Half-timbered, almost Elizabethan farmhouses hid in clumps of willows; piglets, hens, ducks
and goats scratched in the yards. Poplar trees lined the road to
Chengdu, where children waited for the bus home from school.
There were little outdoor cafés in village squares, old faces placid
behind cigarettes, young men playing badminton in a farmyard, two
neighbours leaning to talk over a hedge, mothers cycling leisurely
home with babies strapped to their shoulders, rosy-cheeked children
standing on the saddles behind their fathers. After the winter bleak-
ness round Peking, this seemed a land where it was always spring.
An idyll glimpsed from a bus window, of an ordered, organic, peace-
filled rural world that was at once lovely and unlikely in the late
afternoon haze and mellow setting sun.

Jon looked for the credits to Hornby Model Railways; Bob with
his leftish sympathies was gratified by this vision of human, tranquil
well-being.

Entering Chengdu at twilight, and more acres of building sites
where hundreds of men and women worked with pick and shovel,
mixed concrete by hand, excavated earth in baskets on their backs.
Stone masons straddled blocks of grey stone, we could see the
hammers rise and fall and straight lines emerge from shapeless rock.
'These are serious people,' Sandy commented. Serious but not solemn
as they remake, reshape this vast country. They work steadily, patiently, often 10 hours a day on a six-day week. They have an absolute
guarantee of work, housing, education and medical care; when they
retire, their pension will be paid in full by the State. We laugh
because their Western-style clothes, shops, buildings, technology are
30 years behind us, but deep down we're impressed and slightly
intimidated by their sense of common purpose.

The downtown centre is lively with small private stalls selling
furniture and books, food and toys and clothes. Our hotel is at once
swish and half-built. We walk along a gangway in mid-air to enter
the plush hangar of a dining room. Acrylic blankets, plastic table
lamps, Bakelite telephones, the ubiquitous rose-painted vacuum
flasks of boiling water, the tea caddy and handleless cups, pastel-
coloured Formica. Across the street, near the only statue of Mao
we've seen so far, is an empty lot scheduled for building more
workers' apartments and hotels. In it stands a 100-foot-high sculpture in white concrete, in a pure Art Nouveau style: perched on the
rim of a colossal wheel, as on the lip of a breaking wave, a man
and a woman gaze heroically forward, one hand shading the eyes.

'What's that about?' Sandy asks at my elbow.

'The future, I should think.'

We stand on the balcony as the light fades. Old-fashioned dance music is playing somewhere, two watchfires are burning the last of the rubbish in the empty lot. The flames light the statue and their smoke obscures it. Here they believe in the future. They believe in it so much they may make it come true, like Malcolm's expedition. But our sense of purpose extends only to our personal lives and this self-created drama we're entering. That is how it feels as Sandy and I stand silently in the cool night air until the fires burn down and Jack calls us for the evening meal.

The food that night was more unagreeable than usual, and featured as its highlight '1,000-year-old eggs'. 'So what's this egg like?' Allen asked.

'Um . . . indescribable,' Jon replied.

'That's not what I wanted to know,' Allen returned firmly, pushing back his cap.

'Well, that's all I can tell you, mate,' Jon volleyed back, then added 'In climbing terms you could describe it as "interesting".'

But Allen had been playing these games for years. 'You mean, at the limit of your abilities,' he retorted with just enough stress on 'your' to make and win the point, and just enough humour for it to be conceded with honour. For once Jon had no reply and could only shake his head and laugh. It looked as though he'd finally met his match in verbal sparring, and his respect increased for Old Man Fyffe – not that that would stop him from trying again later.

Mal was unwinding in the short break between his responsibilities in Peking and in Lhasa. When after three Green Leaf beers he picked up and swallowed whole a brown putrified egg, it signalled the beginning of a Session. The tired and sensible began to drift away. 'Get it down your necks!' Jon urged the remainder. He was in high good humour, the good-time ringleader, drinking and partying late at every opportunity. 'Well, when there's this many climbers, you don't feel the same responsibility and pressure on you to perform.'

That night, after a few more beers were downed, Jon told Mal that he and Tony had agreed that their likely role on this expedition would be that of early revvers who would probably burn out quite quickly. This fatalistic attitude upset Malcolm. 'Look, Jon, if you're smart enough to realize you might rev early on and burn out, why not be smart enough not to?'

'That's just the way we are mate. We'll do our bit and then others can take over.' The argument heated up, with Liz, Andy Nisbet and myself as spectators. Liz was tense in empathy with Mal; Andy knew he was of necessity of the 'slowly-slowly' school and wondered if he'd be able to make any contribution on the hill. Tony restated the case: he and Jon wanted to go to 8,000 metres without oxygen and for someone to go to the top. 'Yes, but what if these conflict? What if everyone just wants to go to 8,000 metres and then leave it up to someone else?' There was urgency as well as irritation in Mal's voice. He'd been worrying about this; it could well be that some of the lads had come along for the ride, for a free trip to Everest and a chance to go to 8,000 metres and so break into the big league. Sandy was of the same mind as Mal, had murmured to me in one of his casual asides, 'I can imagine myself on the top – I wonder if any of these other guys do.'

One did. Rick Allen sat reading the New Testament, wondering who'd be prepared to go through the Pinnacles with him, without oxygen. He had a feeling it would come to that. Or could he solo it? He had never yet failed in the Himalayas, and he was prepared to push the boat out a long way to keep that record. On the other hand, he didn't want to die. There was a ridge to walk between under-achievement and unjustified risk; he believed it could end in the summit of Everest. He returned to the Bible.

The argument heated up as Jon accused Mal of having too many preconceived plans and projections and computer flow-charts (of which of course he had none, Jon retorted he was speaking figuratively, Liz said you should be more careful what you say then). After another hour's drinking and arguing they all agreed that one had to have detailed plans worked out in advance, even in the face of the certain knowledge that events would work out differently. If anyone had preconceptions, Liz pointed out, it was Jon and Tony, who still stuck to their picture of themselves as early trail-blazers who would also burn out early. A choir of soloists, I thought, some of them miming, some saving themselves, some refusing to catch the conductor's eye, some selflessly supporting . . .

Jon looked across the table at a ruffled Mal and said, with 500-watt blue-eyed sincerity, 'Yet you know at the end of the day we'll work our balls off to make this trip succeed.'

I left on this harmonious note. Chris and I were woken in the early hours by Jon pounding on the door, exuberant and giggling. 'Duff's on pure babble,' he reported, and collapsed in the corner. We were treated to the unusual sight of Tony 'tired and emotional' as he tried to flop on to his bed, missed, and fell full length on the floor. 'Oh dear . . . I don't think I feel too well . . . I can't ket my heys from my hocket . . .' Malcolm they had propelled into Liz's room with a plastic rose clenched between his teeth, and we could hear them shouting at each other two doors down as we floated back to sleep on a sea of Green Leaf beer.

On the Loose in Lhasa

'Yes we're going to a Lhasa party . . .'

This is it at last. Tibet, the high country, the Forbidden Kingdom, the near-mythical land resonating from childhood books. We stand blinking in the fiercely bright early morning sunlight on the tarmac at Lhasa Airport, and look for fifty miles across the brown Tibetan plateau and its flanking hills. I look up into the depths of the dark blue empty sky. The jet engines wind down.

'This is *the business*,' Jon says quietly.

The four-hour coach ride to Lhasa itself is joy for all except Malcolm and Andy Nisbet. Our leader had distinguished himself by occupying the airplane's toilets both taking off and landing, and now hangs white-faced out of the window, looking down at the dust. 'Must have been that 1,000-year-old egg,' he groans again. 'A thousand beers more like,' Liz retorts firmly, resolutely unsympathetic. The rest of us are raised, light-headed and high, high on altitude and the excitement of the new. The altitude of 3,600 metres has a noticeable effect when one flies straight to it. We begin the three-month discipline of breathing slowly and deeply, moving economically, monitoring ourselves all the time.

The road follows the mirror-smooth river Tsang Po towards Lhasa. Sunlight flashes from the oars of an inflated hide raft; someone waves and the gesture remains etched in the air long after it's over. At every bend in the road and river, every bridge, at the corners of the fields, there are little cairns of stones, and on them prayer flags attached to bamboo twigs. They bob and ripple in the breeze: red, yellow, white against the sky, colours strong and simple as our joy. Our heads are turning, turning, wanting to miss nothing. A flock of miniature sheep; Red Army soldiers looking cool and pissed off in shades as they supervise the road-building, carts piled high with Tibetan road-workers. A tall, shy girl laughs as a young man pulls off her dusty face-mask for the camera. They wave, or stare back at us with equal curiosity. These are mountain people:

high cheekbones, a slight ochre-mahogany about their complexions, strong noses, almond eyes like a classic Buddha's or glimpsed in Archaic Greek statues, long black hair coiled up on their heads. Their racial and cultural connections with the Nepalese, Afghanis and Baltis are evident; they also echo features of the North American Indians. Like other mountain people, they laugh, stare directly, seem unburdened by their hard lives.

Sandy leans forward behind me and murmurs, 'It's getting so I feel more at home out here than when I'm home. The mountain villages *are* my home.' He could be reading my heart, which is full with a sense of returning, of coming home to a world I'd known in Baltistan. Mountain living and mountain people; transparencies of light and colour; clarity of thought and feeling, a way of life uncluttered as the landscape; a sensation of elevation and lightness even while the body is made heavy and weak through lack of oxygen. The mountain villages of Tibet, Baltistan, and Nepal, seem like the last remnants of an original world, one long since flooded, leaving only these fragments clinging on in high places.

Dave The girls have brilliant pink or emerald green head-dresses. They are so alive – mahogany faces with a blank look until you wave or say hello and then they all, without fail, grin all over with glistening white teeth and transformed, pretty faces. And they are very pretty – and shy, many hiding as soon as you produce a camera, with the men young and old asking for their photos to be taken. Total poverty.

A shattering experience – the air – the mountains – the people, all in one morning. The transition from 707 to a dirt track in 160 feet, from an airport to medieval dwellings in half a mile. Yet the most natural warmth I've ever seen, better than the mercenary warmth of Rio.

Meanwhile Sandy muses to himself what his life would be without climbing and expeditions. It's been so long now, he can only remember that ordinary life was not enough. Yet climbing, one expedition after another, can become its own sort of treadmill. Hey, youth, you're nearly 30, what are you doing with your life? These moments of doubt . . . Then, looking out across Tibet, certainty.

We entered Lhasa in the afternoon, a hotch-potch of half-built hotels and wide, planned streets on the outskirts; concrete, corrugated iron, narrow alleyways and traditional Tibetan houses clustered in the old centre. Their walls incline towards each other and would meet at some blue unmarked apex several hundred feet up; the windows repeat that configuration, which at once suggests great sturdiness yet elegance in its tapering line. The colours are strong and simple: dazzling white, black surrounds, ochre, green, yellow, and blue on the eaves and shutters and awnings.

Then someone points and for the first time we see the Potala – former residence of the Dalai Lamas, home of the living incarnation of God, the ancient centre of government of feudal Tibet. It is lodged high on a rock outcrop in the centre of the city, looking like a great ocean liner run aground; brilliant white trimmed with black and a particular sacred shade of ochre beneath the eaves, deck after deck rising to flat roofs on many different levels, topped with what look like gold funnels, glinting in the sun. It is quite unsymmetrical, the result of organic accretion rather than planning, yet the result is harmonious. It is one of those few buildings that transcend building altogether and hit straight to the heart. The coach turns down a wide boulevard and the vision disappears.

Our hotel is a row of rooms strung together along one side of a dusty compound. The rooms are pleasingly plain and clean, but we're being charged £90 per person per night for them. These exorbitant rates are set for expeditions and organized groups, though enterprising individuals can find rooms for around £2. That and the transport charges make expeditions in Tibet prohibitively expensive.

It was here that the famous Chinese efficiency fell apart, precipitating us into our first major crisis. The news was broken in typical fashion. Through Jack, Luo warned us this was the windy season and we should wrap up well going into the mountains. We thanked him for his kind thoughts. Then came the punchline. 'Unfortunately, due to this bad weather, some of your luggage is delayed in Chengdu.'

What?! Why didn't they tell us when we were in Chengdu and could have done something about it? They probably didn't want to lose face and admit something had gone wrong. The luggage in question turns out to be some 200 boxes, including many barrels of climbing gear, the oxygen cylinders, and all our camping gas – the consignment we'd rushed desperately to have sent out a month in advance, because the Chinese wouldn't carry gas or oxygen on internal flights so they had to go by road and rail from Peking to Lhasa.

Jack and Luo are embarrassed, while the local CMA man smirks, unconcerned and unapologetic. We insist on a phone call to Chengdu, from where we are assured that our luggage will be flown promptly to Lhasa. How long will it take? 'Three days' is the reply. This will not only cost a deal of extra money in hotel bills, but also foul up the transport arrangements from here on in. Above all, we are worried about the gas and oxygen. If the Chinese stick to their ban on transporting it by air, then it would take three weeks to arrive by road – in which case we might as well go home. But we dare not ask directly about this volatile consignment in case they've overlooked its nature.

Tense times in the hotel Reception. Dave Bricknell is in his element. As Pilkington's Company Secretary he's been involved in delicate and stressful negotiations all over the world. He knows one must never back the Chinese into a corner where they may lose face. Instead pressure must be applied softly softly, with the velvet glove of compliments and the merest hint of the iron fist beneath.

This sort of thing: 'We in the Pilkington Everest Expedition are very grateful for all the help and co-operation offered by the Chinese Mountaineering Association, in meeting the arrangements made in Peking.' (This to remind both Luo and the local CMA man of their bosses in Peking, and of their answerability if anything goes wrong.) 'Now we are told some of our luggage is delayed in Chengdu.' (The merest hint of a reproach in that 'now'.) 'We accept that this is not your fault.' (He is offering them a face-saving way out, while at the same time that 'accept' as opposed to 'know' hints at the opposite of what it says. He follows this up and underlines the point.) 'We believe that this is because of bad weather.' (Meaning, we don't necessarily believe this at all, but we're prepared to accept your excuse.) 'We need your help in sorting this out quickly, for the protocol agreed on in Peking allows only for two days here. We are confident that you can help us resolve this situation.' (The repetition of 'Peking', reference to our previous financial agreement, the first suggestion that any costs outside that should be met by the CMA, the scrupulous 'confident', at once flattering and sceptical. A masterly performance all delivered clearly, carefully, politely but with considerable firmness.)

The Chinese assure us that our luggage will arive here soon. They suggest we leave on schedule for Everest and our luggage will catch us up. Dave looks at Sandy, who's effectively Leader because Mal's out of it with his hangover. Sandy shakes his head firmly. Without oxygen, gas and personal gear we can do nothing; we can't move on till it comes.

The Chinese assure us again that our luggage will be arriving soon, but ask what alternative plans we have if it doesn't. This is very worrying. Sandy clears his throat 'Our alternative plans are we go home.'

A meeting is arranged for the next morning. We discuss the situation in our rooms; Dave sets out the various power ploys at our disposal. We can threaten to call off the trip – that would certainly look bad for the CMA and the Chinese Government (Dave has casually mentioned the media coverage of our Expedition). Trouble is, they know this is something we have no intention of doing. We can argue that the considerable expense of delay here must be borne by the CMA so it's in their interests to hurry it up – but they can reverse that argument and say seeing it's *our* expense we should set off and let our luggage follow. And there's the ticklish question of the gas and oxygen.

A crisis like this happens on practically every expedition. Very occasionally it means the end. Always it means anxiety. We had begun to think China would not be like that. Sandy sums it up as we disperse for bed, worried and slightly headachy, 'It's not a problem . . . Actually, it's pretty bad!'

We woke to uplifting Chinese music from the army barracks over the wall, and sparrows quarrelling in the dust. I lay with a mild altitude headache, watching the curtain-shadow flicker on the blue ceiling and wondering when I'd lie here again and after what experiences.

Resting at altitude is like convalescing after illness; there's the same sense of light-headed clarity and almost pleasurable weakness. From now on we had to discipline ourselves to drinking at least 9 pints of fluid a day, which, along with husbanding one's resources and not becoming hassled, is the crux of looking after oneself at altitude. The raw, inflamed throats and mucus-filled sinuses, the irritating and inescapable symptoms of being at altitude, had already started though we were only at some 3,600 metres.

I drank three mugs of tea while Allen Fyffe did his daily yoga routine. His self-discipline and quiet organization marked out the old hand. He seemed less grim and forbidding now, gifted with a Scottish, sardonic humour. We discovered a mutual liking for what Jon calls 'old hippie music' and talked for hours about obscure bands of the '60s. If anything irritated or upset Allen, he kept it to himself. Mature behaviour: expressing negative emotions is not appropriate to long expeditions, where tolerance, tact and self-control are more important than emotional honesty.

Over breakfast, Dave Bricknell was cosseted like a prize-fighter for his meeting with the Chinese. In the event, they assured us that our gear would arrive that night or the next day, so there was nothing we could do but wait and hope and acclimatize. And explore Lhasa . . .

The Lhasa bazaar is one of the last great ethnic experiences. It has been going on essentially unchanged for centuries, though it may well not survive the planned onslaught of Western tourists. It centres round a quadrangle in the heart of the old town, backing on to the Jo-Kang temple. It is this mingling of pilgrimage and trading that creates the character of the place.

The people: Red Guards both Chinese and Tibetan, shaven monks in ochre robes, the tall Lhasa girls with jet-black hair and almond eyes, traders and shop-owners, pilgrims prostrating themselves in the streets, local wide-boys dealing in style and black-market currency, nomadic families in from the hinterland on their annual visit to sell skins and produce, going to the shrines, and buying the few necessities they don't make themselves. The varied crowd moves clockwise round the rectangle of streets, clockwise being the religious direction, the direction in which the universe turns. We walk anti-clockwise, meeting Tibet face-on, overwhelmed by colour, sound, smell and sights. Soldier, monk, trader, farmer, nomad, all the immemorial trades jostle here. And now we climbers, the only Westerners in sight. To wander the streets of the Lhasa bazaar is to walk past all the ways your life might once have been.

The nomadic families are sheep-on-two-legs, clothed mostly in skins and smelling strongly of them. They are dark and weathered, at once shy and aloof, as if carrying something of the silence and solitude of the high Tibetan plateau around with them in the midst of this crowd. Many men carry a long knife on one hip and a short skean dhu type knife on the other. Both sexes wear their shining hair long, commonly braided up on their heads with a string of turquoise beads and real or artificial coral. Some wear big lumps of turquoise hanging from their ears, so heavy that a loop is sometimes worn over the ear to stop the lobe being painfully stretched.

We were stared at as much as we stared. Our clothes and beards amused the locals, while crowds would gather round to examine Andy Nisbet's wild red hair. Allen's balding pate was also found to be very entertaining, and several people ran their hands over it with giggling curiosity. We were obviously still something of a novelty, particularly at this time of year. Not for long. The Chinese expect 5,000 visitors to Tibet in 1985, 40,000 the next, 100,000 the next – making one tourist for every ten Tibetans. Thus the huge hotels being built on the outskirts of Lhasa in such labour-intensive, furious haste.

At staging-posts around the bazaar, huge pot-bellied incense burners puffed the smoke of sacred aromatic shrubs into the air already redolent with yak butter, meat, joss sticks and drying skins. We pushed our way slowly into the human flow in a daze of sensory over-stimulation, past the stalls and shops selling daily produce, plastic gewgaws, religious offerings, souvenirs and texts, prayer-scarves and prayer-flags, books, new and antique knives, silver, brass, pewter, bells, bowls, incense-burners, candles, teeth and scriptures and Abba cassettes.

It's a place to which one needs to return several times – once to take pictures, once to haggle and buy, once to participate, once to observe and once for the sheer delight of it. We were frequently approached by money-changers wanting to exchange Chinese *renmindbi* for our official tourist currency to allow them to buy goods in the Tourist shops that accept only the tourist yuan (30–50 per cent extra *remimbi* is a reasonable rate to bargain for). Locals and nomadic men and women want to sell knives off their hips, necklaces and lumps of coral and turquoise, rings off their fingers, yak bells and medallions. We felt ambivalent about buying these personal possessions.

Negotiations attract amiable and curious crowds of onlookers; it is slightly claustrophobic being so surrounded, but in fact the situation was always hassle free. One has to enter into the spirit of bargaining as a game. Prices were written on the back of the hand; one would shrug, register sheer disbelief, regret or amusement at the price, then write another on the seller's hand. He or she would then reel back in smiling astonishment, but quickly come back with another price. At that point one reveals that one knows the difference between yuan and *renmindbi*, and serious bargaining may then take place. They were scrupulously honest, even in the mildly illegal money-changing, which frequently entailed the other fellow holding your money as he bargained and counted out his. A woman pursued me through the crowd to return 5 *renmindbi* change I'd forgotten to pick up.

Dave Elsewhere in the streets you see a mixture of Tibetans in traditional dress, in Chinese dress, and Chinese. But in the bazaar virtually all were in traditional dress of various types – heavy black multi-layered skirts, jackets and aprons, with bright head-dresses; very heavy sheepskin jackets and trousers, marvellous fur hats – some with gold and silver embroidery. Fascinating and fascinated. You only had to stop for two minutes and a crowd was around you, offering goods, wanting to have their photos taken, all happy and delighted to see you. I've never been so relaxed.

Allen, Bob, Sandy, Urs and I all bought cowboy-style hats to protect us from the wind and fierce sun of the Tibetan plateau. They particularly suited the small and slightly bow-legged Allen Fyffe and his larger side-kick Bob, and from then on the duo were known as 'the

Glenmore cowboys' from the outdoor centre at which they both worked.

Expeditions develop their own fashions as well as catch-phrases. On this one it was cowboy hats and prayer-scarves knotted round the throat. They were felt to be 'good joss' and wouldn't be removed till we arrived back in the UK. Most of us had our talismans. Bob's was a felt mouse, a childhood toy of his wife Anna. It had already been to the top of Kalanka and Baghirathi. Mal's was a champagne cork, but for the first time he'd forgotten it in the rush and pressures of putting the trip together. He tried to attach no significance to this. Rick wore a necklace given to him in Kathmundu. With Sandy it was his Peruvian hat, for Jon his Rasta hat. Dave Bricknell had Jewish lucky money from his wife Ilush. One becomes superstitious, reading significance into the smallest event, when life may depend upon luck and an indefinable intuition as much as skill and rational judgement. I fingered the round stone hanging from my neck that Kathleen had placed there with briefly serious tenderness that last night in London . . .

Like a wind out of nowhere, these gusts of absence brushed us all from time to time.

After lunch we visited the Sera monastery, more a village than a building, nestled into the brown foothills near Lhasa. Jack told us it was some 500 years old, but had been 'partially destroyed' during the 'Democratic Rebirth' of Tibet. It had once housed 10,000 monks, who were killed or sent to work on collective farms. But now the Chinese had methodically rebuilt and re-established it as a working religious community of some 5,000 monks, many of them young.

It is at once sprawling and compact, random and ordered. Brilliant white walls trimmed with ochre, golden towers on the flat roofs, a maze of courtyards and alleyways opening on to more courtyards, temples, residences and workshops. In one workshop two very bored Chinese soldiers were helping in the printing of scriptures.

We wandered through prayer halls like dim forests, their wooden tapering pillars hung with tapestries, where a shaft of light from a solitary high window bisected the gloom. Room after room of small shrines lined with paintings, carvings and statues of past Lamas, gods and demons and Buddhas. There were paintings of dragons, snakes and pigs to symbolize the overcoming of the vices of vanity, desire and ignorance. The air was soft and thick with incense and yak butter candles. A solitary monk chanted softly in one corner of a tiny room, another blew his nose. The statues were draped in layers of mouldering prayer-scarves like thick spiders' webs, through which glistened dully precious stones, paint and gold leaf. It was impossible to tell what was made last year or hundreds of years ago, for the dimness and smokey air made everything seem equally ancient, timeless and unmoving. We spoke in whispers though no one told us to, our camera shutters clicked in the gloom.

Outside we came across rocks with shallow depressions and a runnel down the side. They were for the Tibetan ritual of sky-burials. The corpse is dismembered and laid out on these stones to be picked clean by birds and so returning the body (and spirit) to the sky; the runnels were for the blood. It is still practised, though discouraged. It might put tourists off their lunch. To us it seemed at once gruesome and poetic, no stranger than returning the body to the earth. The sky in Tibet is so big it seems to reconcile all things, including the place of death in life. The need for that reconciliation had obscurely brought some of us to mountaineering in the first place.

Nothing sombre in our musings as we sat on these rocks above the Sera monastery and looked across the plain in the direction of Everest, just a sense of shifting a step nearer to understanding.

We woke once more to Chinese opera and announcements on the tannoy. Jack came in to breakfast, excited. 'The Russian Chernenko, he is dead.' He raised his thumbs, grinning broadly. 'Three in two years!' We received the news with casual interest; we were focused on one thing only – getting to Everest and having a crack at the North-East Ridge. It's irresponsible but something of a relief not to read the papers, scarcely to think about politics, money, scandal, world events. The things left behind are part of the pleasure as well as the pain of a long expedition.

We went to visit the Potala. To the Tibetans it must have been Buckingham Palace, Westminster Abbey, Whitehall and the Houses of Parliament all in one, for it fulfilled all those functions. Now it has none of them, and the result is an oddly empty, museum-like feel. As yet unacclimatized, we struggled slowly up the zigzag steps to the entrance. Mal lit a cigarette and, feeling slightly dizzy, threw it away, reflecting that extra time spent here waiting for our gear would at least give us more time to acclimatize.

Kurt and Julie were filming us, so our progress upwards was slow. Sometimes we had to descend and start again. It was with some relief and banging hearts that we finally entered the interior dimness.

Much of it was like the Sera monastery, only scaled up and uninhabited. We were the only visitors. The Potala is said to have 10,000 rooms, most of them dating from the 17th century but we saw only a fraction of them. The same dim chanting halls with immense tapering wooden pillars hung with rich *thankas*, religious silk paintings. Behind the halls were a series of small shrine rooms, each devoted to earlier Dalai Lamas, their cross-legged statues draped with prayer-scarves and studded with beaten metal, turquoise, rubies, lapis lazuli. Dozens of smaller figures lined the walls, each as richly decorated, each individual. In large vats of yak butter burning candles floated, and horizontal prayer-wheels spun silently in the updraught. A distant tinkling of wind-chimes, a muttering of prayers from some unseen source.

We could not take photos; we had to look and experience and remember rather than consume with our cameras. In the room dedicated to the last Dalai Lama we stood a long time in silence, just looking and smelling and thinking in the flickering dimness. We were all touched by something in this alien but palpable holiness. I felt curiously out of myself, looking at our faces in the candlelight: Bob serious, eyes closed and fingers linked; Rick thin-faced, rapt and abstracted; Dave Bricknell solemn but calm, absolutely still. I was not the only one wordlessly praying for our safety through the weeks ahead of us on the Ridge.

We moved from room to room, up one flight after another, thirteen in all, connected by old wooden ladders, past the brightly painted quarters of the Dalai Lama, and came out finally on the roof, into the dazzling light. A sense of elevation up there, looking out over Lhasa, across the plain to the distant hills and tranquil river. The power of the place is in this elevation and the simple purity of its colours. Most of us sat there marvelling, while the others were roped in for more filming. Again, a sense of deep peace, the fullness of the present movement buoying us up as the air buoyed up the solitary buzzard drifting overhead.

Back to lunch and harsh reality. Danny Lewis suddenly collapses from altitude and exhaustion, after toting round film gear for the last couple of days, hurrying after Kurt, not drinking enough. He looks pale and in shock as Urs attends to him. 'I told them so,' Jon says.

Worse, our gear has still not turned up. We'd been assured it had all arrived at Lhasa airport last night, so why is it not here? As usual, the CMA evade the question and thus fuel our mounting paranoia. 'Phone the airport and find out what's happened to it.' Ah, but the lines are down. They don't seem very perturbed. Dave Bricknell tries again: 'If all our gear's arrived in Lhasa Airport – and because you assured us it has, we know that must be true –

why is it not here now?' Perhaps the trucks have broken down, they suggest. Three trucks, *all* broken down? Come off it.

Round and round in circles as the Chinese deflect our questions. Even Dave is visibly tense and angry. The CMA ask us again what our second plan is if the gear doesn't arrive. What are they trying to prepare us for? 'We have no second plan,' Mal says finally. 'Our second plan is we go home.'

They suggest again that we go on to Xegar where our gear will catch up with us. We propose instead to take a jeep to Lhasa airport to find out just what's happening. At this point Jack looks embarrassed, Mr Luo unhappy and the CMA man worried. 'I think someone's been telling little porky pies,' Jon murmurs.

And they have. Mal is finally allowed to talk directly with the CMA in Peking. They admit that not all our gear is at Lhasa airport; in fact some of it is still in Chengdu. We look at each other, all thinking the same thing – if it's the gas and oxygen and they're refusing to fly it, we're done for. Mal blows his top and says quite directly he doesn't like being told lies. He hands over the receiver to Dave before he loses his temper completely. Dave gives them such a firm and powerful statement of our position and intentions that, listening, we feel quite cowed. He extracts and has repeated several times a real, total, absolute assurance that all our gear will arrive here in the next two days. If that does not happen, we will turn round and go home and raise hell with all the publicity we can command. We will stay only if the gear, *all* the gear, arrives on time, on the understanding that we are not liable for the extra expenses in so doing. He gets another promise, but they fudge on the financial responsibility.

Now all we can do is wait. We're tired and anxious, and it takes a typical altitude-affected remark to release the tension. The conversation comes round to silly names. Mal 'Zowie Bowie – what a name to give a kid.' 'That's nothing,' Andy Nisbet mutters through his beard, blinking as he sits on his hands, 'There's a doctor on the West Coast whose name is Donald Duck.'

'Wow,' says Mal, 'it's sadism calling your kid that!'

'No,' Andy replies seriously, 'the whole family were called Duck.'

A pause, then the laughter broke. 'Summit material!' the cry goes up. 'Send that man to the top!'

Late that night, two trucks turned up. When we finished unloading and checking them next morning, one load was still missing. It included the vital gas and oxygen. Had they overlooked it, or refused to fly it? We dared not ask directly. After further phone calls, we were assured the last load would arrive at Lhasa airport the following day. We were beginning to wonder if this was simply bad organization by the Chinese, or a deliberate ploy to keep us here longer and so extract more money from us. The four-man Basque team bound for the North Col route had left here only a couple of days earlier, after a similar delay.

Sandy The day drifted by; Jon, Bob, Jack, Luo, Rick and I went to shop, to the Bazaar. Photos click click click. The mood of the shoppers was very tense at first, everybody wanting to stick their oar in, trying to tell each other that we all knew what we were up to. People seem to find it necessary to remind everybody that they are good at their jobs. I walked in silence, close to the walls, trying to take up little space as Jon and Rick and Bob analysed my shopping list. Once I'd bought a few things they seemed to be much more friendly, realizing perhaps that I did know what I was up to. We bought kettles, spoons, fish-slices and candles, searched for whisks and tin-openers to no avail, drums for fuel, etc., and a couple of sharp knives.

Bob returned to the hotel with a loaded rucksack and the rest of us wandered about, buying odds and ends. Bob bought me a prayer-scarf, a white one, it was a nice and decent gesture. It's impossible to say if we're on the same line or not!

Buying paraffin stoves continued to be impossible. After some bullying, two Red Army petrol stoves turned up. We were nervous of these cast iron Molotov cocktails which sprayed pressurized petrol in every direction but the intended. One refused to work at all. Perhaps we could find some spare parts in Xegar, the CMA man said, not looking too bothered either way.

A game of French Cricket in the courtyard. 'You lot are definitely Summit Material,' a lounging Tinker observed. 'You're all fucking crazy!' And Urs added, 'Medically this is not a good idea, but I hear you laughing, and this is good.' He was fitting in well despite his language difficulty: observant, conscientious without fussing, humorous. We were beginning to pull together as a group; people were still being careful with each other, but there were no troublesome character conflicts. The extra days in Lhasa made time for chat and laughter and exploration. And being here for a purpose saved us from the unease of travelling only to gawp at other people's lives.

Time also for homesickness. Tony still found himself thinking more of his Kathy than of Everest, and hoped that would change when he finally got to the hill. Watching the tall, graceful Tibetan girls laughing as they played basketball reminded us all too much of what we were missing. We envied Mal and Liz, Nick and Sarah. 'If I had Dominique along', Sandy confessed, 'I wouldn't bother leaving Base Camp!' and he wondered how it would affect the others' commitment.

Sandy We spun some golden prayer-wheels today, *ommanipadmehum* under my breath, feeling at ease in that place, but weird and watched. Prostrated persons, brains numbed with faith, can't help but wonder why.
   Long chat with Mal after lunch. We get a lot said in times like this. Andy G. strums and sings, green cap on his head; dust clouds round the hills, cool breeze wafts ethnic Tibetan scents. Danny recovering, actually washes, Bob struts around in his 10-gallon hat. Buds on the trees turning greener by the day, folks at ease, Expedition at a stop. Waiting for gear to arrive – some must come tonight. But life's okay. Drift in a set direction, we'll get to BC eventually.
   Could not help but notice quite a few hoarse voices as people called out box numbers to Dave B. My own throat is sore and red, and my nose runs profusely. I hope this all clears up before we depart or go higher. Spent the afternoon packing my gear. Lists made, more lists, expeditions are made of lists. In and out of rooms, checking people out – feeling at home, semi-getting around to talking. But there's a wall around me you can't even see . . .

Sarah I can't get over the sheer beauty of the place. I think I love the mornings best as the sun lights the hills, gradually warming up, a sharp clarity. Nick and I went through the bazaar eyeing the carpets – then on past the Potala up the hill opposite, on which used to stand the old Tibetan Medical School. Puffing hard to get up there, some really interesting carvings on the rock.
   Nick is really taken with the scruffy dogs. The children at the Potala were swinging from his hands all the way down the steps. He is persevering with my flute tonight – it isn't easy, being made from wood – I find it difficult.
   I guess it's inevitable that people should question my role and purpose here.

No more gear arrived that night, nor the next morning. Writing letters, reading, drinking tea, wandering the intricate alleyways of the old city with no purpose other than being there, alternating between acute frustration and simple delight.
   Then it was crisis time again. All our remaining gear had been promised to arrive at Lhasa airport that day. Mid-afternoon we were told that not all of it would arrive. By tea time this had deteriorated to none of it, and no promises as to when it would materialize. Mr Luo seemed genuinely embarrassed and powerless

as tempers rose. Chinese promises and guarantees had proved worthless; we insisted on one of us flying to Chengdu, finding out what was going on there – had our gear ever actually left Peking? – and return with it if possible. The CMA were dead against this, which made us even more suspicious. We made our strongest threat, essentially that we'd go home and raise hell about it; they refused to say yes and refused to say no. 'Well, what do you think, Jack?' Jack made a face, pushed his spectacles up his thin nose. 'I'm just Jack,' he replied neutrally.

While Mal, Sandy and Dave were locked for hours in a showdown negotiation, the rest of the Expedition let off steam in an impromptu party. We'd been storing up beer and frustration for days, and now let it rip. Jon was the Mad Ringmaster, exhorting, cajoling, producing an endless supply of beer from his barrel. 'More beer! Give that man another beer! Sweet as a nut . . . *Get it down your neck!*' As Reggae crackled from tiny speakers, Allen Fyffe told yarns of Scottish climbing in the early '60s, then others tried to cap them with tales of escapades in Chamonix, death and destruction, fiascos, of characters like Slippery and the Black Knight, Hands and Dirty Alex, of tragedy and comedy on the borderlines of anarchy, Kurt began building a column of empty cans from the floor to the ceiling; the project caught on, it was of the utmost importance that it should succeed. Accelerated drinking provided more empty cans. The more cans we had, the less capable we were of putting them together. Super glue was suggested, but ruled out as an unethical aid. Finally five of us managed to jam a column between floor and ceiling. Not tight enough . . . We inserted Bonington's *The Unclimbed Ridge*, a cassette, five Everest postcards. . . . The tensioned column swayed, buckled, was corrected . . . and held.

Rapturous applause. A metaphor for the trip so far Jon thought, tottering but still together.

Then a seven-foot-high pink rabbit crashed in through the door, pogoed frantically for a minute, posed beside the cans for a photo session, then ran amuck outside, chasing Mr Luo across the courtyard. The noise level was now deafening and the whole scene was beginning to make the Who trashing a hotel room seem like a flower-arranging class. When the ice-axes came out for mooted tree-climbing, it must have been obvious to the Chinese we were getting out of hand, for at 1.0 am they finally agreed to let Dave, Sandy and Luo take the jeep to Lhasa airport to fly to Chengdu.

They drove through the night, Luo shaking with anxiety as they kept the pressure on him. They broke down twice, were stuck once, then blocked by an accident. They reached the airport at dawn, then spent three hours trying to get on a flight. No one had enough cash, the airline refused to take cheques or a credit card. The whole future of the Expedition hung in the balance as Sandy and Dave bullied and threatened and finally Sandy's credit card was accepted as collateral for tickets for Luo and Dave, and he practically pushed them on to the plane before Luo could change his mind. Some collateral! The card alone was worth nothing, and besides, Sandy's financial motto is 'To die in credit is to die disgraced', so he is always heavily overdrawn before setting off on expeditions.

He waved them goodbye, and turned back to the jeep, suddenly weary. This would have to work.

I woke hungover, but forced myself to get up and go with Liz and Sarah on an acclimatization clamber up one of the ridges outside Lhasa. Most of the lads had already been up it to the braided ropes strung with prayer flags across the pinnacles at the top. Now it was our turn.

We took it slowly and steadily. I was reassured to be breathing heavily but not desperately, no altitude headache. I measured myself against Liz, who'd been to 5,000 metres on Mal's first Nuptse West Ridge expedition. We all do that – not always competition, just having someone to measure one's condition against. The young lads in a hurry, especially Jon, Rick and Tony, sped along eyeing each other for weakness and concealing their own. The older lads like Allen, Bob and Mal plodded along at their own pace, getting there just the same.

It was good to be out in the hills again, though the altitude pace was frustratingly slow. But that sense of spaciousness, physical and mental, of being on the move under a huge blue sky, offset the effort. Shattered rock, little cairns, dry shrubs, feet moving steadily up in the wind-silence, ravens drifting overhead. A little light-headed, like mild inebriation. It was peaceful and satisfying up there, like coming home to somewhere one had forgotten was home.

That evening brought no news from Dave in Chengdu. We celebrated Kurt and Julie's combined 99th birthday drinking Chinese sweet red wine and The McCallan whisky, chasing it down with beer and a slimy Chinese spirit amid the debris of last night's party. Things hot up quickly; I bash out a few climbing songs – it feels good to have a contribution to make. We reel next door to Reception to involve and chat up the three lovely, strapping Tibetan girls and soon install ourselves there with booze and music. Girls mean dancing, so I thrash my fingers raw on Julie's Spanish guitar playing rock-'n'-roll while the dancers leap and fall. Just as the girls are losing their shyness and the fun is most fast and furious, the shifty CMA man enters scowling and the girls quickly sit down and go silent. But Uncle Kurt grabs him, pushes him into a chair and pours an enormous whisky into his hand, than gets the girls up and going again. Something of a star, Kurt, absolute authority in a crisis.

So the party went on. The Pink Rabbit appeared, pogoed wildly with the tallest girl, then exited into the night. The CMA man hurriedly had another drink. Across the smokey room Allen Fyffe with a glassy, beatific smile poured himself half a pint of whisky. 'One-pint' Wattie was motormouthing, Mal on 'babble mode', Sandy in seventh heaven, trying to propose to the tallest and loveliest of the Tibetans.

They introduced us to the Tibetan custom of filling a glass, passing it to another of the company who then has to do a turn, drink, and pass it on. This brought out some star performances. Sandy Allan did a bizarre camp Highland scarf dance that left us gasping with laughter; Jon leapt on a table and delivered an inspired anti-Chinese version of 'They're removing Grandpa's grave'; Mal improvised a ditty on Dave's fortunes in Chengdu; the girls sang and shuffle-danced, Urs yodelled. Rick turned out to be hilarious when he lets himself go. Fyffe was unconscious but hadn't realized it yet; Tony, Bob and Nick delivered North of England ethnic ditties, Sarah sang; good to see her getting involved.

In the end the only non-performers were the sick Danny and 'the appalling, disgusting Nisbet', in Jon's phrase. Andy refused quietly to do anything, the lads kept pressing him, he sat on his hands and shook his head. Someone suggested that his turn should be simply to recite his top five unclimbed Scottish routes – a secret he guards like the Crown Jewels. The more they pressed him, the more he dug in his heels, the more they pressed him. Andy Nisbet is a very determined character underneath his diffidence. Eventually – in the first open display of bad temper seen on the trip – he simply walked out and banged the door behind him.

'Base Camp material!' Jon shouted joyfully. Liz criticized us for getting on at him. 'All take and no give,' someone commented. She was partly right, of course, but climbers always tend to give each other stress, it's part of the testing-out. Andy finds it impossible to get his emotions out, to speak of anything other than the purely factual. He's entitled to be like that, but the lads felt that on an expedition he has to try to contribute something. 'Even Dougal Haston could be bloody funny,' Allen Fyffe murmured from a horizontal position.

Not important. The party went on. It was three in the morning
when I finally blundered back to my room, clutching cowboy hat
and guitar and found Allen stretched out like a medieval effigy,
hands clasped on his chest. 'Not asleep, just dead,' I thought, and
gently switched his Walkman off.

'Somebody borrowed my body and abused it,' Allen moaned next
morning. Tony lay remembering the dream he'd had of arriving at
the summit of Everest: there seemed nothing very much to do there,
so he'd clipped into the Chinese tripod on the top and fallen
asleep . . . Chris Watts lived up to his nickname 'One Pint' by being
seriously ill for the next two days. His stomach cramps and acute
dehydration from being constantly sick made Urs inject him with
the most powerful nausea-suppressant drugs he had.

Round midday Dave Bricknell returned in triumph with our
remaining gear including the gas and oxygen. He had discovered
our gear in a room full of freight at Chengdu airport. It had arrived
there a day behind schedule weeks before and no one had got round
to loading it on a plane to Lhasa. If he hadn't intervened, it would
probably be there still. He'd managed to charter a plane, then he
and Luo sat in solitary splendour with the gear all the way back to
Lhasa, trying to figure out just how much this would cost and who
would pay for it in the end.

We'd worry about that later. What mattered was that he'd saved
the day and we were on the move again.

I took a last walk through Lhasa, its streets and temples and
bazaar. It was good to be on my own; most of us would wander
off alone from time to time. On expeditions solitude is something
one has too much then too little of. Behind the Potala is a shallow
lake and a small, brightly painted temple framed by flags and early
apple-blossom. Some nomads were there on pilgrimage: three children were being taught scriptures under an awning by a white-
bearded monk.

I sat by the edge of the lake. A cyclist silhouetted against the low
sun approached an arched bridge across the lake, dismounted; the
black figure pushed the bike slowly over the bridge, light flashed
from the spokes, then he slid back into the saddle and pedalled
leisurely away past four road-workers who stood like a Greek frieze
by the road, their long-handled shovels shouldered like pike. I
thought then of friends and family and the women I loved, all
leading their lives at that moment on the other side of the world,

all distant and separate but now pulled together by invisible threads of affection and memory.

Bob, Allen and I went one last time to the Jo-Kang temple in the bazaar. Though the Potala was the focus of spiritual and temporal authority in Tibet, the humbler Jo-Kang temple was and still is the centre of pilgrimage and religious life. It took us several days to realize that this modest-sized building, surrounded by the swirl of the bazaar, next to a building site where monks wearing gold coxcombs played moaning horns, is the Mecca of the Buddhist world.

The temple courtyard was strewn with men, women and children prostrating and praying. They stood facing the temple doors, fell to their knees and then in a swimming motion stretched flat out full-length, then back up again. This was repeated over and over, a sort of physical Hail Mary, a crucial act of reverence for the pilgrims who had taken days or sometimes weeks to trek across Tibet to renew themselves here. It looked like hard work.

Many of the pilgrims then prostrate their way around the cloisters of the inner courtyard. Those who are really serious about it can prostrate clockwise round the much larger quadrangle of the bazaar itself, through the dust and bustle. The tour-de-force is the outer circuit round old Lhasa, including the Potala, several miles of continuous prostration, advancing three steps at a time. It must take a day or more. But there's a dispensation that allows you, if you have a lot of bad karma to lose and are too busy, stiff or lazy to prostrate around Lhasa, to pay someone else as your stand-in. So we came across professional prostrators, marked out by the pads they carry to protect their hands. As we watched and rather self-consciously took photos it crossed our minds that professional mountaineers perform much the same function for the interested but non-participating public.

Clustered round the temple were stalls selling incense, prayer scarves, scriptures, offering-bowls, clay plaques with distinctly Indian-looking Buddhas, and sacred aromatic herbs for burning. There were also tin badges of the exiled Dalai Lama, which a number of Tibetans now openly wear in the face of their Chinese 'liberators'.

Revolving slowly by the entrance to the inner courtyard was a drum some ten feet high, inscribed with prayers worn smooth by tens of thousands of hands. I brushed it with my hand and passed inside. The cloistered courtyard echoed with the creaking of the dozens of smaller prayer-drums that spin without end as the pilgrims slowly walk by and lovingly brush them, keeping the universe turning. We moved on clockwise, taking in the shadowy cloisters, feeling out of place as the only westerners here yet in harmony with this unselfconsciously reverent place.

At the back is the heart of it all, the inner shrine consisting of two paintings and a gold Buddha that symbolize the coming of Buddhism to Tibet from China in the 7th century AD. The shrine itself was built in AD 652, making it much older than most of the Potala. Here incense and yak-butter candles smoked as the pilgrims muttered prayers and we stood awhile, for once not taking photographs.

We emerged blinking into the dazzling light, feeling gathered in ourselves and ready to go on to Everest and our own painful pilgrimage.

Through Tibet to Everest

17TH – 21ST MARCH

'So much is different now. We are so happy.'

Our trucks thundered into life in the half-dark while the moon set behind the encircling hills. Sandy leaned back in his seat, gave me his rubbery, lazy grin, and said, 'Good value, eh?'

We rattled and rolled for hours along the Friendship Highway that runs from Lhasa to Kathmandu across the hallucinatory high plateau of Tibet. It's an endless expanse of shades of brown, dun and tan, serene and desolate, flanked by distant hills. At this time of year much of it appeared desert, then in the middle of nowhere we'd come on a patch of irrigated fields surrounding a clutch of basic houses, their yak-dung fires uncoiling into the still air. In the wildest country we'd pass a man on a horse, or a child sitting by a flock of sheep, or a group of yak herders and their animals drifting across the plain.

Some hours later we came to a halt. Wind had drifted a foot of sand across the road, bogging down a truck and van coming the other way. We couldn't drive round them because of soft, deep sand on either side of the road. When we tired of watching the drivers footling around ineffectively with a rope, we donned face-masks against the clouds of sand now whistling past and went to push the truck and van out of the way. Then we forced our coach through the drift and re-boarded it, gasping desperately for nonexistent air, our eyes and ears crusted with sand.

The next barrier was a wide, fast-flowing river, where a ferryboat winched itself across on a cable. The captain refused to set off because of a strong cross-wind. Luo argued with him, but the CMA appear to have little clout in inner Tibet, for the captain finally locked himself in his cabin and refused to come out. An hour later, having made his point, he emerged to take us across.

From then on the country and weather became much wilder. Sand storms whirled across the valley, reducing visibility to a few yards. Two yak skeletons poked out of the desert. The road was blocked over and over; each time we wearily put on our masks, went out and pushed, our hearts beating wildly. We came on a virtual traffic jam at one point, where a good twenty drivers and passengers stood around helplessly. Impatiently we pushed their vehicles off the road and got ours through. When we drove off they were still standing there, though with their numbers they could probably have lifted their vehicles bodily. It reminded us that despite the powerful effect of the Buddhist monasteries we were still Westerners, creatures of desire, restlessness and drive. A more laid-back and philosophical approach to life has much to be said for it, but it doesn't get you to mountains, let alone up them.

'Yes, but what about the Sherpas?' someone says. 'They're Buddhists and have been known to climb a hill or two.' These inconvenient questions remain lodged crossways in the mind. We finally entered Shigatse in the evening, tired out and encrusted with sand, but feeling good to be going forward and working well together.

Shigatse is the second largest town in Tibet, but small enough for all that. Like Lhasa it's a curious mixture of traditional Tibetan houses and new concrete, corrugated iron and steel. It is dominated by the Tashi Lumpo monastery that is built up the slope of the hills behind. This was the only monastery not sacked during the Cultural Revolution, because its head, the Panchen Lama, agreed to co-operate with the Chinese. In the Dalai Lama's continued exile, the Panchen Lama is the highest spiritual authority in Tibet – though he has to spend practically all year in Peking, just to make clear who's really in charge.

'Collaborator', one tends to think, but it's not as simple as that. The rivalry and power-struggle between Lhasa and Shigatse and thus between the Dalai and Panchen Lamas, is centuries old. The Chinese have traditionally been drawn in as a counterweight in this struggle, usually by the Panchen Lama. One or other of the Lamas has frequently had to flee the country, sometimes to India or Nepal, sometimes to China. Power-politics, and it's always been that way. It's hard to imagine now, but in the 7th and 8th centuries, Tibet was the dominant military power in this part of the world, controlling large parts of China, Kashmir, Nepal, Sikkim and Bhutan. Then for a long time Tibet was an autonomous region under Chinese suzerainty. The Chinese invasion or Democratic Rebirth, the Dalai Lama's flight and the Panchen Lama's co-operation are nothing new, just part of the continuing story.

The Tashi monastery is very much a working one – though

whether it's a working model of a monastery or the real thing is harder to say. It is one of the few places we saw that was geared up for tourism. It is also very beautiful, ancient, with all the now familiar courtyards, labyrinthine walls and alleys, the casual, sprawling accretion of buildings; the strong, simple colours and lines; the shrouded prayer-halls, the shrines with more detail than the eye could take in, the living quarters and the scruffy, healthy little mongrel dogs drowsing in the sun; old monks regarding us with mild curiosity, with eyes intelligent, humorous or vacant; young novices more edgy and uncertain, staring or giggling.

When we went round this monastery next day, two events stuck in our minds and made us question what this monastery was about – and Tibet itself, for that matter. Once inside, there was a charge and a high one at that, for each room one wanted to photograph. This was new; in other places we took pictures for free, or were simply not allowed to take them. Well, okay, we thought, no reason why they shouldn't profit by our interest. But what made us really uneasy was then being led into an inner prayer-hall to be present at one of their prayer meetings. These meetings are not like public services, they are intensely private, the focus of the community's spiritual endeavour.

So what were we doing there in that low, dim, incense-laden room, hung with *thankas*, among the flickering butter-lamps? The muttered rhythmical prayers and responses of perhaps a dozen monks were interspersed or punctuated by music – a moaning horn, pipes, a cymbal clash, drums. They made formalized, intricate finger movements, as if playing cat's cradle with invisible thread to catch an invisible cat, then suddenly threw sacred grain into the air beneath a portrait of the Panchen Lama. We stood silently in the shadows, feeling fascinated, privileged and uneasy.

Was this a genuine act of private worship we were watching, or a façade for tourists? If it was the former, we shouldn't have been allowed in. We were clearly distracting some of the monks. If the latter, the whole monastery was in effect spiritually dead and might as well not exist. In other monasteries we'd been quietly turned away from the halls where prayer was going on, and this had seemed absolutely right.

Kurt and Julie paid their money and went back to film the ceremony when it started up again. We went on round the monastery and became involved in another awkward incident. Under an awning in a courtyard, a hundred or so young novice monks were being instructed in Buddhist scriptures. Not having paid, we were allowed to take pictures; some of us did surreptitiously, aiming from the hip and trusting to luck. Nick had the misfortune to be the one who was caught by two scowling Chinese heavies in dark glasses. There was a big row and demands for money, while Jack, caught in the middle, looked embarrassed and unhappy.

We were ushered out quickly, under a cloud. To placate them we eventually agreed to pay for Bob, as our official photographer, to go back and take a reel of shots.

Nick It seems to my mind these guys were not true Buddhists – a true Buddhist would ask you not to film certain things, full stop. And other things I'm sure there would be no problem. Here they are quite happy to let us film even the most private of religious events SO LONG AS WE PAY THE MONEY. This is not religion, it is a sham and stinks to high heaven.

There, I've said my piece. I guess I just resent being told I'm wrong.

Was Tashi Lumpo a realistic compromise with financial pressure, or a sell-out? The issue was discussed late into the night, whether it was better to stick to high principles and refuse to go along with the Chinese and/or the demands of tourism, even if that means being unable to practise the monastic way of life, or to compromise on the grounds that something is better than nothing. This was discussed passionately because the same question applied to our Expedition in terms of both the climbing strategy and our financing: purity or compromise? And is compromise realism or selling out?

The discussion broadened as we pooled our impressions of Tibet. I thought of an old woman Urs and I had visited in Lhasa. She was a relative of some Tibetan refugees Urs had known well in Switzerland and Ladakh. We had asked Luo if it was alright to see her, he shrugged and seemed quite unconcerned – itself a major shift in Chinese attitudes.

She was a tiny, bird-like and aristocratic old lady. She sat poised and upright in the large, cool sitting room while her daughter poured us glasses of milky *chang* and Urs passed on the latest news of their relatives. There was nothing forced about her dignity; she was shy and eager for news. Quietude seemed to radiate from her into the sparsely furnished room, shadows of the flowers in the window boxes met and parted on the plaster walls as she answered our questions about Tibetan life.

She'd been sent to Darjeeling as a girl to learn English, which she spoke with bell-like clarity, the Raj English of a bygone age. What she returned to again and again was the speed and extent of the changes of the last three years. During the Cultural Revolution destruction and repression were complete. All the monasteries other than the Tashi Lumpo had been sacked by Red Guards. Jack had claimed that many of these were Tibetans – was that true? 'Yes,' she said quietly, 'many of our young people wanted to destroy things – but they were always led by Chinese.' The same monasteries were now being systematically rebuilt, often with Chinese labour. Even more ironic and surprising, the monasteries are partly supported by the Chinese government.

During the Cultural Revolution all religious practices were proscribed; no shrines, no portraits of the Dalai Lama, no Buddhas, no prayer-scarves. Instead Tibetans had to have a portrait of Mao on the wall, which they hated. Red Guards could walk into any house at any time to inspect it. All foreign literature and contact with foreigners was banned.

I looked round the quiet, sunlit room, at the dozen English books, the chintz settee, the old valve radio, the large portrait of the exiled Dalai Lama. She smiled and said 'Yes, so much is different now. We are so happy.' Her smile of joy in a face lined with illness, age and suffering lingered with me many days. She went on to describe, more in sorrow than anger, how it had been. The 'consciousness raising' meetings they were forced to attend twice a day to confess to being CIA agents and American spies, people scared to talk to each other, having all their movements controlled. 'Prison, yes it was like being in prison for ten years. Now everything is changing so fast . . .' It is no longer compulsory for Tibetans to learn Chinese at school. Boiler suits are out and national dress is back in. And the same Tibetan Red Guards who once had all the power of Hitler's Brownshirts to do virtually anything they pleased were now abandoned by the Chinese, were poor, despised and ostracized in Lhasa. A rare case of bully boys getting their just desserts.

Now she could correspond freely with her refugee relatives; they could even come to visit and leave the country again. She might go to Ladakh for a while if her health permitted. Her happiness was moving.

So what's really going on in Tibet? Is this Chinese window-dressing, to impress the West and develop the huge tourist trade they're planning? Or a genuine change of heart? Is the Tashi Lumpo monastery a façade, or a thriving religious centre? Any visitors must make up their own minds, but to us it seemed that the astonishingly rapid recent changes in Tibet are probably the product both of practical calculation and ideological shift. One only wonders, as the Tibetans do, whether it will last, given China's capacity for abrupt changes in direction.

Tibetans do not like the Chinese. They did not ask to be overrun,

nor for the 'Democratic Rebirth'. The continued exile of their Dalai
Lama symbolizes that protest, and wearing the Dalai Lama badge
is as much a political as a religious gesture. But when we asked our
host whether she thought life for the average Tibetan had changed
for better or worse since the Chinese moved in, she hesitated for a
moment then said 'You see, I must not tell lies. It is better for
nearly everyone now.' The other Tibetans with whom we had an
opportunity to speak echoed her opinion. They recognize that their
ancient, feudal and rigidly repressive albeit picturesque society had
to change. The Chinese razed the foundations of that society – the
absolute authority of the monasteries and the few aristocratic
families – but brought education, housing, sanitation, health, social
justice, and greatly extended agriculture through vast irrigation
projects.

If anything is going drastically to alter Tibet, it will probably be
the anticipated huge influx of tourists rather than the Chinese. So
we concluded and one by one drifted off to bed to put down a final
pint of tea and write up diaries.

Jon In the afternoon me, Rick, and Andy Nisbet went for a walk over all
the tops behind the monastery. . . . Quite windy on top, even did some
bouldering. Rick has been the bloke I've come to know most about so far
– apart from the lads I've been on trips with in the past – and I find him
immensely likeable with very similar attitudes to me – apart from the fact
that he trains!

I am really looking forward to the Ridge kicking the shit out of me – a
bizarre ambition if there ever was one . . .

4.0 am, pitch dark, starry, very cold as our trucks start up and we
stumble aboard half-asleep. Then across the Tibetan plateau in the
mauve and turquoise bleeding light, our minds empty and passive,
merely recording. Immense distances open up as clouds on the
horizon resolve into further foothills. We rattle through a sleeping
village, a dog barks, a stirring of wind or perhaps the draught of
our passing momentarily distorts a straight column of smoke into a
question mark above the flat roofs. We meet a mule train trotting
out of the desert, led by a man and woman muffled in sheepskin
and black cloth. They glance up incuriously, nod then walk on
towards whatever destination. We jolt towards ours, only two more
days. . .

Bob Barton pulls down his cowboy hat, listening to *Blood On
The Tracks*. Dave fingers his moustache, his thick gold wedding ring
catches the low sunlight as he plans and worries about Base Camp

organization. He knows how he wants things done, but his position here is difficult as a non-climber. There's already been some friction with Sandy . . . Sandy opens a beer, looks out of the window, then settles down to a book. Liz is sleeping and her head bobs on Mal's shoulder as he pulls on his first cigarette of the day and stares fixedly ahead, thinking about logistics, personalities, his own hopes. Going quite well so far, he reflects. The extra time in Lhasa has helped acclimatization, but we might come to regret that lost week. The monsoon can come any time after mid-May . . .

We reached Xegar in mid-afternoon, a dusty, casual village of white-washed houses, women spinning as they sit back against the walls, old men carrying baskets of dried yak dung, boys stacking them under the roofs. There's one street, a few concrete and tin-roofed modern additions including a cinema and the post office, where our mail will arrive. Jack goes to check it out: nothing for us. Another four weeks to wait till the first news from home, it seems a long time.

We went to explore the Dzong, the ruins of a sprawling walled fortification built right up a sheer outcrop, a combination of monastery, fort and safe retreat for villagers from the period in the distant past when Tibetan chiefs were perpetually at war with each other. We've seen many stubs of forts like ancient worn-down teeth sticking up out of the desert, but none on this scale. As we scrambled up, feeling the extra altitude at some 4,250 metres, the hillside steepened into a few climbing moves on very friable rock, then a few more.

Soon Mal, Liz, Andy Nisbet and myself were in the position where down-climbing was a bad option and we had to go on with no idea if there'd be an exit. We finally ended up in a broken, near-vertical corner that seemed to offer the only way out. Mal and Andy do it with ease, enjoying themselves. Liz follows with more care. I envy her rock-climbing experience; mine amounts to childhood scrambling and one route in the Lake District. I check out the down-climb again. . . . Seriously marginal. Up's the only way out. How do I get into these situations? One slip and I'm out of the trip. Here goes . . .

Light-headed, heart pounding and slightly sick at the top, gasping for air that isn't there. We eventually made an exit through a hole in the fortress wall near the top. Andy and I found a heap of moulded clay Buddhas under a rock; we picked up a few because they seemed casually discarded, part of the general ruin. But back at our 'hotel' Urs told us they're compounded of clay and the ashes of the dead. Sandy was deeply perturbed by this. 'Look, it's bad joss, youth. We can't afford that on a trip like this.' I tease him for being a superstitious Highlander, but he's in no mood for joking. We decide to return them, hoping ignorance is an excuse in the eyes of divine, if not human, justice.

The sun set and the temperature plummeted. A clear night and the sky studded with unwavering stars. The dining room was a wind-tunnel with all the charm of an aircraft hangar; we shivered over our meal, wearing everything but our down suits. The food seemed even more slimy and intestinal than usual. So it wasn't altogether surprising when the suggestion came from Jon, Rick, Tony and Sandy that we omit the rest and acclimatization day here and go straight on to Base Camp. They're feeling well and are impatient to arrive and get stuck in and start suffering.

The suggestion was considered and eventually dropped, (a) because the majority are against it, (b) because Mal is against it. He holds that going from 3,300 to 4,250 to 5,150 metres in two days was pushing too fast; it might suit some of the lads, but the idea was to arrive at Everest with everyone in good shape. Andy Nisbet for one looked relieved, still concerned about his failure to acclimatize on Nuptse.

This was the first time we'd debated an Expedition decision. Sandy argued that as a group we had to back Mal's decision to wait on; interestingly, Jon agreed. Rick and Tony would obviously still rather have gone on, but the decision was accepted without resentment. It was a good sign that people felt free to make suggestions, discuss them and abide by the outcome. I wondered what would happen, though, if Mal was ever in the position of making a decision that went against the wishes of the majority.

Jon Heart bursting with happiness again. . . . Rick definitely twitchy, Sandy in football-manager mode – talking lots, saying nowt but meaning a lot!

So we spent the following day in Xegar. We drank tea, washed clothes, wrote up diaries and letters, made climbing slings, sewed loops on gear, and lay in the sun. Rick tried to curb his impatience by devoting himself to *Les Trois Mousquetaires*, which he's brought along to keep up his French. There was a sense of drawing a deep breath for the hardships ahead, and enjoying a last few undemanding hours. As we sat and chatted about the route, past expeditions, home, music and future plans, we were preparing our hearts and minds as much as our gear and bodies. By the time we arrived, everything should have been stuffed into the right compartments.

Sandy and I climbed back up to the top of the fort to return the clay figures. We sat there a long time amid the cairns, ruined masonry and clumps of prayer flags, looking out over high Tibet, elevated and at peace.

Another evening huddled in the dining room. 'I think I'll just pop into town and get some I LOVE XEGAR badges,' said Allen.

Sandy Walking out of the dining area it felt cold, very cold with the wind and all. Mal said, 'I hope it's not this cold on the hill!' My thoughts hit me, made me feel nervous in anticipation. Yes, I said to myself, won't be too cosy creeping out of a snow hole at Camp 2. Shivers ran down my spine. Don't know if I'm looking forward to it or not. I think I am, even trying to throw egotism to the dogs. Been trying that a lot lately. Dominique said climbing is selfish, I'm trying to see if it is or not. I wish it was not. But it must be, we climbers must be selfish.

Sure, being in the hostile environments makes us and helps us to *really* appreciate the finer points of valley life. But can't work out why we leave all that just to climb – and as I write this I know that I'm psyching myself into thinking, Yes fuck it, this route is hard but as a team we can climb it and even if we can't then *I* can . . . How the hell can I believe such a statement? But we have to, I have to. I imagine before a woman gives birth she must feel, Well how in hell can a baby so large come out of me so small? And then some fear, then some confidence, then birth, some loud screams, then OK, *Inshallah*. Perhaps it is the same with us climbers.

But I want to go there, to try, even to the point to die (I won't die though). But I'll push to beside death, till I can smell it. . . . But that's the art in the game, I guess, to recognize when to step back. . . . But on a 8,000 metres technical route. . . Well, one and one's mate have to walk close with death for many paces – that's when life is seen so close to. We may then be able to compare them, life and death, and see what's what. I cannot tell which one I'll choose – or will be chosen for me – death is probably the easier of the two for me – but I don't want it – I want life. Maybe I'll find it that way!

*   *   *

You're a bumblie, Andrew, an incompetent wazzock. You must have known a pint of water wouldn't be enough for a day going from 4,250 to 5,150 metres. Nine pints a day, man! So stupid . . . The tent's moving up and down again. I feel sick. Drink! Another litre to go. I'm going to throw up. Wish I could see properly, instead of out of focus and grey round the edges. This headache is not so much an ache as a Frankenstein bolt through the head. You're a sick man, not entirely in your right mind. Drink! So this is what cerebral oedema feels like . . .

That was what mild cerebral oedema, water retention in the brain, felt like. A crushing headache, absolute physical weakness and the mind wandering in its own labyrinth. Like childhood 'flu when a dressing-gown on the back of a door momentarily becomes a monster – the same worrying sense of unreality, as if the world and oneself were a leaky boat about to come apart at the seams and sink.

Lying alone in the claustrophobic world of my tent that first night at Everest Base Camp, I struggled to keep a grip on myself. I took Urs' pain-killers and anti-nausea tablets at regular intervals, then lay back and waited for the relief. Whenever I came to myself enough to remember, I drank my way through the flasks of luke-warm coffee Julie had brought over. I was angry at myself and my body for getting into this state, and well aware that if I didn't get better by morning I'd be facing a drive back down to Xegar with Urs to lose altitude and recover – unpleasant and embarrassing. Even *in extremis*, the ego still defends its self-image.

One of those seemingly endless nights. No question of sleep even if it were possible; I had to keep drinking. I tried reading but my eyes played tricks. The Walkman made the headache worse. Looking blankly at the ceiling was claustrophobic and there was something unsettling in the way the weave of the fabric bulged and shifted. I drank more, propped myself shivering up on one elbow and forced myself to record the last day of our journey to Everest in a shaky hand by the light of two flickering candles. . .

. . . Stumble out into the freezing dark of Xegar, dazed and half-awake. The moon burning white and brilliant as magnesium, the stars unwavering. Blow-torches roar under the trucks as the drivers unfreeze the engines, hunched figures moving in the shadows. Unreal and vivid as a dream, this final setting out. Finally the trucks shudder into life, echoing back down from the ruined fort. Most of the lads clamber into a Mothercare-type playpen of mats we'd constructed in the open back of a truck; Danny and I each climb into one of the other trucks as driver's mates. A wave and we're off.

My truck gets 100 yards from the compound then breaks down. A broken battery lead; the driver cobbles it together while Danny and I joke and stomp up and down to keep warm though we're wearing everything we've got. Dawn turns cobalt blue over the mountains, the star fades, the first dog barks.

An hour later we're on the road again. My truck is the oldest and slowest, breaking down with monotonous regularity. More desert, more moonscape, tiny villages with grey fields that will be green when we come this way again. And what will our harvest be? Irrigation streams, raggedy children, an old woman with a hen tucked firmly under her arm. This is the last of natural human society we'll see for a couple of months. Our existence on the mountain is completely unnatural and can only be temporary. Maybe that's why it seems so precious and so intensely experienced, like the last sight of a woman's bracken-tinted hair, or another **waving goodbye in a London dawn . . . I want to journey on and on like this till I become completely amnesiac, living in the eternal present of expedition time.**

Mid-morning we abruptly turn off the tarmac Friendship Highway onto the 'road' to Everest. It's scarcely a road, more a clearing in a boulder field. The truck grinds on in its lowest gear, bouncing us about like dice in a cup. The Chinese extended this road right to Everest Base Camp to bring in supplies for their 1960 expedition. It's indicative of their methodical approach and colossal manpower. They may also have been anticipating the potential tourist trade, though anyone going to Everest Base Camp on this side of the mountain for a quick look around is going to feel distinctly unwell.

At the far side of a river, which the trucks ford only after some difficulty – it can be completely unpassable – we all meet up again and open up Expedition supplies for the first time: luncheon meat, tinned peaches and oatcakes. They taste wonderful because we've all had enough of Chinese food. We talk and joke, take off layers of clothing. A few of the lads admit to the first ghost of an altitude headache and I'm light-headed myself, but we're all very raised behind our attempted casualness. In a few hours the mountain, which we regard more as our testing-ground or theatre than an adversary, will show itself. The weather is perfect; surely it can't stay like this all the way to Base. We're all aware that Bonington's expedition arrived in very hostile conditions.

. . . 'See you, Jimmy! See you . . .' My driver rehearses over and over his only English phrase as I coach him in the authentic, aggressive Glasgow gutterals with which we aim to astonish young Tinker. For nearly two hours now we've been grinding up towards the 5,000 metres pass from where we should see Everest. The cab's stifling, stinking of diesel; the wheel leaps like a fish through the driver's hands. We share cigarettes and the contents of my one water-bottle. Should have brought more . . . Danny's truck is way up ahead, the other is out of sight. This is endless, want to get to the top and see Everest, want to get to Base and put my tent up. Mal and Dave have planned exactly what's to be done in which order so that it'll not be everyone for themselves when we arrive. Hope the lads stick to that; it'll be a test of how co-operative we're prepared to be. Not another breakdown, please . . .

We creep round a bend. 'See you, Jimmy!' I nod, speechless.

Spread out before us now are the true Himalayas, a surf breaking on the horizon and leaping into the sky. Or a necklace of teeth that happens to be some 200 miles long – and smack in the middle, unmistakably and unarguably, the biggest and wickedest canine of them all.

Our trucks have gathered at the top of the pass. We jump down and stand and stare. Kurt and Julie are filming us, but we don't need to fake our reactions. We'd been prepared for disappointment, knowing Everest doesn't look impressive from the Nepal side, but from here it's a towering, squat pyramid gleaming with promise and threat, putting all other mountains into their proper place. But what other mountains! We identify them: the giant Makalu, the classic white triangle of Pumori, the sprawling magnificence of Cho Oyu, Chomo Lonzo . . .

And our ridge, the North-East Ridge? To our amusement, Dave Bricknell corrects Bob and Allen's identification: the long, tapering left-hand skyline is our target. It doesn't look too steep, is Andy Nisbet's first thought. Most of us share a degree of relief; at first sight it doesn't look outrageous. What it does look, Mal thinks, is very, very long. That's going to knock the stuffing out of us, the amount of work we're going to have to do over 7,300 metres.

'A piece of piss!' Jon laughs.

'A serious challenge,' Sandy replies. 'But then – we're Serious People!' But to himself he thinks how poorly his down suit fitted him when he tried it on, how cold it's going to be up there.

'Just as well WE'RE SHIT HOT!' the chorus goes up – and then we fall silent again on the high pass, looking over at our future. Mixed feelings of exhilaration, confidence, uncertainty, apprehension. We are very impressed; it is mammoth, absolutely worthy.

There were still several hours left in the journey to Base. It must have been this stretch that did me in, for my water was finished. Everest was getting bigger all the time, breathtaking if one had some spare breath to take. Down into the valley, past the last primitive village of outer Tibet. My truck was dropping further and further behind. Finally we were into the Rongbuk valley, the truck grinding and lurching from one boulder to another. There was a pile of ruins on the left and in front of it one tall chorten was still standing. I recognized it from the pre-war photos – the Rongbuk monastery, where expeditions used to be received and blessed by the Lama there. They all came this way on the long march from Darjeeling: Shipton, Tilman, Odell, Norton, Mallory, Irvine. And the eccentric Maurice Wilson, who aimed to climb Everest on the strength of rice and meditation but instead died on the lower slopes of the North

Col, he sheltered here. For even the most blasé of us, Everest is special; to be here is to live among history and legend, to climb here is to become a permanent addition to the Everest story.

A few miles more of sand, rubble and frozen streams, then the truck pulled up. In something of a daze I took in a scene of purposeful activity. Bob and Allen had gone ahead in the jeep to choose a site and start putting up the Mess Tent. Already barrels and food boxes were being unloaded from the trucks, tents were going up, stoves being carried into the Mess Tent. We were lucky with the weather; anticipating a freezing gale, probably snow and a real struggle to organize ourselves, we had instead a warm, still afternoon and time to take care of the essentials at a leisurely pace. But we didn't hang about because as soon as the sun went down it would be another story.

I knew I wasn't quite well, should have said so and sat down for an hour to rest and drink. But not wanting to be a wimp – maybe everyone else feels as bad and they're all working away – I retrieved my barrels and rucksack, dragged them over to a flat spot and started putting up my Vango tent. Bob, always helpful, gave me a hand, then we did his tent and I dragged myself over to lend a hand with the Mess Tent.

The sun went down, and all the clothing went back on. Waiting for the brew and supper, I had a stabbing pain in my neck, felt sick and grey. I slumped down, nearly knocking over someone's plate. Sandy spoke sharply; he probably wasn't feeling his best either and I was too far gone to care. Dumb animal passive suffering, unable to respond or listen to the chat, too sick to eat or drink, I stared helplessly at the plate in front of me.

It was Julie who came over, took one look at me and efficiently took charge. When it matters, she and Kurt are on the ball. A vague memory of being led to my tent, helped into a sleeping bag, my head propped up. Two flasks of coffee appeared. 'I want you to drink this, all of it. If you don't, you'll feel very ill.' I want to say something, like thank you or yes, but just nodded, absorbed in my pain. 'And if you feel worse, call out. Don't keep it to yourself – I did that on Nanga Parbat and got very sick.' I made some kind of gesture, stared at my mug and with considerable effort steered some of its contents towards my face. And again. Cerebral oedema, I was sure I had it. Urs appeared, looked me over and said oedema was exactly what I had, 'not too awfully, I am thinking,' repeated Julie's instructions, gave me some pills and went away. He's the right kind of doc, neither alarmist nor dismissive.

It's 4.0 am. I feel desperately weak and weary but semi-normal now. It's been a long night but I should be okay. A last drink, put away the journal. Blow out the candles and pull the draw-string tight. Lie in the dark and say it to yourself: *I'm at Everest Base Camp.*

Boy Racers & Old Farts

'Rule 5: All moraine is terminal.'

I woke feeling weak, washed-out, and thankful for the light of day. Drinking some water from the bottle stashed inside my bag to keep it from freezing overnight, I slowly took stock of myself: trace of a headache, throat burning, nose and head thick with the mucus the body produces at altitude in an effort to protect the lining of nose and throat. Breathing shallow and snatched, pulse faster than normal. Sitting up too quickly makes my head spin. Don't feel wonderful, but as well as can be expected for a first morning at 5,150 metres.

Running through the check-list of the body and mind like a pilot checking out an aircraft before take-off, was something each of us did every morning, automatically. Call it hypochondria or self-monitoring, either way it's essential. In the mountains we're obsessed with every aspect of our bodies and our mental condition. It's banal, yet that perpetual self-awareness adds to the intensity of the experience. Ironic how in the midst of the world's most huge and awesome scenery much of the time we are preoccupied by the coldness of feet, colour of urine, replacing suncream, adding or removing another layer of clothing, drying out socks. Other than that one is usually aware only of the most immediate aspects of the outside world – the ground underfoot, the brew in one's hand, the hissing stove. Only once in a while do we lift our heads, relax our attention, and for one unforgettable moment take in where we are.

We lay in our tents that first morning at Base Camp, each coming awake and going through the check-list. Most of us felt headachy, off-colour, throats burning from the dry air, had slept poorly – though the lads would hardly ever admit at the time to feeling any less than 100 per cent.

But it would be a while before we went climbing. There were another six days to go before the yaks were due to turn up to take our food and equipment up the Rongbuk glacier to Advance Base

Camp. We'd need all of that time and more to acclimatize and organize. Chris Bonington's team had two weeks here before they moved up to ABC. Unfortunately, due to our later departure from the UK and the delay in Lhasa, we didn't have that much time – even at this early stage the arrival of the monsoon around the end of May was in the back of our minds. From now on we were on a countdown, never knowing how many days we had left.

We'd discussed the strategy of the Base Camp phase of the trip on the way in. We had to establish a base that was as comfortable and orderly as possible, for it would be to here that we would return at intervals from the hill (always called 'the hill' not 'the mountain' – makes it seem smaller) for Rest and Recreation. ABC at 6,400 metres was too high for recovery. We had to acclimatize. And there were many days' work in preparation for the next stage: sorting out all the gear for the yak runs – packing it, calculating how much food and gas we'd need for ABC, making dozens of two-man hill-food packs for Camp 1, then lighter ones for Camp 2 and beyond, sorting out our own barrels of gear. All this done at the geriatric pace of altitude, for here at 5,150 metres there were about half the normal number of oxygen molecules in the air, which is roughly half one's physical energy – and mental, too, it seemed to me struggling with my first *Sunday Express* report.

As Base Camp Manager, Dave Bricknell had drawn up day-by-day work-sheets assigning our daily responsibilities. Some of the lads, being used to small and self-organizing Alpine-style expeditions, found this degree of planning risible, while recognizing it was probably necessary. Difficult for Dave, who had never been climbing, to give orders to experienced mountaineers, and difficult for them to accept it. A certain degree of irritation on both sides, everyone testy from altitude, but we recognized the uncomplaining and valuable contribution he was making.

Moving slowly, I pulled on my boots, hat, gloves, a layer of pile and a down jacket before emerging from the tent. The morning was blue, windless, bitterly cold for the sun hadn't yet risen over the hills that channelled the Rongbuk valley up towards Everest. Though some ten miles away, its squat pyramid of rock and snow slammed down across the head of the Rongbuk valley, dominated Base Camp. This morning spindrift flew horizontally from the summit, pale and gauzy as a prayer-scarf.

Mal came over, we exchanged good mornings and stood looking. Sunlit, every detail of that near-mythical mountain stood out clearly – the West Ridge, the 'Yellow Band' of limestone that ran across the North Face, the Hornbeim Couloir, the First and Second Rock

Steps on the summital East Ridge where Mallory and Irvine had disappeared, the last Pinnacle where Joe and Pete may be . . . 'Christ, I wish I was going for the Summit today,' Mal said. 'It's a perfect summit day. It can't last. The 1938 Expedition who used this site arrived in perfect conditions like these and then they failed because of sustained bad weather.' He seemed more relaxed and communicative now we'd got over our second major hurdle and actually arrived at Base Camp with all our gear and everyone in reasonable shape.

In the Mess Tent the lads on cooking rota had breakfast well in hand: brews, cereal, biscuits and cheese. 'A regular hotel, this,' Nick said, smiling. There was a line of tables and stools up the middle of the two interconnnected box-frame tents, a cooking corner, where Chris Watts crouched thoughtfully over the two moody petrol stoves, which were already playing up, washing-up bowls, kitchen rolls, a box of books, bags containing our personal utensils hanging along the sides. . . . Dave had organized an oasis of comfort and order in the midst of the elemental chaos around us. These pristine standards inevitably dropped as time went on and we became more frazzled and weary, but Base Camp never ceased to be an ideal place for R & R (Rest and Recovery in this case, though there was Rock 'n' Roll later when we were fit enough to sing).

At 10.00 am the sun hit the tent and the bitter chill quickly lifted. Time for work. Urs, Bob and Allen went to dig out a latrine – and never was there a Superloo with such a view, looking across to Everest as, cord in hand, one hung out over the abyss. Those on the cooking rota washed up and set off across the ice-lake nearby in search of water. The others began the long task of laying out and opening up 120 boxes to set up loads for ABC. Urs had excused me from work that day, so I had time, feeling slightly guilty and apologetic, to sit around and take stock of our surroundings.

Base Camp was sited on a broad, flat expanse of stones and sand, the residue of the retreating Central Rongbuk glacier whose snout ran across the valley some 300 yards away. Beside us was an ice-lake where we could chop through to pools of water. Bonington's expedition three years previously had used the same site, while the pre-war expeditions had tended to use the more sheltered area half a mile down the valley where the four-man Basque team were camped. Immediately behind our camp was a hillock of rubble. I wandered up it with legs that had all the resilience of blancmange. Along the crest were half a dozen stone memorials. Placed as they were, we could never cease to be aware of those cairns. Everest in front, the memorials behind, we in the centre. We all went up there many times, to pay our respects, to reflect and to hope.

And these were just the post-war casualties. Jon came back that afternoon from visiting the Basques with a broken stone slab that read 1921 KEL. They'd found it near their camp. We worked out it must have been to Kellas, the doctor and climber who died, probably from pneumonia, on the 1921 reconnaissance expedition. It had come from a large memorial where the names of all the pre-war casualties were recorded, though we were never able to find and restore it.

The summit spindrift had grown to a mile long white flag, and it was certainly not one of surrender. These expeditions are little wars of their own. 'Of course, climbing is pointless,' Mal once admitted as he frowned into a pint of Clachaig lager. 'It doesn't change anything. Except ourselves, which is the whole point. Just because I do something well which anyone could do if they put their mind to it, and it doesn't make a blind bit of difference anyway – well, there's nothing brilliant about that, is there?'

From that little hillock, one could deduce something about the nature of our Expedition from the lay-out of Base Camp. The imposing Mess Tent was the focus, but the rest of the tents were scattered about at random, according to each occupant's choice, some distance from each other. Mine was at the outer edge. Bob's was nearest the mountain, and only his had the entrance on the Everest side ('I know it's draughtier, but I like to be able to look out and see the hill'). And apart from the two couples' tents, only Tony and Andy Nisbet shared. The rest of us had a tent to ourselves. That was pleasant, a luxury. Only in retrospect does it seem symptomatic, and perhaps unfortunate. Privacy is important on long expeditions, but it could be we had too much of it. Like our tents, we were a loose, scattered group.

Kurt and Julie's tent was set apart from the others round the corner and out of sight. The same arrangement was to be repeated at ABC, where they again chose to isolate themselves. In the preparation stages it had been unclear whether they were part of the Expedition or filming it. Now it was beginning to seem that they were an expedition in themselves who occasionally happened to film us when they weren't away doing other things, who were mainly to be seen at meal times. Still, I wasn't going to forget it was Julie who'd noticed and acted when I was ill. Right now she, Kurt and Danny were filming aspects of Base Camp. The lads were still not enjoying this, partly because they felt phoney and partly because of the extra effort involved in the repeated performances of their activities. Even those who respected their achievements and understood the necessity for the filming had serious doubts about it.

Later I shuffled down the frozen lake to a melt stream. Washed socks, my hands aching with cold, then lay in the hot sun and day-dreamed of home, and success here. My socks iced up and my face was burned, a typical Himalayan combination. Still feeling weak and headachy, the short walk back to camp exhausted me. Then I looked around and saw everyone was moving very slowly, as though the air was a clear, thick glue.

It was good to sit all together at the end of the day, get brews down, eat and chat. Supper was courtesy of Wide Boy Productions (Jon, Rick, Sandy, Tony); a kind of cannelloni-glue followed by stewed apples and custard. 'Hey, this is good!' said Mal. Sandy grinned 'That's what they all say – at first.'

Bob and Allen came in late, Bob indignant. 'You said we were going to eat at 8.00.' Jon gave his most angelic smile, paused. 'We lied.'

He was Membership Secretary for the Alpine Climbing Group, and that evening wrote Chris Bonington a postcard. *'Dear Chris, Remember your ACG membership is coming up for renewal.'* We all signed it and dropped it in the mail bag. He was only 20 miles away with the Norwegians on the other side of Everest, yet our card would probably travel hundreds of miles to get to him.

Mal in a philosophical mood says, 'Life is like a tin of shortbread. . . .'

'Yeah, I'll give you two Yorkies for it, mate!'

So much laughter on these trips as we sound each other out, entertain ourselves, forget today's stresses and tomorrow's uncertainties for a while. And it is almost impossible to explain later what was funny.

It was suddenly too cold to stay in the Mess Tent any longer, so we separated for the night. Wild out there – pitch black, a bitter, gusting wind, ten degrees below. Suddenly comfort is a struggle. Find tent, grope around for head-torch, then zip up the flap, boots off, massage some feeling back into feet, take off one layer of clothes and into the bag. Weak and breathless, lie there a minute. Then put my kingdom in order: light candles, water bottle and socks inside the bag, pee bottles, pen, journal, Walkman, munchies, salve for cracked lips, batteries in gloves under my armpits. . . .

The early days at Base Camp took on a rhythm. The weather had a definite pattern: clear and windless in the morning, warm over lunchtime, then cloudy and windy in the afternoon, very cold at night. We'd assemble over breakfast, then get on with our assigned work till lunch. In the afternoon there'd be some time for washing and gradually sorting out one's own gear for ABC, perhaps a short acclimatization walk. Then supper, banter and planning the next day, till the sudden cold drove us out to our own tents.

Jon Up at 8.0 for a pre-yak recce – me, Rick, Tony and Nicko (the young and stupid team). Up the pleasant path to the turning to the East Rongbuk glacier.... We went on to about 5,450 metres – three hours' walking – then back for lunch. I had a bit of a headache, but it went after a few brews.

Andy Nisbet looking like a Muppet with his wild red hair, very pale. Perhaps it's not just the suncream. Bob exasperated with the Chinese stoves, tongue between teeth in concentration. Allen peeling potatoes, 'I think I'll go off and do something really useful now, like look at my tent ceiling.' Kurt comes across as an irascible old bull; partly because he is, partly because his brain works faster than his (excellent) command of English. Muttering to himself, peering over his grandad glasses, looking like an East European bishop in his woolly hat. Andy Greig humming 'She's got perfect skin' as he types. Rick doing a seminar on radios – heavy Motorolas again. Chris looking not too good at the moment – lucky he's a professional dark horse.... Everyone's face beginning to show the strain of altitude – psyches recede as people realize the pressure.

The Basque lads came up for a brew and stayed for supper. One, Juan-Jo, seemed ill, his first time in the Himalayas. Antxon was cool – he's got a good British sense of humour. Juan, the young lad, switched on, did Jannu by the French route. Mari, the leader, wizened, 40, climbed on K2 with Roger Baxter Jones; like an army NCO, puffing on cigs, slight twitch in the left cheek. Good men and true.

A secret. In the Himalaya, people who have some spirit left over for their mates are the most valued companions of all. . . .

Bob My thoughts go even more than usual to Anna and Alex and little Eliane, and I look at their photos often. This is the first big trip I've had since we've had children and I do feel different – I don't think I'm more held back from risky situations, because I never was a necky climber, but I feel like I've got a more stable core, a reference point, and that my feet will stay on the ground even if, God willing, my head is in the clouds. . . .

The first Yak Run has been scheduled for the 28th and the team has been divided or has divided itself as follows:

OLD FARTS   BOY RACERS
Me, Allen, Mal, Andy N., Jon, Sandy, Rick, Tony
Andy G., Chris Watts.   Brindle, Nick.

Dave Bricknell appears to be hyper-fit as does Urs, and so they are allowed to feature as Boy Racers despite the constraints of age.

The Old Farts have a leaning towards hypochondria (Andy N. got sunburnt in Lhasa and ever since has been walking around with his face inches deep in cream). We prefer leisurely acclimatization, and we think the route is going to be pretty hard.

By contrast, the archetypal Boy Racer won't admit to fatigue or head-aches, can't cope with all this hanging about, and reckons that Bonington's team would probably have done better if they hadn't been O.Fs!

Tony A rest day for everyone. I spent most of the day in the tent 'cos it was very cold today – writing letters and thinking of home and Kathy. Can't wait for the 8th when Terry is expected with the jeep and surely some mail. By then I will have been away a whole month without a word from Kathy – seems so long. Liz has been nice, knowing my plans more than the others do and very understanding.

This is a whole new ball-game for me, thinking about the future rather than just the next month or so . . . amazing how much strength one can draw from such a close relationship. . . .

I am beginning to retreat a little again into my shell – have been aware of this on other trips, but am finding it hard on this one to do otherwise. I don't like to make relationships too quickly with people I know so little about and understand even less.

Afternoon in the Mess Tent. Kurt and Julie film Mal and Dave discussing the route from Base to Advance Base (pre-war Camp 3). On their fourth take and getting more and more stilted. 'Silence with the Mars Bar!' Kurt commands. Off-camera, Jon mimes a silent Fuck Off.

Liz and Sarah make up sachets for hill-packs. Jon and Tony peel apples, Rick fiddles with the petrol stove. Chris and Nicko are poring over the photos in Bonington's book. Urs sorts out his drugs into a Base and an Advance Base barrel. Yesterday we all got our hand-outs of aspirin, sleepers, pain-killers, suncreams and salves, tubes of vitamins. 'Typical Himalayan wimps, we are,' Mal commented. 'Have you seen the avocado hand-cream anywhere?'

The Basques drop in on their way down from ABC. They look tired; Juan-Jo, the least experienced, is absolutely done in and the others have to carry his rucksack. 'The pressure of a small expedition,' Jon remarks. Their presence makes the Boy Racers more restless, eager to get to the hill.

Kurt trains an enormous lens on Everest and we all have a long look. The spindrift is like the sky bleeding milk. Sandy glances through the lens. 'Well, that's it,' he says cheerfully, and sets off towards his tent, 'I'm going back to Lhasa!' We are thoughtful and impressed. There are not really three Pinnacles at all, more like five.

And a hell of a way from there to the summit, the jet-stream into your face all the way.

Sandy Oh, magnificent to be here! Everest looks huge. We've got our work cut out but mean to go easy over the next few days to keep it all in perspective, to become acclimatized, to feel and be one with the environment here, with the team, with life. I think for me that feeling of peace with the surroundings is the most important point in Himalayan climbing. Then one can begin to feel confident and then move up on the hill and feel at home there, as though approaching the house of a friend rather than heading for an interview or interrogation. . . .

. . . Yes, keen. Realize the route is quite desperate and way beyond our previous experience – well, the 8,000 metres part of it, but still think that if we all work together, don't get panic-stricken and take things cool, we stand an OK chance. The wind is what frightens me. Really frightens me.

We're lucky people! We've got a licence to go crazy on the N. E. Ridge of Everest. . . . Are we fit to be here or are we counterfeit? Joe and Pete. . . . Who the fuck do we think we are? So keen, so keen. . . . Pity we couldn't have got a 8,000 metres peak in after Mustagh Tower. We're not quite ready. I see that as we sit around the Mess. We're close. . . . We'll need luck. . . . We're almost there. We're sort of vulnerable – but it's not unconquerable. . . .

Feel so distant from the lads, bit of a drag, don't mean to – but man! Like 40,000 miles away. God only knows what the reason for this is, can't seem to slip into conversation, probably something to do with . . . Yeah I used to love her, but it's all over now . . . Joe and Pete. Passed by their memorial again tonight. Strange, trying to prepare myself for meeting their bodies. Not a nice thought. Christ, really I'm not looking forward to that. . . .

We need some JOLLIFICATION. No bull-shit, just real regular JOLLIFICATION.

Nick . . . The Basques seem to be moving really fast. I felt I'd rather be with them today, going lightweight, fast and mushy, instead of snail-like, hampered by the media bullshit. . . .

Had a bit of a go at Kurt – he was being really stupid and awkward. Folks were generally sorting things out in the Mess Tent – he then decides his film barrels and other gear have to take up about half the Mess Tent space, despite the fact he has an empty Vango near. I suggest this. 'Oh no,' says Kurt, 'maybe somebody steal things from it – nobody sleep there.'

I just couldn't keep a straight face. The guy must take us for a bunch of idiots. To have the audacity to think that the film gear is more important than any other thing, e.g. medical and for that matter climbing gear. After all, we're here to climb a mountain. I think some people seem to forget that.

Andy G. You wouldn't expect on a big expedition to have so much time on one's own, something like 16 hours a day in the privacy of our tents, alone with our cassettes, books, letters and diaries. Alone with our thoughts of home and the past, our hopes and fears about the future. It's quite unlike the intense companionship of a small expedition. We're finding this hard to adjust to. Only Allen has experience of a big expedition, on the South-West face of E. with Bonington's crew ten years back, and he said today that they'd had a long walk-in to become close. Implying, quite rightly, that we're not. Still, early days, and in truth we do get on remarkably well.

One's tent can be a sanctuary or a prison, depending on mood. Tonight it's freezing and wild outside, the tent rocks and is battered like a small boat. Some evenings I crawl in here and dislike the thought of the many solitary hours of broken sleep ahead. As Dave remarked today, what one misses most, even more than bacon or beer or sex or a shower, are the few people one is used to sharing one's life with. Intimacy is what we miss.

There can be value, not deprivation, in this solitude. Climbing may be an escape of sorts, but not from oneself. Whether face-to-face with one's own fear halfway up a route, or in these weeks and months away from everything familiar, mountaineering is one long adventure or ordeal in self-knowledge. And self-possession, the quality these lads have so strongly, tends to make them hard to know. They often scarcely know each other outside of climbing.

Tonight, wearing all my daytime gear and only just warm enough in this bag, with munchies, water-bottle, old man Fyffe's Taj Mahal tape (we've similar Old Fart musical tastes), tonight I like this tent. I'm physically, mentally and emotionally comfortable. But we need action and movement soon to pull us together. The first hints of boredom, irritation, broodiness. Like our tents, each a certain distance apart. Each contained in our own orange glow, and the freezing dark between us. We're separate kingdoms in a temporary alliance.

So many stars at night, it's hard to pick out the constellations. Hanging back on the rope over the shit-pit, looking at Everest in the silent moonlight, I've a brief, farcical vision of myself as a charioteer riding this earth as it thunders through the void.

The days passed. We finished all our Advance Base preparations and waited for the yaks to turn up. Word came they'd be two days late. A small delay, but added to our earlier ones it could be significant. 'Where's the sense of urgency?' Rick asked himself.

Graffiti began to appear on the Mess Tent. By the entrance *NO MORE HEROES ANY MORE* and *NOT A SECOND TIME.* Above the kitchen area *DON'T GIVE ME THAT GOLDEN STUFF* and *HOW DARE YOU CRITICIZE MY CUSTARD?* Near the ceiling *WE SHALL STAMP TO THE TOP WITH THE WIND IN OUR TEETH* – heroic stuff, unfortunately it comes from one

of Mallory's last letters home. Jon took a broad felt-tip pen and scribed THE AUSTRALIAN RULES OF WALKING:
 1. *If you have all day to get from A to B, you take all bleeding day.*
 2. *Never, ever, break into a sweat.*
 3. *Never do anything twice.*
 4. *(Of course), there is no 4th rule.*
And after his first time up to ABC he came down and added a heartfelt:
 5. *All moraine is terminal.*
We were beginning to occupy this space, to make it our own and express ourselves in it. Our expedition was acquiring its own mythology, history and language of private jokes. Now we were ready to begin exploring further, and at our own pace began taking acclimatization hikes. Bob and Allen packed their gear and went for two overnight bivvies in the hills above our valley – typical Glenmore cowboys, no fuss, very methodical. The Boy Racers went for a preliminary recce up the trail towards ABC. Chris Watts wandered off by himself. Mal stayed in his tent, reading and planning and sleeping, in a manner reminiscent of Achilles, another believer in static acclimatization. Liz, Danny and I made our own forays. Acclimatization is not like hard training at sealevel; pushing yourself tends to do more harm than good.

*   *   *

'You'll never learn, mate,' says Jon, shaking his head and handing me a brew. I take it, grey-faced and shivering, fighting nausea and a crunching headache. And I'd felt so good just hours earlier. . . .

. . . Heavy-headed and slow as I am every morning here, I pull on salopettes, pile and down jacket and crawl out of my tent. A perfect morning, Everest flying its customary white flag. Sounds of zips, pissing, a clatter from the Mess Tent.
    It is Jon's birthday, he shambles in late to affectionate abuse and applause. We gradually wake up, conversation begins to flow, sun hits the tent. 'Let's go climbing!' from Sandy. 'Oink, oink,' Jon replies.
    I want to move today, so I find Andy Nisbet and persuade Dave he deserves a day away from Base now that everything's under control here. We set off – water-bottle, camera, suncream, munchies, the routine is automatic now. We work our way up the initial slopes of scree, rock, loose blocks, gasping at first till we slow to a more sensible pace, perhaps 1 mph. It's all the body can do; the problem

is the mind's frustration, its impatience to get somewhere. Remember the Australian rules. . . .

It feels good now. Everything super-clear (is it the air, or light-headedness?) Happy being up here and pushing myself a little. I take my pace from Dave and Andy. An hour passes, two. We're in no hurry. Moving up is an effort, then as soon as we stop we feel good again. Cho Oyu starts to appear, a sprawling beautiful-ugly massif. New angles on Everest. This is the business, clambering in the Himalayas' thin air and hot sun. Dave and I exchange smiles of pleasure.

We see a figure below working his way up towards us at an astonishing pace, at least twice ours. . . . Mr Rick Allen, Boy Racer incarnate, neat and trim. The gaunt, foxy face, his nose as sharp as a pen; the cockerel quiff of his short red hair; the precise economy of his words and movements – everything about him is honed to a cutting edge. 'Thought I'd come out for a stroll,' he says with just a hint of self-mockery, and leads off in front. Mal's restless energy appears in his large gestures, enthusiasms and impulses; Rick confesses himself to be just as restless, but he channels it within an absolute discipline – physical, mental, moral and emotional. It will be interesting to see which of them goes further.

We follow him on up for another 40 minutes of geriatric boulder-hopping, then Andy Nisbet announces this is far enough for him. Like Allen Fyffe, he's very much preoccupied with his failure to acclimatize, and is determined to take things very methodically. I'm impressed at his self-control; it must be hard for a very pushy climber like Andy to let Rick and two bumblies go higher than him. I should have learned from that. . . .

But I follow Rick and Dave on to the crest of the ridge as we work our way awkwardly up towards an ever retreating 'summit'. Going very slowly now, monitoring an incipient headache like a huge thumb gently pressing my temples. Thoughts of home, of success on the hill, of getting to my personal summit, drift through my mind like the slow nebulous clouds above.

Finally we stop, take photos, drink and chat. Around 5,770 metres, Rick says. I translate this into feet and realize it's possibly a new height record for me – even more so for Dave, who's never been over 4,000 feet before coming out here. He's as ecstatic as I am. It feels wonderful to be alive, sitting on these warm blocks looking out over the deep blue and glittering white of the Everest range. This sense of elevation is more than physical.

'Half a dozen of us could get to the top without oxygen,' Rick asserts. I remind him of the track record for oxygen-less ascents of

Everest. 'Well, getting down again would be a different matter,' he concedes, smiling as he stares hungrily over at our summit. If he wasn't so absolutely sane, I'd say he was mad as a hatter.

Our descent is exhausting – scree-running, awkward traverses, feeling suddenly sick and wobbly. Rick thoughtfully waits at intervals to guide Dave and me down. As we finally trudge across the flat moraine to Base Camp, the tents are bobbing in and out of focus. . . .

'Yes,' Jon concludes sadly, 'you'll never learn. There's no point in trying to keep up with the appalling Rick Allen.' The Boy Racer, looking very relaxed, looks up from his *Les Trois Mousquetaires*, grins. Tinker-stress bounces off his armour-plating. 'You've got to find your own pace and don't let anyone distract you from it,' he observes quietly, and goes back to his book.

I mumble something and drag my abused body off for a long night's penitence in my tent. Violent shivering all the way from knees to throat, nausea, boom-boom headache. The worst is not being able to breathe regularly, as if breathing were now an effort of will. Whenever I start to doze off, I jerk awake gasping for air. A touch of claustrophobia. This time, surely, I've learned my lesson.

Sarah Atmosphere is very good at BC, people get on most of the time – only the odd niggle – nothing serious. A free day – I went down to the Rongbuk nunnery with Nick. It takes about an hour to get to – an hour and a half back up – however small the incline, it's still up! Nick is a lot fitter than I am – but I'm not doing so badly. It was very pleasant just to sit in the sun, drink our water and eat a few munchies. Across the valley, a herd of sheep were being shepherded along, bells gently ringing.

Julie must have spent a long time making beefburgers – probably the most memorable meal, special effort for Jon's birthday. Beefburgers, chips, peas and tomato sauce, followed by sponge pudding and custard. . . .

On 27th March the yaks and their herders or 'yakkers' finally slouched and tinkled their way up the valley. They'd come from the nearest villages, two or three days away. They pitched their basic tents, brewed up, and soon the air was full of the surprisingly fragrant smell of dried yak-dung fires. Lots of less fragrant fresh dung from the morosely grazing yaks. They were slow, shaggy, moody creatures who seemed entirely unenthusiastic at being in this godforsaken place. They probably had altitude headaches too. The gay ribbons pleated into their tails and manes by the yakkers must be an ironic joke. There is nothing festive about a yak at altitude.

Their owners were 'real heavy-duty ethnics', as Sandy remarked.

Clad in layers of sheepskin, turquoise stones in their ears, knives on their hips, long black plaited hair, they were as curious and inquisitive about us as we were about them. We kept all valuables out of temptation's way, and nothing went missing.

Except the yaks, which scattered overnight to the four winds. We woke to find a few on the slopes, the rest had disappeared in the direction of the Rongbuk nunnery. A yakkers' ploy to gain a paid rest day, another day's delay for us. Negotiating with them was difficult, because Jack spoke no Tibetan and they claimed not to know Chinese. This was compounded by the problems of democracy: each yakker had an equal say in the proceedings, even the little 12-year-old boy. This was impressive, but it made arriving at an agreement virtually impossible.

However, they eventually agreed to round up their yaks, and then the pantomime began as they inspected our carefully weighed packages. Eloquent gestures of disbelief, despair, manifest impossibility. One of the yakkers was struggling to lift one of our loads, grimacing horribly, when Liz came along with a cup of tea in one hand and casually hoisted the package with the other. . . .

So the yaks stood about resignedly and we lay back with equal resignation and let the yakkers, Jack and Urs get on with it. No point in getting worked up. The yakkers would know how late they could afford to set off and still make the first night's camp site. But Urs was astonished at our laid-back attitude, and confessed that had this been a French, German or Italian expedition there would have been hysterics, shouting, rage and 'the having of kittens'.

Lunchtime came and went, and fewer than half the yaks were loaded. Endless disputes between the yakkers, each trying to minimize the burden of his own beasts – for now they actually own them rather than being part of a collective, they take great care of their yaks. And when we handed out their sunglasses, we saw another example of local egalitarianism: the shades had different coloured rims and each yakker coveted the same ones. So they took off a brightly woven garter they wear, laid out the shades and asked Jack to pair them at random with their identifying garter.

Jack sat down beside Mal and I, complaining mildly about how hard it was to work with yakkers, partly because of the language problem, and also because they keep saying yes and then doing nothing, or they raise a new problem. We had to hide our smiles, because this was exactly how we felt about dealing with the Chinese.

In the late afternoon they finally lurched into motion and the yaks drifted vaguely towards the glacier snout with the yakkers whistling, shouting and occasionally clouting them. One yak load fell off after

100 yards. They were moving very slowly indeed, and the lads
obviously had some hours ahead of them. We stood and watched
the Boy Racers, with Dave and Urs, Kurt and Julie, trail away.
Bright yellow Libond suits, ski-goggles, ski-poles clicking among the
boulders. We all rather envied them but there were simply not
enough yaks in that part of the world to take all our gear up in one
run. Anyway, it seemed more efficient use of time to have the team
operate in two groups, alternatively being on the hill and resting at
Base. This pattern was to determine the structure of all our efforts
from now on, and probably had a decisive influence on the outcome.

'Leave something unclimbed for us!' Mal shouted.

'Look after yourselves,' from Liz.

We watched till they disappeared round the edge of the glacier
snout, then went into the Mess Tent, envious and restless.

It would be another four days before the yaks would be back and
ready to set off again with the remainder of our gear. In the mean-
time we took more walks, ate and drank as much as possible, and
wondered how the Boy Racers were doing. They'd taken a radio
with them, but we'd picked up nothing on our Base Camp, which
surprised us. The Motorola radios had communicated across greater
distances and out of line-of-sight on the Mustagh Tower – that's
why we expected them to work for BC/ABC contact. Perhaps they'd
just forgotten to transmit at the set time, or the radio was broken.
(It wasn't. Despite setting up a Base Station with a more powerful
receiver and battery-pack, we were never to have a radio link between
BC and ABC. That lack of communication, with the logistical and
psychological distance it created between the two camps, made impossible proper organization and utilization of our resources and was
a decisive factor in determining the character of the Expedition and,
finally, its outcome.)

They were due to take three days going up to ABC, and there put
up the Mess Tent and some personal tents. Dave Bricknell was in
charge of setting this camp in order; it had to be a good one. Then,
if they felt up to it, the lads would try to explore and wand the
crevasse-riddled glacier across to the foot of the North-East Ridge
and maybe even make a start on it. They'd do what they could then
come down; we expected to meet them on our way up. It would be
hard work for them, arriving unacclimatized at 6,400 metres. For
both parties the first time up would be an acclimatizer and preparation for the serious assault the next time round.

The weather began to deteriorate in the following days. Everest
disappeared in cloud. Conditions could be rough at ABC –

Bonington had told us it could be quite desperate in a storm. We'd have to wait a week to find out. But. . . .

Allen Fyffe Surprise time! Two figures on the moraine. Urs and Sandy back down from ABC, Sandy with cerebral oedema probably caused by working too hard as the yaks kept shedding their loads. They went to ABC then back down some way; today tried again for ABC but Sandy bad again. . . .

I think some people have had a rude awakening. Sandy's always been the 'strong man' type and for him to fall ill is a bad sign. However it may wake everyone up to what this is all about; Everest is a dangerous place, even the bottom bits.

Sandy looked deeply tired; his eyes were slightly glazed and his face was swollen with water retention. As we plied him and Urs with brews in the Mess Tent he tried to be cheerful and philosophical about it, but it wasn't too hard to sense that he was deeply disappointed and shaken. He'd never thought himself to be a superman, but his body had never let him down like this before on occasions when he'd been higher.

Sandy So we got all the gear loaded, leaving BC behind. East Rongbuk glacier is where we travelled, the yaks really sure of foot, some loads came off, naturally enough. One yak was ill so the yakkers unloaded it and carried half themselves! We moved on up a steep moraine bank of sand and small stones. Rick's barrel fell off and I held the yak as Urs and the yak-driver re-loaded it. . . . We moved on up beside a frozen river and then had to cross over the ice. Kurt and Julie were ahead and filming the two yaks in front of me as they stepped really quite confidently on to the white, slippery and smooth ice. Then noses down looking for the rougher parts. Cows in Britain never walk on ice. One or two fell but managed to get back up on to their knees then their hooves and waddle on. Julie did not look really effervescent so I asked if she were OK. Unfortunately she had the runs and also felt very tired, I hope she'll mend.

So at 6.30 we reached the old Camp 1½ and pitched our tents. There was tension – no need for it. Nick, Jon and Dave were really quite annoyed at Julie and Kurt. As we had only three stoves and three billies, the lads suggested getting inside the Phoenix tents and brewing up in groups of three and four. But Kurt and Julie said no, we'll wait for you guys then take the stoves. . . . I do not want folks to pair or triple off at this point in the trip, but it is the best way to cook and live efficiently when in transit.

My head throbbed but I felt in control. Lots of brews and intermittent sleep.

Round noon the next day we departed, and oh it took an age on the way. Yaks dropping loads, yak drivers trying their utmost to get the yaks to cross over ice bridges. Urs, Nick, Rick and I loaded, loaded and loaded yaks. Sometimes we had to carry loads across. Eventually Kurt and Julie helped too.

We reached pre-war Camp 2 round 7.30. My head was really pounding with the extra work. Tony handed me half a cup of tomato soup, 'Share it with Nick.' I was most pissed off that the lads didn't help with yak loads, etc. I said to them that 'they had let the side down and they were a bunch of egotistical fuckers.' Jon said 'Well, do we get to speak in our defence?' I said 'No, fuck off – say fuck all!' Went back outside to find Urs and Rick with a yak in a crevasse, Jon and Tony did not even help. Dave B. was out there, giving what little he could but he gave.

I was knackered. Urs saw this. Jon obviously realized too as he came and helped Urs pitch our tent. Tony and Jon came later with our rations. Urs went for water and returned very annoyed. 'Those young guys have not even cut a water hole!' Kurt came and said he found it difficult to believe Jon and Tony had sat for three hours and had not found water. He was very wild.

Jon Antxon, the Basque, had asked me to make sure the yak-men didn't steal anything from the tent they had left at 11. Flogged behind half a dozen of them, in my exhausted state sensing a pinko conspiracy. Seeing double by the time we got to their amazing blue brolly tent, parked next to an ice pool. Luckily they'd left a store so managed to get some liquid. Tony and Dave staggered in. 'Why do we do this?' Much later the rest came in, having had an epic time with the yaks. Only Rick, Kurt and Julie civil, the rest blazing with self-righteousness and fatigue. Just cool out, we've got to live together for a long time yet.

Sandy 30th March: up early. Urs did most of the work as I was out of it. Stepping along felt nice, following the yaks up the steadily steepening moraine, then the NE Ridge appeared. Ace, man! Really . . . Stopped for a brew, then another drink stop. Me, I'm saying to Urs, it's fantastic, what do you think, looks hard but not impossible – but look, you can almost see the wind on it . . . Dave comes, sits on a stone, looks at the Ridge and starts to cry. Me, I think it's altitude and pour him a cup of hot tea.

Dave As the ridge came into view and the lack of oxygen made me light-headed, the emotion of the last few months really got to me and I sat down and cried. What was an ordinary man with an ordinary job doing just below Everest Advance Base at nearly 21,000 feet? The years of dreaming and months of planning and the uncertainty all culminated in total emotion. Sandy, Urs and Jon were concerned, but it was hard for them to understand how a non-mountaineer could feel in this environment . . .

Sandy When we decided on a site for ABC, we all went into the teams which were naturally formed on the route here. Urs and I constructed a good stone platform for the tent that we'd been using on the way up. Urs went to get the tent from the yak and it was not there – Jon and Rick had taken it. This did not appear to be a problem at the time, but once Urs and I got the other tent out, we found it was a completely different shape . . . This meant we had to reshape our base, which took a lot of energy, of which we did not possess any extra. I said to Jon that he should have told us that he was going to use 'our' tent, then we would not have spent so much time arranging a base to suit it. Jon said, well they were not allocated to anyone in particular. I agreed . . .

We got our tent pitched about an hour later than anyone else, but it kept getting blown away as we had pitched it sideways into the wind to save totally rebuilding the platform. Kurt helped Urs build a wall to protect our tent from the wind, I crawled inside and made a brew . . .

During the night my head became very sore. I asked Urs for a tablet, took one and my head went away but came back later, feeling about three feet thick so I took more pills. 'I must go down, must go down' going through my head. I was very uncomfortable . . .

Morning came. Urs arranged all: radio, food, stove and Kurt and Julie's high-altitude tent. We walked down the hill from ABC for an hour, then pitched the tent, brewed, etc. Urs did everything, I am grateful for his help. Dave Bricknell came down to see me. 'Well, I thought it would be me who would have to go down,' he said. 'Oh well, a stitch in time,' I said. He probably thought I meant the old proverb, but I meant, well, Everest has been here a long time and we are just the stitch, just a stitch in time . . .

So they dossed about all day at their lower site, brewing, chatting and reading. A touch of cerebral oedema was Urs' opinion; it might go away with a day's rest. They both strongly wanted to return to ABC and get into the action. But Sandy woke next morning with a pounding head. He pushed away anger and despair, took some painkillers and waited. No improvement, so he tried a drug called Diamox – this was a major concession from Sandy and indicates that he was extremely concerned, because he's not at all keen on taking drugs on the hill.

Sandy I was not too impressed with it. Tingle, tingle, tingle went my body. The plan was to go back up to ABC, but inside my head I felt that it would not work. Urs was keen to go up, so at 4.0 pm we packed up the tent and headed for ABC. But I felt so bad, sat on a stone, said to Urs, 'Sorry, but I know I'm going in the wrong direction. I've got to go down.' And down we went ever so slowly . . .

So that was that. Urs' diagnosis was cerebral oedema, then some pulmonary oedema. Now Sandy was down at BC he felt much better, but would need some days to recover fully. Our first casualty among the lead climbers. Given my oedema on arriving at BC, I resolved to go very carefully up to ABC, drinking all the time, very slowly, monitoring myself. It was almost a relief not to be the only person who'd got ill.

Bob I think it strikes a bit of a chill in us all, and I feel that this, this is the moment when the real expedition begins. A feeling reinforced by the deteriorating weather, snow squalls lashing the Mess Tent. So far everything has been rather casual, but suddenly the holiday is over. We are in for a hard couple of months and must hope that fortune smiles on us.

The Boy Racers' first night at ABC was wild. The site is exposed, perched on a long rib of rough moraine running all the way up to the foot of the North Col route. The surrounding hills seem to act as a wind tunnel rather than a wind break, but all the pre-war expeditions used this rib as their Camp 3, as did Bonington, for there's no obvious alternative site.

Jon Oh so impressed by the ridge. Is this the best unclimbed ridge in the high Himalaya? Dave burst into tears on arrival. My eyes were suspiciously moist . . .
  Put up the ABC MacInnes Megabox – a huge system of colour-co-ordinated scaffolding with a Vango orange outer slung on top. We felt much better after it was up. Later on Rick wandered in and said he'd found part of a body . . . It was a pure white piece of bone, part of a human skull.

Rick Found the top part of a human skull 1,000 yards below ABC. Said a few words and dropped it down a deep crevasse. Mallory? Irvine? A yakherd? A reminder of our own mortality.

Jon Nicko found another part a bit lower down the moraine. Took a photo for posterity, stood silent for a while thinking a few words, then Rick reburied it. We did *not* tell Kurt and Julie – they can play around as much as they like but our defences slam shut when a serious subject arises. We didn't need to discuss this.

So they spent the rest of the first day setting up the kitchen, the stoves, organizing the boxes, which the yak herders had dumped anywhere on the moraine, brewing and acclimatizing.
  Another rough and sleepless night, then the usual morning head-aches, slowly clearing with aspirin and brews. Then they set off across the vast white bowl of the glacier that leads to the foot of the North-East Ridge. Nick and Tony led, placing wands as they plodded. These wands were used both to mark out the wider crevasses (often indicated only by a slight fracture-line in the snow) and

to mark out the route, because there would inevitably be times when we'd be stumbling across there, exhausted, in a white-out. The others followed, Jon reflecting that it looked reasonably safe, but that there were some very hollow-sounding sections. We were always very watchful crossing it, and quite often roped up in pairs for additional protection. Why take any more risks than necessary? was the feeling, particularly among the Old Farts, who fully intended to live to grow older still.

Yetis: something we'd often joked about, the majority of us sceptics. And yet, as they tramped across the great wilderness, they came to a line of large prints running across the glacier. They stood and looked at them in silence, knowing full well they were the first **expedition there that year, and indeed the first since Bonington's three years previously. The Basques were going for the old North Col route, and hadn't come anywhere near here. So . . .**

'Saw what looked like Yeti prints,' Jon noted casually, 'and I ain't a believer.'

At the end of the glacier, just past the foot of the North-East Ridge, is the Raphu La pass, one of the great Himalayan viewpoints. After two hours of plodding they stood as near to the cornice edge as possible and looked out over Nepal . . . From right to left they could see Kangchenjunga (some 100 miles away, so thin and clear is the air), Jannu, Chomo Lonzo, Makalu, Lhotse Shar, Lhotse. Evocative names for anyone, but for mountaineers, visions that excited desires, dreams and plans for the future. From where they stood they could also see the upper part of the awesome Kangshung Face (the East Face) of Everest – several thousand feet of wildly fluted snow, ice and rock that defined the far side of our North-East Ridge. Clouds and spindrift boiled up from its depths. Was that where Pete and Joe had gone, or were they, as Sandy feared, still somewhere on the Ridge?

The wind was strong. They shivered and turned for home.

The next morning Nick and Jon felt particularly rough, so it was Tony and Rick who set off back to the Raphu La to reconnoitre a route up the initial pyramid of the Ridge, accompanied by Kurt and Julie and their film equipment. They were filmed crossing the small bergschrund, the characteristic fracture-line at the bottom of a big face. It was crossing the Rubicon – a small but decisive act of commitment. They were finally on the North-East Ridge.

A brief grin, then they began methodically climbing the snow and ice slope, most of it between 40 and 50 degrees, while the camera whirled at the bottom. Tony carried a coil of fixing rope and Rick some snow stakes in his sack. For experienced mountaineers it was reasonably straightforward, so they both soloed. The névé was sound, there was little fresh snow and their crampons and a single ice-axe were quite sufficient. At intervals ribs of rock run up the face; they dumped their gear at the second of these and continued up to the crest of the Ridge, around 6,660 metres. The Kangshung Face, Tony noted, looked even more absurd from close up – but that didn't stop them from at one point sitting right on the crest, one leg dangling over either side. Then they set off down, pleased and suddenly very tired.

As Tony and Rick make our first moves on the mountain, the Old Fart Collective sets off on the first day's trek towards ABC. It snowed at Base the night before, the moon a sickly yellow through the swirl. The yaks look even more mournful than usual this morning as they slump like vast sheep, white in the snow. The yakkers roll balls of tsampa in their tents and light the yak-dung fires as we stumble through the day's first brew.

We finally leave mid-afternoon, after the usual yakkers' pantomime. After Sandy's illness, we're all resolved to go very slowly. It seems to be not so much altitude gain as effort expended that brings on mountain sickness. So our initial steep climb up on to the moraine bank – some 200 feet – takes nearly 30 minutes, with several stops.

An enjoyable day's walk into the wilderness. Rubble, sand and ice. Wind-silence, the click of ski-poles, yak-bells and the croaking of a chough. After an hour and a half we make a left turn and plod step by step up the slope that takes us into the East Rongbuk glacier that leads to Everest. It's easy to see how the 1921 exploratory expedition missed this turn-off, for it looks most unpromising. They ended up having to go 100 miles round the way into the next valley, the Karta valley, before climbing up to roughly our ABC site and then realizing the way they should have come. Each expedition builds on the experience of the last, just as we hope to learn from Bonington's expedition here, and those who come after us will learn from us. We climb, at times literally, on each other's shoulders, like those Chinese acrobats in Peking.

We pass the remains of rock-enclosures which the pre-war trips used to shelter their Camp 1. We stand and consider them in silence, thinking of those who came this way before us. Everest is as much a myth as a mountain, this place is full of ghosts. This stream, this slowly changing view, these very stones under my feet – these are the same our predecessors knew . . . Altitude and silence making me light-headed, dreamily contented through the hours of painful effort.

At length we cross the frozen lake in the light of the setting sun, pitch our tents and start brewing up. Suddenly it's dark and the temperature plummets towards −20°C. Andy Nisbet and I crawl into our bags and organize our evening meal. Good to be with Andy; with our shared history of altitude problems we're both concerned at doing everything just right on the way up; we monitor each other, help each other out when one of us suddenly isn't up to it. I'll never climb at anything near his standard, but on this trek we're equals, partners.

Sweet-and-sour pork and instant potato, tea, chocolate and coffee. We're feeling more substantial now, though both slightly light-headed and headachy. Before settling down in the hope of sleep, I look outside. Moonlight not silver but white; yak-bells, clatter of their hooves, laughter from the yakkers' tent; the air very cold and absolutely still, sweet with smoke; ridges soar in the moonlight on either side, ice-towers glimmer up ahead where we're going tomorrow. This is the essence of adventure for me, camping some-where new on the way from somewhere to somewhere else, the past distant and the future unknown.

We all had a poor night, but Bob's coughing and chest pains were bad enough next morning for him to wait for Urs to catch up from Base Camp. Possibly bronchitis, was the verdict, but not oedema. Bob decided to push on.

It was a long and very demanding day of endless ups and downs on glacier moraine, of hurried traverses through stonefall-prone areas, of chivvying recalcitrant yaks. We seemed to have been going for hours when we met the Boy Racers on their way down. They seemed sickeningly fresh. Only Dave was finally showing the strain, though he'd coped extraordinarily well. They gave us an update on their doings: they had accomplished less than we'd hoped for, but quite a lot just the same. That was to be the pattern throughout, we always seemed to fall short of our aims – typical of altitude climbing. Jon cheerfully told us the worst of the day lay ahead. 'Purgatory, mate, bleedin' purgatory.' In our innocence we thought he was just winding us up . . .

Purgatory it is. I must have done something terrible in a past life to merit this punishment. Hour after hour anting our way along a medial moraine bank that ran like a disintegrating highway between ranks of surreal ice-towers, into the teeth of a freezing wind and swirling snow. These ice-pinnacles, fins of ice some 200 feet high, are unique to this part of the Himalayas. Allen with his geography degree explains their formation is due to the combination of intense sunlight and very dry air, which causes the ice to 'sublimate', i.e. pass straight from solid to vapour. We take pictures, another water-break and stagger on.

We're grim and silent, strung out along the moraine. Chris has the joyless Joy Division on his Walkman, Allen tries in vain to find fresh impetus from ZZ Top's driving rock. I retreat into a world of vague memories and fantasies, force myself to remember and recite the whole of that damned *Men On Ice* which got me into this mess in the first place. Don't look up, don't wonder how much longer this is going to go on. This present step is bearable. And the next. And the next . . . Don't *force*. Always keep something in reserve . . .

But we were all running on empty by the time the yakkers finally halted at an inhospitable and exposed spot in the gusting snow. Andy had somehow got our tent up, so we started melting ice and making brews for everyone. My only comfort was that the others looked as bad as I felt, all staggering about like zombies trying to locate the barrels of gear we needed for the night. Liz suddenly started crying in sheer exhaustion and frustration, angry at her weakness. Mal sat on a rock with gloved hands under armpits, vomiting while he went through the agonizing hot-aches as circulation returned. Sarah was very pale and silent, feeling worse than she'd ever felt and missing Nick after meeting him earlier in the day. She resolved to go back down the next day and cheered up a little. Bob felt not so much exhausted as downright ill, was coughing feebly and wondering if he too would have to go down. Only Urs and Allen had any energy left in them, and gave it generously like the good team-members they were.

Hard times in the freezing half-light, trying to wrestle shelter, warmth, and sustenance from our grim surroundings. Finally into our sleeping bags, change socks and gloves. Another brew boils, we drop our food-pouches into the billy and cook by the light of our head-torches. Andy is suffering after his earlier efforts and I'm largely in charge. We have a final brew with aspirin and a sleeping pill. I insist on making another. We wake from fitful sleep and brew up again; I glance out and see two other tents glowing by stove-light. Insomniac Brewers Incorporated . . .

Bob Had a dreadful night with coughing and a headache and about 4.0 am I resolved to go down. Regrettably I got some broken sleep after that, felt good enough to start off, albeit very slowly. This was a bad mistake, and the final moraine slopes to ABC were a torture – I'd got violent chest pains and a severe headache and just collapsed into a tearful heap when

Urs came to get me. I was rustled off to a tent immediately, vomited several times and then managed to doze for a while. Urs is very reassuring, but indicates that I might have to go down tomorrow. If I hadn't been such a damn fool I'd have gone down this morning anyway.

Mal . . . passed Bob Barton who was lying down on the moraine, which seemed strange but he said he was okay (mega mistruth!). Turned a slight corner and there facing me was the NE Ridge in entirety. Big – a very inadequate word. Fucking enormous. Emotionally I was buzzing. One of the few mountains that have affected me that way. Goose pimples or the shivers down the back of my legs. Pete and Joe up there somewhere. The Ridge is too big for just a couple of people. Mammoth.

   Tears in my eyes, yeah sure, but who or what for? Apprehension even fear for the people I've brought across the world to do this thing.

We all finally straggle into ABC in various stages of elation and distress. Bob takes nearly an hour to cover the last 200 yards. 'Summit speed,' Allen thinks. Bob's face is swollen, his vision blurry and his lips blue – as they were to remain for the next six weeks. In the Mess Tent Julie is doling out soup. An hour's rest till we summon the energy to put up our tents. Kurt and Urs generously go round helping build tent platforms amid the jagged, sloping rubble. I'm in a daze, working on automatic, but my monitor tells me I am in better shape than on arriving at BC.

   As I sink nose-down into broken sleep I think of 'our' Ridge, seen in entirety today for the first time. It's an 8,000-foot-high wave of rock and ice, soaring out of the flat calm of the Raphu La. A wave nearly three miles long. This mountain just gets bigger and bigger. Looking at it was a blow to the pit of my stomach. But immense satisfaction at being here. And some optimism – the general opinion is the Ridge is monstrous but climbable, given the right conditions.

   And then I look inside myself, and at my friends, and our ambitions seem laughable. Here we are, crawling to ABC on the last of our strength, at a mere 6,400 metres, and we seriously think – !

Going Up

'Totally shafted but grinning from ear to ear.'

ABC was grim. Nobody liked it. It had neither the excitement of being on the hill nor the comfort and comparative ease of Base Camp living. Our tents were much closer together there, but since we were usually knackered they could as well have been 100 yards apart.

All the lads' diaries list the same discomforts. 6,400 metres is high for a base one might use for ten days at a time, too high to fully acclimatize to, too high for recovery. So we slept badly due to the lack of oxygen, all suffering those endless uncomfortable insomniac nights that drain energy and commitment. The usual lethargy, incipient headaches, nausea. Pronounced loss of appetite too, which wasn't helped by our cooking arrangements. The petrol stoves, bad enough at Base, were a disaster at ABC. There always seemed to be someone crouched cursing over a dismantled stove. The small gas stoves made cooking and brewing slow and awkward. In retrospect, we needed a full-time cook at ABC; that would have made life there much less wearing, and kept climbers' energies for more important work. No one wants to get up first thing in the morning, hack out a barrel of ice and start melting it; no one wants to set up breakfast or any other meal for another eight – it takes a serious amount of energy and good-will, both of which are in short supply at altitude. The result was invariably late morning starts, often by people who hadn't had enough to drink, and patchy evening meals. All too often we'd huddle shivering in the Mess Tent, finding that a kettle of luke-warm water didn't go far among eight, each individually trying to hack open a tin of fish or corned beef that was permafrost rigid in the middle and mushy at the edges where we'd tried to defrost it over a flame. All too often plates and pans and mugs went unwashed – for who could spare precious hot water, and who would make the effort? Liz and Sarah were both to do more than their share of ABC work, making their contribution to the Expedition, but when they weren't there or were exhausted from assisting in load-carrying, conditions went downhill.

One element entirely out of our control at ABC was the extreme cold. Minus 20°C to −30°C most nights, often freezing and blustery by day. At night our breath would condense on the inside of the tents then turn to ice, which would shower down like snow when the wind shook the fabric or one brushed against it – ice which would then melt and make sleeping bags and clothing damp. Most of us had a stove for insomniac and morning brews, making us both more self-sufficient and more separate. My most vivid memories of ABC are of my numb hand groping out of my bag in the dark to fill a billy with ice, warming the lighter for a few minutes till it would work, then lying back watching the ice on my tent glitter by the stove's blue light. Wondering what the hell I'm doing here, will I stay up another day or go down tomorrow? Is anyone else awake? For that matter, is there anyone else anywhere? And so one would wander down the solipsistic labyrinths of the oxygen-starved brain till the water finally boiled, then laboriously make the brew and drink, propped up on one elbow, staring into the mug and thinking of nothing at all.

ABC was grim. We never liked it.

But the adrenalin was flowing on 6th April, when after a rest-day we set off in force for the hill. Bob had had to go down, and Liz was worn out after working hard tidying up the Mess Tent the day before, but the remaining seven of us all put loads in our sacks, strapped on the crampons, picked up ski-poles, adjusted shades, smeared on barrier cream and set off for the Ridge.

Andy Nisbet and I rope together. As slow acclimatizers, we're carrying our loads – gas cylinders, a stove, hill-food bags – only to the foot of the Ridge. He asks me to lead, which I appreciate. It's good to be given some responsibility. Today I'm raised, for the first time feeling myself to be actually on Everest. The early section sounds hollow in places, with many crevasses obscured by snow. Luckily they're mostly only a few inches wide. Still, one could easily break an ankle or a leg here, so I go carefully, prodding with the ski-pole, scanning the snow ahead.

I like this ... crunching slowly across the glittering expanse. Everything's yellow through glacier goggles, very high-contrast. Flat clouds steam over the North Col on my right, spindrift birls skyward from the North-East Ridge in front. Sudden gusts send the loose snow scurrying past our ankles. I look back at Andy, he nods slightly so I stop and wait till he comes up. We rest, leaning on our poles.

It's wonderful to feel so small yet fully in control, so relaxed yet so purposeful.

We plod off again towards the next marker wand. Black specks in the distance. Another marker wand. I'm in no hurry to be done, this could go on forever. Only when we hit the final incline after an hour, a modest 15°, do we start to wobble and have to stop every few minutes. We finally crest the slope and see the ape-like figure of Danny standing in a forest of ski-poles, wands and loads. He grins broadly, openly exhilarated. The 'novices' show their emotions much more. Together we move the gear out of reach of any avalanche coming down the initial pyramid of the Ridge, make a stash and wand it so it can be found after snowfall. Then we sit on our packs, take out our water bottles and settle down to watch the action on the hill . . .

Which was very slow, dreamlike, like a minimalist movie where at great length almost nothing happens. Mal had decided that we'd take up Bonington's suggestion and fix ropes up the initial pyramid to the crest of the Ridge. That 1,800-foot snow and ice slope was not technically difficult for experienced climbers in good conditions, but Bonington had felt it to be avalanche prone, and his expedition had found the descent unpleasant, wearing and worrying in bad conditions. With our kind of heavyweight expedition we'd be going up and down there many times carrying loads; fixed ropes would make going up easier because one can pull with the arms as well as push with the legs, and make descents much more quick and secure. There had been some muted disagreement over whether fixed ropes were necessary, but that quickly disappeared once everyone had made an exhausted, bad-weather descent. In the end, they probably saved the lives of one or more of us.

It was Allen Fyffe who crossed the bergschrund and led off the first 700 feet of the blue polypropelene rope, climbing slowly and methodically. He banged in a snow stake, secured the line and rested while Mal and Wattie came up the rope to his stance. Meanwhile Urs and the Pink Rabbit ('Who is that masked rabbit?' 'This silver carrot will reveal my identity!') led out the next bale of rope. They veered gradually to the right, by this time tiny specks on the huge face. The scale of the Ridge started to dawn on us as we realized this initial pyramid was merely an introduction. The Pink Rabbit led up an ice-bulge, where the slope steepened to some 70°, then crossed to a rock rib and found a belay there among the fractured blocks. Mal, Chris and Urs clipped on their jumars and laboured after him with their loads. At 6,800 metres, the rock rib was their high point for the day. They half-buried their loads and set off back down.

'Pretty tiring for a first effort,' Mal recorded. 'Nice image of Fyffey enveloped in spindrift as we went back across the glacier, like one of Bonington's pics and just what you would expect on Everest.'

Meanwhile Andy and I were finding the way back to ABC long, and the last mild incline up to ABC was sheer hard work, as it would always be to knackered climbers returning from the hill. Finally we got up to do what we knew we had to – hack out a barrel of ice. Boom-boom headaches, irritation, absolute weakness. But with two brews the greyness departed, and we began melting more ice for the lads' return.

Half an hour later the Old Farts clambered wearily up the moraine bank. Mal looked particularly beat, while Urs and the Pink Rabbit were revoltingly cheeful. Then Jon and Rick turned up, having trekked from Base Camp in a day, eager for the fray. Lots of Boy Racer stress – 'What have you done?' 'Why do we need fixed ropes?' 'When are we moving up to Camp 2?' and so on. With Tony, Sandy and Nick due up the next day, I decided I'd head down the next morning, along with Urs and the Rabbit. Lack of tent space was the excuse I gave myself, but in truth I'd had enough for my first time up.

Bob Another dreadful night persuades me of the inevitable and I pack up and set off down, tormented by doubts of whether I'm doing the right thing – if I'm fit enough to walk down then surely I'm fit enough to stay at ABC? I feel bad but do I really feel worse than anyone else? I almost turn back but rationality prevails. I feel terribly isolated from the rest of the expedition and Jon and Rick powering their way back into the fray seem in a different world, and for the first time I feel badly homesick. I creep shamefacedly into Base Camp at dusk to a kind, warm welcome . . .

I've noticed quite a bad defect of vision in my right eye, and Urs says this is a retinal haemorrhage due to altitude, annoying but probably not serious. Daunting to think that this sort of damage to blood vessels is also going on in the brain.

Sandy About 4.0 pm I strolled out of the Mess Tent, Jack called to me 'Hey, Sandy, come with us!' Mr Luo, jeep drivers and other liasion officers were with him. They walked in the direction of the memorial plaques behind our camp. I went along as Jack told me that today, 5th April (our Good Friday), is the Chinese mourning day and they (this group I was now unwittingly involved with) were on their way to pay their respects to the dead. The Tibetan jeep driver put little piles of rice in front of the memorial plaques and sprinkled some rice over the cairns. He did it to them all, including Pete and Joe's, as we followed in a close group behind.

Then Luo and I stood in front of Pete and Joe's memorial cairn and Jack
went to take a photo – I thought 'What's the point, Jack, they're dead,
Everest is hidden in the normal afternoon cloud and you can't see a thing!'
Jack rushed forward and pushed a Holy Bible into my hands, I held it and
just as Jack moved back and took the photo a weird, really sad feeling
overtook me. Tears semi-swelled up in my eyes. I choked them off, not
wanting to show the Chinese lads this was upsetting me.

Dave Bob arrived soon after at Base, very despondent, bad head and chest
cough – oedema? Kurt and Julie arrived later, having enjoyed the trip
down, playing among the ice fins and sliding down the frozen river. Long
chat about news and plans with Sandy cooking for them (he is marvellous
like that – he will cook for latecomers, look for things when it's cold and
dark – he is very generous with his energy). His remarks can be very
cutting, but it's usually to deflate bullshit, and at heart he is generous. He'd
got over his oedema, at least at this altitude, and seems much more relaxed
now, maybe it's the smaller group – in many ways I like Sandy the most
of the group, he is certainly more open and less self-centred than the rest.
   I can relate to Kurt and Julie easier than the Boy Racers, and I enjoy
sitting up and talking – what a waste to bury your head in a book as most
do, even at meals, and disappear to bed with a Walkman . . . There is an
antipathy towards Kurt and Julie from the younger set, who seem to think
that the filming is an intrusion – bloody daft – without its money they
would not be here at all – so grin and bear it when Kurt says 'Vun more
time . . .'
   I try to fill my days here – a 12-hour day does seem such a waste, and
the amount of idleness around me makes me sure I could never be a
mountaineer – and I don't believe they are 'saving their energy' all the time
– leisure time can still be relaxing if it's filled – but Walkman and trash
novels!

Another bad night all round, and everyone was washed out the next
day from their exertions on the hill, or by coming up from BC in a
day for the first time. Allen showed his determination and commitment by forcing himself to carry a load with Andy Nisbet up to the
previous high-point, where they re-aligned the rope and added a
couple of snow stakes. Andy went slowly, monitoring himself carefully. He was now well above the height where he'd got ill on
Nuptse, he was into the unknown. Liz went with them carrying a
load to the stash at the foot of the Ridge.
   The others rested. Nothing gained by burning out at this stage,
Mal thought as he warded off a mild pang of guilt. It's so hard to
know when one is being prudent or merely lazy.
   Which was exactly what I felt, wandering alone down the 15
miles to BC. Urs had long since disappeared into the distance. Should

I have stayed on? Both Mal and Urs had said that the pattern should be: go on to the hill, make your contribution for as long as you can, then come down to recuperate at BC. With our numbers we could rotate, pace ourselves. Yet still that lingering doubt.

I met Sandy and Tony on their way up. How often on this expedition people were to meet each other for only ten minutes on that trail, exchange news and pass on. And we nearly always descended alone. I asked Sandy how he was while Tony grumbled about fixed ropes. 'Pretty good, actually. That summit is MINE!'

A long descent, happy to be going down and on my own, slightly worried when I lost the trail several times. A driving snow made footing awkward and life unpleasant. It was with pleasure and relief that after seven hours I stumbled across the flat moraine towards the Mess Tent, dumped my sac and pushed in. My journal entry is fairly typical of how we all felt whenever we returned to base.

Andy G A very warm greeting from Kurt and Julie, Bob, Dave – hi, Terry! He arrived from Lhasa a couple of days ago, is delighted with life. Gives me a big grin and (a) a packet of chocolate Easter eggs (when was Easter?) (b) four packets of cigarette papers (c) two letters from Kathleen. A star. He's also brought old Sunday papers and magazines as diverse as *The Economist, New Musical Express* and *Face*.

It feels warm, friendly, relaxing being back at BC. Lots of big oxygen molecules about; not in a mental clench any more. Huge meal of real potatoes, curry, fresh oranges, and the first cigarette for days. Oh yes, yes! Much laughter, we're much livelier down here. Feel so grey and stupid at ABC. Still, should be better next time up.

Now in the warm world of my tent, reading the fashion magazines – clothes, records, social trends, etc. Not so much a foreign country as another planet. Hard to imagine I was once interested. Do such things really matter? But then – does this? Read Kathleen's letters several times, they're funny and tender, talk of us taking a motorbike holiday in Spain when I get back. Not something I can afford to think about now. Take my pill and wait for sleep. Christ it's good to be back here. Like spring after winter.

Terry Can't believe I'm here, that I've really made it. Feeling a bit headachy but looking forward with trepidation to heading off up the mountain to at least ABC. I am determined that I will contribute as much as I can . . . I'm frightened to death of being the worst member of the team.

Mal 8th April. Off eventually at 10 am with Chris, Jon and Rick behind. Plot was for Chris and myself to collect gas, stoves, food and tent from top of fixed rope and fix more as far as possible. I was going like a heap of shit (major will-power to avoid packing it in), Chris seemed in good form as were Jon and Rick. Eventually fixed across the huge couloir and up a spur to find a small wand in the snow! Further investigation led to the discovery of Bonington's First Snowcave – exactly three years after they'd chosen the site.

Jon Chris dug out a Karrimat blocking the entrance, then I look over. Feeling a bit like Howard Carter at the entrance to King Tutankamen's tomb, I hacked a hole through . . . There was just a cup or two in sight in a small, compressed chamber. 'Anyone fancy a Nikon camera?' I said facetiously. But later excavating revealed a pair of down boots, down mitts, Pete Boardman's red windsuit, some food, an onion and . . . an XA Olympus camera, still working after being buried for three years! It was all a bit creepy, like the *Marie Celeste*. Got a good two-man doss excavated and slept like the just.

Finding the snow cave was a piece of unlooked-for good luck. For the price of an hour's work, it gave us a ready-made extra camp on a ridge notoriously short of good sites. Our original intention was to put our Camp 1 at Point 7090 on the crest of the Ridge, but as the snow cave came to be used regularly it was eventually known as Camp 1 or simply 'CB's'. Mal and Chris set off back down the fixed ropes in a blizzard, while Jon and Rick slept in the cave in preparation for going up the next day to locate a site near 7,090 metres (roughly 23,400 feet) for our Camp 1 (later known as Camp 2 or simply 7090).

There was a lot of movement off the hill. Nick, Sarah and Dave arrived at ABC; Andy, Allen, Liz and Danny descended with the latest news. The weather was wild on the hill, and mild and lovely at Base. Terry and I played guitars in the sunshine, Bob made bread, Julie typed film notes, Tony peeled apples. We washed our clothes and ourselves, spread damp gear out in the sun to dry. Urs was busy, first with a poisoned finger of Kurt's. The legendary 8,000 metres hero was pale and quiet as Urs took out his instruments. They both had a stiff whisky to fortify themselves, then the finger was pierced, drained and bandaged. A whisky to celebrate. Then the Rabbit came in with a grossly swollen and septic big toe. 'What I need,' muttered Urs, 'is a trombone.' We looked at each other. 'A trombone?' 'Oui, oui, a trombone,' he said firmly. It seemed our effervescent Swiss gnome had suffered brain damage till we discovered 'trombone' is the French slang for paper-clip. So Urs and the Rabbit had a tumbler of whisky each, then Urs held a needle by the 'trombone', heated it red-hot in a candle-flame, then slowly pushed the glowing needle right through the nail on the Rabbit's toe. At this point, as blood and pus began to ooze out, the onlookers also required a medicinal dose of whisky to steady their nerves.

By evening we were all feeling quite mellow, Urs particularly voluble as he celebrated an interesting day's work.

Bob Later had some good conversation about mountain romanticism (my view – Whillans was a crypto-Romantic!), baked some bread, and at last life seems to be worth the candle again. This evening Terry and Andy played and sang together and we drank a little . . . All in fine spirits. I think we may be what the books call 'a happy expedition'. Two nights ago it was −32°C at ABC. Why am I so keen to get up there?

Andy G. Looking round at us relaxed and laughing, feeling this tent in the wilderness of the Himalayas to be the last word in luxury, I wonder if we have to keep undergoing difficulty, suffering and deprivation before we can appreciate what we've got. To be able to wash, or sleep without ice falling on one – to sleep at all! – to eat fresh bread, to have a song, these things seem so wonderful to us down here. It's like being in love, when for a brief time everything seems miraculous. How can we make it a state of mind that will endure, that is not the plaything of circumstance. Firm foundations is what I seem to be looking for on this trip . . .

Urs said he's never read a book which has captured the mountaineering experience truly – either too romantic or too factual. So much of climbing is so physically banal and demanding there's little time for reflection and spiritual uplift. And yet of course it's there, for all of us, from time to time. Urs talked of being alone at the top of the fixed rope and the wind suddenly dropping as he stood looking across the Himalaya into Nepal . . .

'Yes,' said Terry thoughtfully, 'everyone who comes here is looking for something inside and something outside, in different proportions.'

Jon 9th April. Away by 10.0 am to get to Point 7090. Rick first then me on a climbing rope. Last bit I took over. Pulled over a lip, an almost Scottish finale, on to the horizontal bit of the Ridge leading to Bonington's 2nd snow cave. Flattish, not knife-edged. Rick came up with a whoop for the view of the Buttresses and Pinnacles. Very very inspiring.

Feel great. Photos, then wandered along the ridge a bit to recce the 'holes' there for potential snow caves. No joy, so abseiled down the climbing rope to a cave about 100 feet down. A natural hole, which we enlarged. A bit spooky, as we didn't know if the floor was okay – a big hole at one end. I left Rick to it for the last hour and went down to CB's to get the brew on. Soloing, facing out, concentrate . . .

And so our Camp 1 (which became Camp 2 or 7090 – confused? So were we!) was manufactured inside not so much a cave as a crevasse formed by a cornice fracture line just below the crest of the Ridge. It was not ideal, being draughty and lacking a floor in places.

But it would have to do, for the Ridge has few snow banks one can dig a cave in. We felt it far too exposed for tents, and the only alternative was to dig a cave into the ice, as Bonington's team had done for their Camp 1.

Kurt and Julie set off in the jeep to explore Karta and the Karma valley. This surprised us, as they had not yet gone beyond the bergschrund or filmed us pushing out the route. Their film, we now realized, was going to be only partly about our Expedition. The weather blew up into a full-scale gale that evening, at both ABC and Base. We sat in our respective Mess Tents, hanging on to the sides, once or twice stumbling outside to strengthen the guy ropes. Mal and Chris returned from ABC, hoarse and weathered. Wine, laughter and music at BC, harder times further up the hill.

Next morning it was clear no one was going climbing. Jon and Rick descended, bantamweight Rick getting blown over several times while crossing the glacier to ABC. Everywhere we battened down hatches for the day.

At Base I was quietly finishing an *Express* article while Bob and Danny were locked in a titanic chess struggle when a whirlwind hit the tent. One side blew out, the whole fabric lifted and quivered, the air was thick with dust and papers and outside we heard a great Whumph! followed by crashes and bangs. We rushed outside and found the Chinese tent had simply disappeared and barrels and pans were rolling over the ice lake. Dave Bricknell's empty tent was flattened, as if a yak had fallen on it. Worst of all, from my point of view at least, was that my precious article was flying down the valley in the general direction of Xegar.

Much boulder humping, replacing and adding guy lines. With some improvization we managed to restore most of the Chinese tent. The gale blew the rest of the day but there would be no more whirlwinds.

It was on this day 38 years earlier that the Canadian Earl Denman had arrived here at Base Camp, intending to make himself immortal by being the first man to climb Everest. He had entered Tibet illegally and secretly with the soon-to-be-famous Tenzing Norgay and Ang Dawa. Shivering at Base with their pitifully inadequate equipment, he looked at Everest and still believed he could climb it despite his minimal climbing experience. All one needed was idealism and will-power . . .

The next day brought the first signs of spring at Base. A few bees droned laboriously by, working very hard to stay up in the thin air. Between the rocks one would come across little patches of moss or miniature shrubs. We'd already seen some game-cocks and chamois-like creatures, even a couple of rabbits, and it astonished us that they could live in this apparently absolute desert. Base Camp had also gathered its own flock of pigeons, which the Chinese spent hours trapping, and a number of choughs. Water ran freely from the ice-lake, making life a lot easier, and the lake itself was evaporating both from above and below, leaving the surface wildly pitted and in sections ice hanging a foot or so above absolutely dry stones. There was no slush – somehow that seemed typical, everything in Tibet was simple and extreme, uncluttered. There was rock, ice, snow; a great deal of sky and a great deal of silence.

But at ABC the weather was still wild and we lost another day's climbing.

Nick Should have carried a load today – weather very windy, no good on the Ridge. But eased off later and Sarah, Dave and the Rabbit went to Raphu La and on to climb summit 6823 on left-hand side of the Col, same hill Kurt and Julie climbed (to film Tony and Rick on their first outing on the Ridge). I'm impressed – Sarah obviously worked hard – though technically not hard, it's quite high – Dave obviously thrilled to bits – good on him, a great climax to his time here. He goes to BC tomorrow then off home. I think in many ways we'll miss him. He's been a great asset – organizer and morale booster.

Dave And to think we nearly didn't go. It was very windy again overnight, very severe gusts making the whole tent move, but it survived very well. I woke up thinking 'that's it, nobody will want to go up today,' but over breakfast the Pink Rabbit said 'Shall we go?' and Sarah and I both said 'Yes,' and it was decided – the rounded peak (6823) to the left of the Raphu La, all 22,385 feet of it. We were off at 11.30, only an hour over the glacier to the cache, me carrying about 15 wands and flags, which I then dumped, and then a two-hour plod up to the summit. Not a problem, I felt very fit and Sarah was struggling a bit so there were plenty of breathers, all very easy and no risk – a slip would take you on a toboggan run back to the Raphu La.

We got to the summit about 2.30. The views were fantastic; as we climbed, the whole of the Kangshung Face opened up, including the well-named Fantasy Ridge: enormous fluted and etched buttresses rising in a series of crests to just below the Pinnacles. Lhotse and the ridge to Lhotse Shar . . . far away were Kangchenjunga and Jannu . . . Chomolonzo and Makalu were much closer, and further round Changtse showed its true elegance.

Sarah and I felt very smug, only Jon and Rick have gone higher on this trip! and for me it was a proper climax. To have bagged a peak was more exciting than to have done a part-carry on the far more dangerous Ridge. Anyway, I had promised Ilush I would do nothing technical above the Raphu La.

Back to camp about 4.30 – Urs had just arrived and there was no brew ready – of course – mountaineers at rest must be the idlest people around. A long chat with all of us waiting for a cook to volunteer.

I'm not sorry to be leaving tomorrow. It's been exciting up here but I could not follow or out-do today without real climbing . . . Good sleep and rapid progress back home will be a welcome relief. I've made the managerial contribution, now it's down to the order of load-carrying and who is to do what – only Mal can do that as team leader. I only hope he does because it's pretty anarchic at present.

Meanwhile Bob, Urs, Andy Nisbet and Terry set off for ABC to get back into the fray.

We'd lost three days to bad weather, but Mal wasn't too worried. We had to expect some storms at this time of year. What was crucial was would the weather improve in the latter part of April through May when we'd be working high on the Ridge. That was the normal weather pattern in this part of the world, with increasingly stable conditions right up to the monsoon, which could arrive any time between the last week in May and the end of June. The monsoon's arrival was always a great unknown and we had to work on the assumption it would come early.

So when Jon and Sandy came down with Dave to BC the next day there was need for a general tactical discussion. But when they walked into the Mess Tent Mal was sitting reading a book with his headphones on and just carried on while the rest of us caught up on the latest news from the hill. That astonished me, and pissed off the lads no end, though they kept it to themselves. Jon thought Mal would have to start reconciling his role as a climber and shuffling dosser with being the leader of a large expedition. Everest was not like the Mustagh Tower scaled up, where one could just let things work themselves out between a few climbers who were with each other constantly. This trip needed active, even dominating, leadership, that was just not Mal's style nor in his experience.

'For fuck's sake, Duff . . .' thought Sandy. I tried to paper over the cracks by being hyper-enthusiastic in getting their tales of doings on the hill. I'd seen this before in Mal. When he is absorbed in something – a book, newspaper, climbing, TV – nothing else exists, his concentration is absolute. That is one of the reasons why he is such a good and safe climber. Liz would try to point out it was rude to carry on reading or viewing when friends dropped in, but it never made much difference. I felt it wasn't my place to suggest he needed to show more evident interest. Liz might well try to but would probably be told to mind her own business . . . followed by an apology later. It wasn't as if Mal wasn't thinking about the Expedition most of the time, but he had got into the pattern of spending BC days in his tent or reading, as if entirely oblivious of everything going on around about. What he thought or worried about, he seldom confided. I could see it was a strain, this responsibility and isolation. He seemed very abstracted much of the time. This mirrored Sandy's prevailing mood, for he too often felt apart from everyone, ill at ease among the numbers, thinking of Dominique in the South of France, his future, the meaning of what he was doing, Joe and Pete.

In retrospect, incidents like Jon and Sandy's return from ABC were indicative of the nature of the Expedition. There's no doubt it was a 'happy Expedition' without bitter internal divisions or confrontations; we got on well, worked together, shared some laughter and conversation – but we never quite gelled. We lacked the cohesive commitment and the disciplined, organized unity of purpose required for the hardest achievements. We took our cues from each other, and the dominant personal sense of isolation we felt probably came initially from Mal and Sandy.

It wasn't till the next day that the necessary discussions took place, over many brews in the Mess Tent. I sat in on it, partly as a recorder and also because the lads seemed to feel that precisely because I wasn't a lead climber I could be counted on for objective comment when required.

Sandy Chats and discussions with Mal, Jon, Andy G. Jon and I both notice Mal seems protective and defensive when we mention an idea. We mention this to Mal and he settles a little – I don't think he looks too well, I wonder how he is, he has not got a nice job, plus the BBC recording and all. Yeah, he's a little bit stressed and I get the feeling he needs to crawl to some quiet place . . . We've all got such places . . .

The talking helped, but there was little we could resolve. We needed a permanent ABC manager and we hadn't got one. Sarah, Liz, myself and Terry were all prepared to do what we could up to a point, but Terry and I were needed to do some support climbing, together with our other responsibilities, and Liz wanted to climb too. Sarah had paid her own way so had no responsibility to the Expedition; as it turned out she did a great deal, but ABC living was too hard and thankless for her to stay up all the time. Perhaps when more of the lads were sleeping on the hill it would be less necessary. As for standardizing and directing loads, Mal pointed out most of us were at different stages of acclimatization. Bob was clearly struggling desperately, we'd discovered Nick was still suffering from the amoebic dysentery he'd picked up in Nepal, Sandy was having to go easy. He suggested we carried on as before, people picking up from ABC whatever they felt up to carrying that was obviously needed on the hill. Jon gave a slightly cynical grin and remarked on Mal's touching faith in his climbers' conscientiousness. Who would willingly wear themselves out carrying big loads when they would then lose the chance of getting out in front, of making 8,000 metres, perhaps getting to lead into the Pinnacles?

So the conclusion was pretty much carry on as before. But it was agreed that the next three weeks were crucial. We had to carry something like 30 loads up to Camp 2, start acclimatizing to that level by sleeping there, and push the route out along the Ridge to establish a Camp 3 either before or after the Rock Buttresses. Only then could we start moving the oxygen, stoves, food, climbing gear up to near the Pinnacles. This carrying would be punishing and thankless, devoid for the most part of any interesting climbing – only the 1st Buttress offered technical interest. It had to be done as quickly as possible yet without burning ourselves out.

The conversation later turned to fear, something mountaineers seldom openly discuss. 'There's different kinds of fear,' Mal said. 'There's fear on a rock route, gripped out of your skull when you're in fact only ten feet above a bomb-proof runner. Then there's fear on an ice-route when you know if you fall off or give in to it, you're dead . . .'

Jon and Sandy nodded. 'And big-mountain fear is different,' Jon added, 'more of a dull ache than a sudden stab. A certain level of anxiety, always there.'

So Dave left for Lhasa in our jeep, taking with him our thanks, momentary envy, TV and newspaper reports – and most important, our mail. He shook hands all round, took a last lingering look, then set off on the jolting journey back to his normal life, back to family and suits and desk, wondering if he'd ever be able fully to adjust to them again.

Sandy Let's go climbing! With an ice-tool and hard blue ice . . . me, I can see the crystals, place my pick there, oh gently, and rise up to a new crampon hold, points gripping delicately. I like that . . . millions of crystals, and spaces between them for us folks who know how to find them . . . That's my game. I wonder what Dominique plays right now. It's difficult trying to love an independent woman. But guys like us (thinking too of Andy G.) probably need independent women. With heads, ideas, dreams and convictions of their own. That's how I like to think it anyways.

Long black hair spread on a pillow . . . But having said that . . . Let's GO CLIMBING!

We went climbing. This was the consolidation stage of the Expedition, the time when much of the unglamorous, repetitive and exhausting work gets done. 'Himalayan thuggery' Jon calls it. Crawling out of one's pit, brewing, then gearing up for the day, gather a load and set off . . . Returning wiped out before sundown; brew, eat, chat if one still has the energy, into one's pit, take a sleeping pill maybe, then thoughts of home or tomorrow till broken sleep comes . . . then waking and struggling again out of the warm sleeping bag.

The following ten days were as productive as they were unspectacular. The weather wasn't wonderful – still tending to blow a lot in the afternoon – but we only lost one day to it. It was very freewheeling, everyone doing what they felt able to. We quickly found that two consecutive days of carrying from ABC to Camp 2 and back to ABC were the limit. Often a big day out necessitated a restday. As people burned out, they went down to BC for a break, and others came up.

Our loads were primarily gas, stoves, hill-food bags, some climbing gear and rope. The 12 oxygen bottles meant a lot of extra carrying – one was a reasonable load, two very hard indeed. There were no scales, everyone just picked up what felt possible on that day, but our loads probably varied between 20 and 40 lb. It doesn't sound much, but at altitude every pound feels like a kilogram at best, a stone at worst.

As well as carrying loads, everyone needed to aid acclimatization by sleeping at least once at Camp 1 or 2. That meant carrying up a sleeping bag and a few extra bivvy items, which greatly reduced the payload one could carry.

I have the Roll of Honour on my desk now, pieced together by Sandy. It's scrawled in blunt pencil on the notebook we kept at ABC as a log, cross-hatched with arrows, corrections, Sandy's calculations of what was now stocked at each camp, how many loads there were still to go. It's crumpled, coffee-stained, abruptly broken off –

April 12 Nick, load to CB's. Hammered with dysentery. Tony, Rick carried to C2, completed fixed ropes. All back to ABC.

April 13 Urs, Andy, loads to C2. Urs put a shovel straight through the floor of C2 and found himself looking straight down the Kangshung Face. Bob knackered at 6,400 metres, left load there. All back to ABC. Nick, Sarah to BC.

On this day Earl Denman, after a desperately cold and sleepless night, set off with Tenzing Norgay and Ang Dawa for the North Col. As far as one can judge by his account, they managed to get only a few hundred yards up the slope and were brought to a standstill by a freezing, howling gale. Unlike his equally single-minded predecessor Maurice Wilson, who'd persisted and died there in similar circumstances in 1934, Denman saw sense at this point. He realized his dream was hopeless, and he turned and practically ran back to their Base Camp, away from the now hateful mountain. What makes, for me, this fiasco something more than a farce is the extent of his bitterness and disillusionment – from being an obsessively anti-materialistic idealist, after Everest he concluded that the majority of people had been right all along, and the only worthwhile objective in life is the acquisition of material wealth. As Terry said, we all came here looking for something – recalling the Denman episode I was reminded that what we find may come as a shock.

April 14 High winds and extreme cold. Allen, Tony, Terry carried oxygen to Raphu La. Mal and Chris arrived in blizzard, Mal in particular verging on serious exposure. He'd fallen through the ice near 'Camp 1½'.

April 15 Urs, Andy, Allen, Bob, loads to 7090, back to ABC. Good day for Old Farts. Unspoken rivalry with Boy Racers. 'Huh, they didn't do much!' Andy G., Liz arrive, Tony down.

Allen Breakfast is shortbread and cider-flavoured Cremola foam – my appetite is shot! . . . A monotonous plod across the glacier despite the superb scenery all around. We pick up loads at the Col dump, then off up the ropes. It's slow, monotonous, numbing work. The angles of course are wrong for everything! A few steps, a rest and so on. We lunch above the ice-bulge, where the going improves and at least it's new ground for me, following the crest up and right to CB's, then more of the same, but the steps are better now and easier to follow. You can't use the jumar properly though, only as a safety runner. Then eventually the crevasse cave after six hours. Had a bit to eat and drink then went down, which was very fast on the ropes. C2 is not as bad as I'd feared but does need some work on it. Then back across the glacier which had grown considerably. Arrive at

ABC wrecked. Took me all my time to eat and drink. Bob kept nodding off during conversation. Really, really exhausted but satisfied.

April 16 Andy N., Urs, loads to C2 (two days running). Also home improvements on C2. Mal, Chris and Danny, loads to C1 and back. Andy G., Terry, loads to Raphu La. Basques dropped in.

Mal Wattie and I off with two oxygen bottles, awkward bastards but felt really good for the first three rope lengths. After that, a complete collapse. Just made it to CB's. Met Danny coming up – totally shafted but grinning from ear to ear.

A mental review of things: generally OK, but a lack of action since I was last up.

April 17 Bob, Allen, loads to C2, also climbing gear for Andy and Urs. Danny and Terry down to BC. Jon, Rick arrive – forces a bit thin today. Liz, Chris, Andy G. sorted out ABC.

Bob Allen and I set out to do another carry to 7090 . . . I'm feeling really awful. After dozing at the ice-bulge for a while I feel a bit better and press on to CB's, where I meet Allen in descent. Commonsense dictates that I should dump my load there, but I decided to press on until 5.30 pm, which is just enough time to get me to C2. I'm really weary and have to be pathologically careful with the ropes on the descent. Rick kindly comes out to meet me with a hot drink and a rope for the last ten minutes before ABC.

Terry '*The genteel art of using a pee bottle*' (Male version).
1. Night-time.
2. Cold – goes without saying – but usually rime covering everything in tent.
3. Urgency about your nether regions.
4. Windy outside tent.
5. Typically snowing – powder snow.
6. You're usually camped on the side of a cliff with a sheer drop.
7. You're asleep.
8. No you're not.
9. You go through the mental check-list above.
10. Night, cold, YEOUW my nether regions! Skip the rest of the above.
11. Action quick!
12. Try to get out of my sleeping bag without waking 'Charlie'.
13. Sod Charlie. The zip's stuck – how the hell can I get out?
14. Wriggle, that's how!

15. No, stop that quick! It makes things more imminent.
16. No Charlie, don't roll over on that bit or you might get a surprise!
17. Thank God, he grunted and turned back over again.
18. Nearly out of the sleeping-bag – the relief.
19. What's all that wet stuff on my face – is it snowing in here?
20. Where's the head-torch – oh shit, the battery's nearly gone!
21. Thank goodness, it's only the rime off the inside of the tent.
22. Where's the tent zip?
23. Oh Christ it's snowing out there (as powder snow avalanche falls in through zip opening). I remember what happened last time I had a pee in a storm like that; I had so much snow inside my layers my knees got frostbite.
24. I know – the pee bottle. I've been meaning to use it for ages!
25. Ohh – don't tell me I've left it at home!
26. I know (whew!), the '5 Pint' is almost empty.
27. Dart to back of tent where food and stoves, etc., are kept.
28. Scrabble about – urgently now as the immediacy about nether regions is becoming more imminent by the second!
29. Find bottle – the mental relaxation makes the urgency more urgent.
30. Tear at zips, layers, etc., in clothing with one hand. Flip top of '5 Pint' bottle with other.
31. OOOooo
32. OOO – I forgot my thermal undies!
33. A quick adjustment and the fountain of golden liquid (very dehydrated) finds its way into the bottle where it belongs.
34. Oh bollocks – this isn't the empty bottle. It's frothing up! It's coming over the top!
35. Sorry Charlie – didn't mean to lay a trail all along your sleeping bag.
36. It's bloody difficult to waddle on your knees with one hand between your legs to the front end of the tent again.
37. With spare hand manage to unzip tent and fly.
38. Hold member in one hand.
39. Try to empty frothing '5 Pint' bottle into snow outside tent.
40. Fall flat on face in snow.
41. Feel silly, but let go with neither hand.
42. In this more rational frame of mind, possibly brought on by the snow-in-the-face trick, one has a decision to make!
43. Do I let go with one hand and pee all over the place (mainly me), or let go with the other and the pee bottle empties itself all over our doorstep – where do I get the brew from in the morning? This ledge is the only snow catchment for yards up and down this face.
44. The brain at altitude struggles to decide . . . For the next instalment, tune in next week at the same time.

Now the atmosphere at ABC was one of strong, coherent purpose, of non-competitive co-operation among the Old Farts. Mal was quite different up there, more actively engaged. Listening, asking questions – can C2 be improved, how's your head, what do the Rock Buttresses look like? – frowning at the ground, smoking. An unstated sense of rivalry with the Boy Racers was an incentive for both teams, each trying to cap the progress of the other. Chris and Mal had formed a strong partnership – watching the one lanky figure and the other more thickset one set off across the glacier, I mentally nicknamed them 'the Spider and the Fly'. Chris would return hoarse, whispering and grey, sit for an hour in the Mess Tent in what seemed to be a coma of suspended animation – but he always found fresh energy and commitment the next morning. He and Mal had started sharing a tent at ABC while Liz moved out – this caused much ribald comment, but was indicative of the closeness they felt necessary.

Danny Lewis was revealing himself as something of a star. Unlike Kurt and Julie, he was now very much part of the Expedition. He earned many Brownie points from the times he spent cooking, brewing and washing up. We teased him a great deal, but increasingly appreciated his boundless humour and good-will as he stumbled about the tent grinning, knocking things over, laughing. His effort in carrying a load to CB's was an achievement for a 19-year-old rock climber with no winter experience who had never been higher than 4,000 metres before.

Andy Nisbet and Urs had emerged as a strong team; the unlikely combination of the chortling Swiss and the reserved Aberdonian worked out well. Mal was delighted that his gamble on Andy's ability to acclimatize had paid off – as it had with Allen Fyffe. That counter-balanced disappointment over Bob and Nick, and Sandy's set back. There was still uncertainty as to how high Andy could go. But he'd find out soon enough, because Mal decided that with more than a third of our loads now up at C2, it was time to push out the route further, over the Rock Buttresses.

April 18   Mal, Chris, loads to C1, back. Urs, Andy to C2, stayed and
            improved snow hole. Liz, Andy G., loads to ice-bulge . . .

I wake at 8.30 after a long night drifting in and out of sleep. Sun on the Pinnacles, ice inside the tent. Hear voices and stoves. Then I remember – I'm going on the hill today! The Bumblies' day out . . .

Leave around 11.30, roped with Liz. Still get a kick out of the glacier – soothing, other-worldly, serene. We actually gain on Mal and Chris. Feel good today, all doubts and hesitations gone. Yes, that slope looks big but it's a perfect, calm, blue day, no objective danger at all. Just up to me.

Clip jumar to sling and sling to harness. Clip jumar to fixed rope. Add a back-up krab just in case the jumar twists off the rope. Extra sling and krab to clip into snow-stake at change-overs. My first time jumaring so I'll do it by the book as the Glenmore Cowboys tell it. Wait for Mal to get beyond first stake. Okay, let's go . . .

The ground is roughly 40° ice with snow patches. Need to place crampons firmly, axe not necessary. Push with the legs, pull on the jumar. Initial adrenalin settles down, find a rhythm. So much of it seems to be about rhythm in movement and breathing; no sudden effort. Minimum effort. Count steps up to 100, take a break, start again . . .

On it goes, pure doing, little thinking, glancing up for the next snow-stake, at Mal above and Liz below. Methodical change-overs at snow stakes. The slope steepens as it swings over to the right. The rock rib comes nearer, the ice-bulge glitters. Take a break just below it to collect myself and finally look around. To my surprise, no drastic sense of exposure – a 50-foot vertical drop makes me feel much worse than 1,000-foot slope. The scale of this place sinks into me, standing on this vast, sparkling slope, watching spindrift boiling up the Kangshung Face and ripping off the crest of the Ridge above, while huge stately clouds steam over Nepal. Way below, the dots of ABC, and the East Rongbuk glacier like a white curving motorway. An intoxicating agoraphobia, I feel the boundaries of myself dissolve into this openness. Up here there are hours of lethargy, deprivation and struggle, then minutes of euphoria or peace that soar above them. This tiny summit on a great mountain of unpleasantness.

Fuck me, I'm on Everest! I wave to Liz down below. She's coming on very slowly, but coming. She waves back, wishing she'd trained more but sustained by the astonished awareness she's probably the first British woman to climb on Everest. It's a long way from the Insurance business . . .

Right, let's do this ice-bulge properly. Maybe 30 feet high, under 70°; straightforward compared to Scottish routes, but being at 22,000 feet makes nonsense of that. Take out my axe and front-point laboriously up . . . Pain, pain, no not pain just fighting against the body's leaden drag. Sand in the legs, heaving chest, heart pounding and sick in the stomach. Nearly there . . . Mal's sitting watching me, don't fuck up . . . *There.*

'Well done, youth,' Mal says as I slump down beside him. 'Pretty shitty, isn't it?' I agree, get my breath back, feel on top of the world.

Long way down, must have been on the go for two hours now. I feel tired but not exhausted, in control. He suggests I leave my load here 'in view of the time' (3.30, actually been four hours, where did it go?), and the threatening weather now sweeping down the Ridge. The long couloir traverse to CB's is still ahead, which could prove awkward in bad conditions. Andy Nisbet had already taken a flyer on it, penduluming across the slope on his back, attached only by a safety krab. Also Liz is way below, and he wants me to tell her to stash her load where she is and go down together.

So, slightly disappointed, mildly relieved and well content, I set off down. Treat the ice-bulge as a proper abseil, facing in, then down to Liz. I give her Mal's message, but she isn't prepared to stop having pushed this far. She says she's not exhausted, just pain-fully slow. I look at her, believe her, we grin at each other. 'The Right Stuff, Liz,' I joke. 'I'll wait for you at the bottom of the ropes.'

'Thanks, I don't want to give up.'

'Yeah, sure. . . .'

Using two krabs as a friction brake the way Sandy had shown me, I zip on down the ropes, still making myself do everything by the book at changeover points. Then sit for a cool hour at the bottom watching Liz struggle on to the foot of the ice-bulge, climb it, leave her load and follow on down.

The last uphill section to ABC was hard going. Jon's ready with brews then food. Sandy's arrived very cheery. Sit and listen to the crack, have a cigarette, feel wiped-out, whole.

That evening, as Chris and Mal lay in their bags in CB's snow cave, they jerked awake, hearing the sound of jumars being pushed up the rope, and footsteps. Suddenly the cave seemed full of ghosts. The jumars stopped just below the cave. They waited for the Karrimat blocking the entrance to be pulled aside. . . .

No one entered. A long silence. Mal and Chris looked at each other. Neither of them was going out to investigate. Turn over and try to go to sleep. Don't think about it.

Urs and Andy also slept badly that night at Camp 2. The crevasse/cave was a regular wind-tunnel; they wore thermal underwear, pile, down and their Libond suits inside their bags and still shivered much of the night. Andy admitted later that excitement probably also kept them awake, the prospect of breaking new ground tomor-row, their first chance to attempt some technical climbing at altitude. . . .

April 19 'Heavy-duty pastry day,' as Jon says. Biggest number on
the hill yet.
Jon, Sandy, Rick, loads to C2 and down.
Mal, Chris, loads from C1 to C2, down.
Allen, load alone to C2.
Andy G., load to top of ice-bulge, down. 'Dead on arrival
– trying too hard.'
Bob to BC.
Andy and Urs, fixed 1st Rock Buttress. . . .

This is the account of Andy and Urs' day as I gleaned it from
them on their return to ABC that evening. As they talked – Urs
excited and voluble, Andy hesitant and self-effacing, sitting on his
hands and talking through his beard – the long icicles hanging from
their beards dripped on to the floor and froze again.

Urs wakes at 6.15 and starts the laborious process of melting ice
for the day's first brews. It is bitterly cold. Two hours later they
emerge from the cave, slowly pack their sacks with ropes and
climbing gear. They sit outside making slings, waiting for the sun
to rise and warm up their world. Here in the lee of the ridge it looks
like a perfect day. The rope vibrates, five minutes later Chris Watts
appears round the corner, carrying a massive load up from C1. Time
to leave, Andy thinks, and leads up the last steep 100 feet to 7090.
The wind is a shock, battering straight into their faces, so cold and
spindrift laden as to be nearly impossible to peer into. Heads down,
they taper their way carefully along the gently rising ridge. It's
straightforward yet always potentially tricky, angling down to their
right. The rock slabs covered with loose snow are unpleasant so
they try to keep to the snow alongside. A stumble or a slip here and
they'd probably go all the way down. Essential to concentrate but
hard to, with the gale blowing them this way and that. 'Easy ground,'
Andy thinks, 'but there's really no such thing up here.'

They carry on, peering round carefully when they reach the dip
in the Ridge where Bonington's 2nd snow cave had been. It would
be a great boon for us to find it, but there's no sign. They've been
going for two hours now; it seems like an eternity and the day's just
begun. Urs' feet have gone numb, 'They were feeling awfully, so I
dance for ten minutes. Then they are painfully, then OK.' They
decide they won't try to do both rock buttresses today, so dump a
bale of rope and some snow-stakes and carry on along the steepening
slope towards the first Buttress.

Finally they arrive, take a breather then rope up. Andy takes out
his second ice-axe, as a gunfighter straps on two guns before walking

out for the high-noon showdown. Technical climbing at last. He feels well and makes an effort to remain level-headed and treat this as another day's climbing in the Cairngorms. It's a very Cairngorm day in fact. Urs is rather more taken aback; he's been high before, but doesn't like this weather at all. As Sandy once remarked 'Climbing in Scotland is great training, not because it's good but because it's terrible!'

Andy bangs a peg into a crack for their initial belay – which promptly splits open. Rotten rock. He finally gets one in and sets off, Urs belaying him, diagonally right up a snowfield leading into the Buttress. The incline here is about 45° to 50° and the soft snow makes the going hard and insecure. He gets in a friend, then a snow-stake and feels better. It's with a sense of surprise that he spots some frayed red climbing rope half-buried in the snow – he'd almost forgotten someone had been here before him. At the top of the snowfield he uses that rope as dubious further protection to make a move across on to rock and, hanging from one hand, puts in a peg. 'Quite tricky, really,' he admitted later, with an apologetic laugh. He shelters there as Urs jumars up to him, suddenly realizing he is heaving with exertion and sweating for the first time that day.

The most interesting section lies ahead, in the narrow gully that splits the face of the Buttress. The first 20 feet are soft snow, being in the lee of the wind. His axe shafts sink right in, his legs too as he forces his way up, running on adrenalin now. This initial bulge rates as 'a wee bit hairy' on the Nisbet scale. Then the slope lies back a little and the snow improves. Halfway up he spots an old peg in the left wall, tests it . . . sound. He thankfully uses it as a running belay, then bridges up a groove between the snow and the rock.

'Rock and snow, it felt quite familiar . . . Hairy because of panting and weakness. . . . I felt isolated, really alone, like I was the only person on Everest – really exhilarating!' he concluded with a rare burst of enthusiasm. 'It was definitely climbing and not plodding.'

The gully curves left and comes out near the top of the Buttress. No good anchor there, so Andy traverses right, across to some bands of loose rock. He has seen another old peg, thinks 'Great, an anchor!' but wisely tests it and it comes away in his hand. 'So I put it back in, and added a friend. Then more bulges, so I kept going and finally put in a peg which was very bad and a nut which was quite good, then tied off the rope.'

He is now at the top of the first Buttress, back into the gale. It looks like easy ground ahead to the second Buttress. But that is enough for one day, time to go home. 'When I stopped I felt really good, on a high. . . . Felt really optimistic that I could go to 8,000 metres without oxygen. Really chuffed. I'd been maybe one and a half hours on the gully, but really I haven't a clue. My only thought now, as usual, was to get back down as quickly as possible.'

So he abseils back down to Urs, and together they set off back along the Ridge to 7090, then on to the fixed ropes. 'Needed them, had to really concentrate just to get down. I felt my legs would buckle if I stumbled.'

There was a very positive atmosphere in the ABC Mess Tent that night. Everyone had had a hard day, general exhaustion all round, but we felt the Expedition was moving forward. Load-carrying is grim and demoralizing, and a surge forward is a great morale-booster all round. Particularly for Andy, who'd finally broken any remaining physiological and psychological barriers he had about altitude. The only set-back was the failure to find Bonington's 2nd snow cave, and the lack of obvious other sites to dig one. That would be the next task. Chris and Mal brought us down to earth by pointing out we still had some 30 loads to get up to C2, which meant a hell of a lot of work before we could go forward in strength. There was no point in pushing the route out a long way ahead of our supplies. Mal stressed that we really needed all the oxygen, tentage, gas, cooking gear, food and climbing gear at the foot of the Pinnacles by early May – and that was only three weeks away. Put that way, we were on course, but only just.

But my enduring image of the day, possibly the whole trip, was not of Andy's adventures. I'd overestimated my stamina and set out again for CB's; I felt fine at first, but suddenly below the ice-bulge I was running on empty, my body choking and spluttering, losing power. I struggled on to the top of the ice-bulge and I knew I'd had it for the day.

Back at the bottom of the fixed ropes I slumped down, for the first time really beginning to appreciate what the lads had been up to. The Sultans of Pain, that's what they were. Though stronger and fitter than I, they're not supermen, they suffer and struggle just the same. . . . And yet they drive themselves on. Sultans of Pain. . . . If they were supermen they wouldn't be half so impressive. It's because they're all heart and flesh and blood that they impress and move me so much.

I watched with fascination the tiny red dot that was Allen Fyffe inching with appalling slowness across the couloir above CB's with a load of oxygen. He was stopping more and more often, his suffering evident across the distance between us. Once he stopped moving for a full ten minutes. Was he going to accept the inevitable and come

(above) Jon Tinker, Pink Rabbit, Mal Duff at Base Camp

(main picture) Liz Duff, coming on slowly below C2

(above) Everest at dusk, N.E. Ridge on left

(right) Mal Duff at ABC

(top) Jon Tinker leading towards Camp 1

(above) N.E. Ridge from moraine below ABC

(above) Camp 1, below crest of N.E. Ridge, 6850m

(left) Terry Dailey on fixed ropes below C1

(opposite) The First Pinnacle, from C4, 7850m

(right) Danny Lewis, immaculate and tidy as always, below fixed ropes

(below) Rick Allen crossing the bergshrund

(bottom) Old Farts stepping out beneath ABC: Chris Watts, Andy Nisbet,
Allen Fyffe, Liz Duff

(right) The Potala, Lhasa

(below) Pilgrim in Lhasa

down? My heart lurched as the tiny figure turned forward again and put one foot in front of the other, then the next. . . . At this rate he had another two hours of punishment coming to him. I thought: if we succeed on this route, it'll be because of that kind of self-over-coming, the irrational refusal to pack it in. And even if we don't succeed, something quietly magnificent is happening here. I'm seeing the will push the body to its final limits.

And I remembered sitting with Mal in South Queensferry watching Steve Cram win his gold medal. As Cram kicked off the final bend and went for the line, Mal had tears in his eyes. Nothing to do with patriotism; it was the will's transcendence that moved him so.

So it was with me. Those brutal days on Everest, filled with banal bodily weakness and pain, linger still as curiously spiritual events, in the image of Allen Fyffe relentlessly forcing his suffering body towards Camp 2, step by step.

A rest-day followed. Urs, Andy and Allen went down to BC. I considered going down too, feeling burned-out after a week at ABC and also because there would likely be mail waiting. Yet I found myself surprisingly indifferent to the prospect of letters, which so dominate one's mind at Base. ABC was rough, but at least one felt involved there and lived very much in the present, however demanding it was.

I had a long talk with Mal about how he felt things were going at this halfway stage in the Expedition. His assessment was we were very slightly ahead of the game, due to hard work and the recent spell of good or at least climbable weather. 'But we must be in for some nasty surprises. Sooner or later this hill is going to show its teeth.'

Carrying loads to Camp 3 and above the altitude was going to become decisive. Everyone would be operating above their previous height limits. Above 7,500 metres one is into the 'Death Zone', the area where on most great peaks one would expect to spend only a day or two – going for the summit. We had to carry loads several times to the base of the Pinnacles at 8,000 metres before we could even start getting into the crux of the route and some real technical climbing. The siting of Camp 3 and load-carrying were the central issues now. There were still some 18 carries to do to Camp 2, and then 20 to Camp 3, somewhere beyond the Rock Buttresses. Or was that too far; would we have to somehow make a Camp 3 on this side of the Buttresses, and have yet another camp beyond them, near the Pinnacles? A large proportion of those loads would be the oxygen which we'd committed ourselves to bringing in order to have a real chance of making the summit. Mal was worried that tired climbers might think 'sod the oxygen' and decide just to push on as far as possible. It was just possible that we might climb the Pinnacles that way – Rick, Tony and Sandy believed it could be done – but if we abandoned the oxygen we almost certainly abandoned any real chances of going on to the summit.

Everyone wanted to break new ground, to get to 8,000 metres without oxygen, to get in among the Pinnacles. As always on a big trip there was a tension between personal ambition, the husbanding of one's own resources, and commitment to working for the good of the Expedition. Ideally, both come together when a pair finally set off for the summit. If they make it, then all the others' selfless work is justified, as is the summit pair's ambition. But if they don't, 'well you've a lot of pissed-off knackered people.'

The lack of communication with BC was likely to become an increasing problem. Not only in case of emergency but also for maximum efficiency. Today was a case in point – the weather was ideal for climbing, but no one at all was in a state to climb, having either just arrived or just come off the hill.

Something was obviously seriously wrong with Bob; his lips were still blue, his right eye blurry and his chest pains bad as ever. Sandy was still suffering headaches most mornings and having to go cautiously. Nick was hammered with dysentery; Chris wasn't complaining but clearly suffering. Jon spent most of the night coughing ('What, me? Can't have been me, mate. . .') Mal felt only natural competitiveness was keeping him with Rick. Rick was OK, but had been husbanding himself. Allen – the old man had probably carried more than anyone and clearly needed a break now.

'It's been too easy so far,' he concluded. Easy, I thought, this is easy? These lads are suffering! 'It's going to get a lot worse, you'll start to see it. But, sure, I'm quietly optimistic – but that's just the way that I am! We'll just let it roll for a few days.'

Andy April 2 Mal and I both slept badly. Diarrhoea in my case, a curious, numbing jaw-ache in his. In the morning I felt drained and decided to go down. I was just getting weaker and was obviously not going to make CB's let alone 7090 this time up. Mal forced himself to set off with Chris, Sandy, Rick and Jon to carry crucial loads to C2, but. . . .

Mal Bad toothache for some reason, got worse as I went across the glacier. Dropped my load at fixed rope and doubled back to Base. Hope it's easy to cure and not some weird jaw infection. I'm a bit worried as it seems to have affected the edge of my tongue also. Now listening to Bob Marley and the Wailers, which seems appropriate!

The other lads completed their carry with extra-large loads (Rick struggling with two oxygen cylinders, a load that the few who tried it found to be at their limit). They all got to Camp 2, brewed and descended to ABC to find Mal packing to go down. That was a blow, but Mal's jaw had got worse all day and he needed Urs to sort it out. It was not apparent at the time but this was a decisive moment in the Expedition.

That blow was counter-balanced by the appearance of an exuberant Tony with mail that had arrived with the jeep that had taken Dave Bricknell out. I'd met the diminutive one at the halfway tent, he was bobbing like a helium balloon, his spirits inflated by a batch of letters from his Kathy. He babbled on about her, the photos of her he carried all the time, the wonders of Everest, how well he felt – 'I suppose I'm lucky having a natural physiological advantage.' It was innocence rather than immodesty, but the kind of remark the lads would jump on him for. It's alright to believe you're stronger than anyone else, but you're supposed to keep it to yourself! And a particularly unfortunate remark in the light of what was to come. But he certainly looked well, and was as optimistic as Urs and Rick, feeling half a dozen of us could get to the top. He remarked how big expeditions were good in a way – for instance, the rotating rest periods – but it was difficult to maintain interest and commitment. 'But it's a beautiful mountain, and such a pure line!' He grinned, waved and steamed on up the glacier moraine, like a cheery village postman.

The mail as always brought joy, surprises, pleasure – and crushing disappointment for Chris Watts, who received nothing from his wife Sonja. She had clearly not forgiven him for going on this trip. He was very quiet as the others exclaimed over their letters and slipped off early to his tent. Quantity counts as much as quality in expedition mail, and Rick came out ahead with a whole packet of letters from an entire class of schoolchildren. Jon opened his parcel to find a very squashed hamburger sent from New York by an off-beat climbing client of his known simply as *God* – no one could top that. No one could eat it either.

We always look forward to mail so eagerly, yet it probably does as much harm as good. Mail scratches the itch of homesickness. It reminds us of what it might be better to forget, that the world we have left behind still exists. This inevitably to some degree distracts us from the present. Perhaps on an ideal expedition there would be no communication whatsoever with the outside world. In the same way as a severe monastic order might isolate itself entirely from the

world to concentrate on the Divine, an expedition might do well to
devote itself to the mountain. Then again, it might go nuts.

It must be the extra oxygen as I descend. My mind is waking up,
clearing for the first time in days, like wearing goggles that you
hadn't noticed were steamed up until the moisture suddenly evapor-
ates. This is what we all feel coming down. I look back at Everest
and Nuptse and for the first time in days notice they're awesome
and beautiful. I see patches of moss, rabbit droppings between the
stones. A red and black bird swishes past. I'm coming back to the
world again.

On impulse I switch off the Walkman. That's better. Wind over
the rocks, the distant sound of running water. I am the Walkman;
the world around and inside me is sufficient entertainment.

Spring is arriving down here. I scurry past two sections where
stones now fall regularly, the 'Rockfall Alley' that made Charlie
Clarke sweat three years ago. It's no longer safe to cross the ice-
lake beside Camp 1½ – Mal fell in here a week ago. Everything's
coming loose. Those firm foundations I've been thinking about, they
seem exemplified here in this world of loose scree, melting ice,
stonefall and shifting moraine. There are no firm and utterly stable
foundations within or without, the only certainty is being alive now.

You can trust the mountain to be itself; you cannot trust it not
to fall on you or shrug you off. Same with other people. That's not
their fault. The fault lies in the unspoken, unstable bargains we try to
make with the world. Sandy would say if you accept the mountain's
unstable and learn its nature, you can go almost anywhere on it.

Take a break, fill the water-bottle at this stream. No hurry, got
all day. Why do these white clouds fascinate so? All expeditions are
sustained inner meditations, speeded up and intensified. If you don't
change and learn something on a trip but only climb another mountain, you might as well not be there. That's what Sandy's wrestling
with: what am I doing here, why for, what is it all about?

These clouds . . . I'll never forget the sky in Tibet. This chough
croaking overhead, the lingering smell of yak, the water running
through my fingers. This, this, *this*. So clear and absolute. Trust the
untrustworthy, yes go ahead and climb and love and risk and write.

Tired ankles, leg-weary now, round the corner of the moraine and
there's the scattered tents. Drop my rucksack by my tent, no one
about, and savouring the moment, stroll over to the Mess Tent, past
*THERE IS A RIGHT SHAPE AND SIZE TO EVERY PHYSICAL
IDEA* and *NOT A SECOND TIME* scrawled on the flap, push my
way in. All the faces looking up – Nick and Sarah cooking, Bob

and Danny locked in a chess match, Andy watching, Urs sewing, Allen reading.

'Is this "the White Hell of Base Camp" or the Costa del Sol retirement home?'

Attrition

'This time I could hear the choir singing . . .'

What's doing on the hill? The eternal Base Camp question. Every morning we'd get up and study the mountain, trying to judge the wind speed up there by the spindrift, and see if more snow had fallen overnight, even though we'd already learned that BC weather was an unreliable indication of conditions on the hill. All we could do was wait and wonder, wash our clothes and ourselves, sit inside the Mess Tent and speculate. It was hard to maintain a sense of involvement and commitment at Base. Towards the latter part of the afternoon we'd find ourselves glancing more frequently up towards the edge of the glacier snout where a descending figure might appear . . .

By 8.0 pm the next night we'd given up expecting anyone when Mal and Liz walked in. He had the distant, preoccupied look of someone in extreme pain. He was also ill, because the abscess that Urs quickly diagnosed was letting poison into his body. Problems with teeth are quite common on expeditions – the lowering of pressure causes any tiny air-bubble inside a filling to expand, with extremely painful results. An abscess is far worse, particularly under a wisdom tooth. Urs had no drilling equipment; he'd have to extract it or leave it. Mal went even paler at the prospect. Like Kurt and some of the other climbers, he is a self-confessed coward when it comes to dentists at the best of times ('I have to have an injection before I can take an injection!'); the idea of having a wisdom tooth wrenched out up here with only a heavy dose of painkillers by way of anaesthetic . . . He accepted a glass of The McCallan malt whisky. Was there an alternative to extraction? Urs hesitated, then said he could try a high-dosage course of antibiotics, which might possibly kill the infection, together with heavy-duty painkillers to make the pain bearable while they waited to see if it would work. 'But I have to say, with these drugs you will not be feeling very sensibly, hein?' No matter; Mal grasped the reprieve gratefully, finished the whisky, took Urs' pills and staggered off to his tent. We'd see very little of him for the next few days.

Still, BC had its distractions while we waited for further news from the hill. There was Nick and Danny's bread, ingeniously and painstakingly baked inside a pan that sat inside another closed pan on a layer of stones, on top of the wildly unreliable Chinese stoves. However successful or otherwise the results were, the bread always tasted wonderful to us and seldom lasted more than half an hour.

The Basques dropped by for a chat and we exchanged news. They'd established a camp on the North Col and had now pushed up the ridge to 7,500 metres, but were finding conditions very rough up there, with high winds and loose snow on the sloping rock slabs.

There were guitars (Urs's and Julie's) to play with Terry, delving further and further back into our Old Fart past, through the '70s into the '60s, finally back to the late '50s. Like myself, he'd played semi-professionally in many types of bands. Playing music together you can get as close as climbing together – so many shared musical jokes, discoveries, accidents. It was good to laugh, and bring laughter back to the Mess Tent.

And there was washing, which is like a baptism and re-birth. I peeled off my thermal vests and longjohns for the first time in three weeks. I was very white and thin. I'd almost forgotten I had a body and a skin under these perpetual layers of clothing. In normal life scarcely a day passes without even the least appearance-conscious person seeing themselves in a mirror; on a trip like this you can go for a month without glimpsing yourself, and you start to lose the notion of yourself as someone seen by others.

On impulse I asked Liz for a mirror, and stared with curiosity and delayed recognition at the strange person therein. He looked half-mad. Hair in knots, burned patches on the cheeks, pale circles round the eyes where glacier goggles had blocked the sun, split lips, and those eyes much, much too intense. He looked angry and primitive, a creature from another culture. I wouldn't care to meet him on a dark night in the Himalayas. 'Thanks, Liz. I think maybe I'll wash and comb my hair.' She laughed, 'It might be an idea, Andy. I didn't want to say, but . . .' She was looking thin and well.

Base Camp was further enlivened by the eruption of a full-scale argument one afternoon, the only such occurrence on the entire Expedition. Inevitably, it involved the two most volatile characters, Nick and Kurt – and Terry, who is a strong character, very determined to have his way. One of his roles here was business and communications manager, for a lot of money and credibility rested on our film and newspaper reports getting out on time, and in making sure all our product-promotional pictures were taken.

Nick Kurt's film barrels back in Mess Tent – Terry says 'Hands up those who want them out.' Most agreed, so out they went. Later Kurt storms in, 'Where are ze barrels?', angry and fuming – puts them back – pushing me out of the way – I think maybe he thinks I did it, he was looking for a thumping and by God he nearly got it – I would like to feel respect for this 'famous' man but cannot. Anyway, Terry calmly argues the resentments of all the people here – me, I just got angry and shouted my mouth off – they think they're so important, and their film. I think a lot of our grievances are based on K. and J.'s attitude to others – I don't speak just for me – oh God I'm fed-up with this bitching . . .

After much shouting and argument, some kind of compromise was eventually reached over the barrels. As Nick indicated and Terry agreed, the real cause was probably Kurt and Julie's separation from us, the way Kurt never involved himself in cooking or washing up, their refusal to tell us anything of their plans and intentions in filming. Terry would press for some idea of what they were saying in their film reports. Julie would reply she hadn't transcribed her commentaries. 'Well, I can just listen to them, then.' But somehow one never got the opportunity to. Such evasiveness inevitably breeds suspicion and resentment – as did their Karma valley jaunt from which they'd recently returned.

Still, the argument cleared the air somewhat, and Terry managed to extract a commitment from them to stick by their agreement and make five ITN film reports, and give some idea of their future plans. They intended to go to ABC soon with Danny and finally for the first time go up the fixed ropes to film some of the action there.

Liz: 'How do you fancy the Pinnacles, Allen?'

Allen: 'Oh, I'll jumar anything!'

Four days passed and no returning figure was seen rounding the corner of the glacier snout. It had become much colder and windier at Base. A monstrous scarf of spindrift was flying not only from the summit of Everest but also from the whole upper North-East Ridge. Mal had left Sandy instructions to try to create a Camp 3 somewhere on or beyond the Rock Buttresses, and if that turned out to be impossible or too far from Camp 2, try to find one just before the Buttresses. We knew that would be hard, for camp sites are a major problem of the North-East Ridge. There are few snow banks for digging into and the Ridge offers little protection for tents. At the same time as pushing out the route, many more loads had to go up the hill. It was up to Sandy and the lads to juggle these priorities according to conditions and how they felt.

So what was going on up there? Had no one come down because they were going so well, or were they stormed in on the mountain and having to eat precious hill-food? They could be nowhere, or in striking distance of the Pinnacles. Mal lay in the woozy, pain-filled world of his tent, trying to read but unable to because of the questions crowding his mind. And was this damned abscess clearing up, or would Urs have to pull the tooth?

Base Camp emptied out as Nick and Sarah, then Kurt, Julie, Danny, Terry, Bob and Allen, went up to ABC. Again, radio communication would have told us if it was worth their going up; they could be simply overcrowding the camps on the route, or completely wasting their time if the hill was unclimbable in this weather. But they couldn't afford to wait till the Boy Racers came down and then set off for ABC, for that would mean three days of climbing lost. So on 26th April there was only Liz, myself and Mal left. Mal was on his feet now, stomping about with his jacket over his shoulders like a grizzled confederate general. The antibiotics seemed to be working. That evening the tent flap parted and Chris Watts staggered in. 'Hello,' he whispered. His voice was shot from days of coughing, and he had 'Panda eyes', the huge circles left where his goggles had protected him. He looked as if he'd been imprisoned, starved, beaten up, and then shut in a spin-dryer. In a way, he had been. He slumped down in his characteristic zombie, arm-dangling, empty-eyed manner, and after accepting a brew, hoarsely told his tale . . .

The 22nd, the day Mal and Liz had descended, was a rest-day at ABC as the BRs recovered from the big carry of the day before. Next morning they set out in a stiff wind: the sports plan was for Sandy, Tony and Chris to sleep at Camp 2, then try to fix any necessary section of the second Rock Buttress; Jon and Rick would sleep at C1, then follow the others' steps to try and site a Camp 3 beyond the Buttresses. This would be a major step forward.

Sandy I was wearing longjohns, fibre pile and Gorètex windsuit. In my sack was a sleeping bag, down boots, spare gloves, head-torch, down suit, two Gaz, one 'deadman', slings, snow-stakes, radio battery, packet of Jaffa cakes, one roll of film, and my Karrimat. Camera round my neck; suncreams, some sweets, bog-roll . . .

Chris and Tony were moving very slowly, Tony coughing and I honestly wondered how he was getting on and why he was there, he appeared to me to be very tired. Me myself had a very slight sore head, just a pain passing now and then in the right front section of my forehead like a carousel going around . . .

Chris told us he'd been going his usual Old Fart trudging pace and couldn't understand why Sandy steamed ahead so fast. There was a hollow-sounding section on the glacier that Mal had earlier remarked felt like walking over the dome of St. Paul's, aware of a vast cavern beneath. 'You weren't kidding,' Chris said hoarsely. 'This time I could hear the choir singing!' There was 'a slight fracas' on the fixed ropes when Chris realized the BRs were jugging up the same section he was, contrary to all safety practises of fixed-rope climbing. After a short exchange of words he pointedly unclipped from the rope and let them go on ahead and he didn't follow till they'd passed the next snow-stake. He finally arrived at the Camp 2 to a strained silence. Tony and Sandy seemed to have been getting on each other's nerves a lot of late, and the tension had finally come to a head. They'd had a short argument, concluded by Tony saying this was the last time they'd climb together – and then Chris appeared.
    Next morning . . .

Sandy I went out to move my bowels. Put on my crampons and took down my clothes, then a huge gust of wind came and almost knocked me over. I was not tied to anything, so pulled up my suit and jumped head first into the snow hole – had a vision of Tom Hurly, who died two winters ago on the North Face of the Droites, he had a shit on a bivvi ledge, fell off, died . . . I was shaking when I came to rest in the cave.
    . . . Then on up the fixed rope; once at 7090 I waited for the others, but they did not come so I went on, it was still real windy. Once I reached the first gully I had been blown off my feet three times and then one gust came and let me down the face a bit, I stopped with my ice axe into the nevé . . . Looked back and thought, no, this is no good. Walked on a few metres to some rocks, left my load there and came back, met Chris. 'Desperate, ain't it?' We all retreated to C2. Gust of wind, 'Fuck!' Chris runs out . . . comes back five minutes later, very composed. 'My rucksack's blown away.' He had tied it to a shovel, in the gust the shovel had come out and his sack went down the hill. He was most upset, I was impressed by his impassiveness and calmness. He packed his gear into a plastic bag, just 'See ya,' and went . . .

Terry Just stepped outside Mess Tent when a stumbling, staggering figure approached the edge of the ice, hardly able to put one foot in front of the other. Instantly dumped my gear and dashed out onto the glacier to see who. The figure was to my line of sight carrying no gear, no rucksack, and my mind went into instant overdrive thinking about catastrophes etc. and that this was the sole survivor. When I got close enough I recognized it as a severely knackered Chris Watts. His face had a sort of zombie expression and he admitted that he had lain down three times coming across the glacier in order to have a sleep. I took his stuff-sack and had to guide him up over the moraine to the Mess Tent. Fed him lots and lots of drinks till some semblance of normality returned to his eyes . . .

Fatigue, bitter cold, a full Everest gale – little tensions, little mistakes. Jon and Rick battled up the fixed ropes to C2, agreed no further progress was possible, and went back down to C1 to doss for another night. Sandy and Tony tried to warm up in the snow cave – the wind chill factor on the Ridge had numbed them to the core. They worked on blocking up the draught, argued some more, finally improved things somewhat and went back to their bags. Two hours later they were still shivering, accepted the inevitable and packed up and went down. Crossing the glacier Tony was blown off his feet several times and even the heavier Sandy was being cuffed around like a kitten by the gale.

Sandy 2.00 am. Watching the flame of this candle, trying to block out the rattling tent and wind. Drifting for a long time between the tumbling and ice-axe braking of this morning, the cold toes as we built the walls of the snow cave, Dominique, and wishing Tony and I would not argue. Hoping that Jon and Rick are OK, that there's not too much spindrift blowing in their tiny cave. High-altitude mountaineering, it ain't a simple way of life.

Tony Genuinely homesick tonight – a big hug would work wonders just now, from the right person.

The next day, Chris continued, he went back to look for his sack. The wind was still outrageous.

Chris Determined to find my sack I wandered on to the glacier alone to below the face in the area of C2. I lay and scanned the face with Urs' binoculars until I spotted a tiny dot of red lying on a ledge very high up. I then climbed up the face, carefully picking the easiest line since I did not have an axe. Balancing delicately on my front points and clawing with my bare hands on to stones embedded into the ice. Only slight damage to the sack, so I extracted my axe from it and climbed back down feeling I had achieved something despite the risk.

Jon and Rick returned to ABC after carrying on up to C2. No further action on the hill. Nick and Sarah came up. That evening they all sat in the freezing Mess Tent and had a long discussion.

The mountain had decisively put them in check; where did they move from here? They could stay put and conserve energy – but for how long? They could in most weathers still carry loads up the fixed ropes, but the route needed to be pushed out as well. In the end they decided the priority was to fix the Buttresses and establish a Camp 3. So Sandy and Tony would climb together again (each privately resolving to try to get on better with the other), go to CB's and try to fix the second Buttress next day. Then Jon and Rick would come up behind and set up a Camp 3, somewhere . . . The wind had dropped as they left the Mess Tent that night to go their separate ways, tired but resolved and hopeful.

Sandy Just been out squatting, cold, deep-dark sky, stars, some tumble brightly, moonshine on North flank of Everest. Glacier cracks as ice settles. Jon coughs. Me, feeling of being watched in this semi-eerie place. Mountain looms big, shall be up there tomorrow night with Tony! Wonder how Chris Bonington and the Norwegians are getting on on the Nepali side . . .
    Crawl back inside, a carousel goes round my head. Candle flame is straight, no turbulence, peaceful here tonight, only occasional sounds from the glacier and the rustling of my Gore-Tex-covered arm as I write. The pen, as it sounds a full stop.
    Who are we, what are we? A rasping cough from Tony's tent . . .

And that was as far as Chris's story went, for he'd set off down to us at BC that morning. He could only add that Bob Barton had arrived at ABC in very poor condition, with an intense pain in his right shoulder to add to his blue lips, fogged vision and chest pains. He was feeling desperately weak and demoralized, and it was doubtful whether he should or could carry on. Mal grimaced, nodded. Poor Bob, he was having a bad expedition, but there were bound to be more falling by the wayside, that's why we had brought ten lead climbers.
    In a way he was almost relieved. Everest had finally shown its teeth, as any great mountain must. The lads had obviously been shocked by the numbing ferocity of the wind. 'I'm not worried, youth, totally expected. Now we can get down to some *real* Himalayan mountaineering . . .'
    Mal lapsed into a thoughtful silence, lit a cigarette and sat there in his characteristic hunched-forward, elbows on knees, frowning stance. I caught his eye, he grinned ruefully. He wanted to be up there, but still wasn't fit to go. Wattie had crawled away to his pit. Mal restlessly picked up and started to reread Tom Wolfe's *The Right Stuff*, which had become very popular on the trip. 'What's it about?' he'd asked when I first suggested it. 'Mountaineering.' He'd

come back and said delightedly, 'You're right, it *is* about mountain-eering! These pilots were crazy in the same way as us!' But now he tossed the book aside. 'It's time to put that shit away.'

More waiting days at Base. The weather changed. The wind dropped and Everest was white and shrouded, like a gigantic piece of furniture in an empty house. Snow began falling at Base. We spent much of the time lying in our tents, wondering and worrying, listening to Chris cough day and night. Luo began to press us for a departure date, explaining that the arrangements for yaks, trucks, drivers and hotels had to be made well in advance. Mal gave him a provisional date of 31st May, reckoning that if we hadn't made it by then it would be because we couldn't. It seemed very far away.

Two days later, 28th April, I saw a small figure staggering slightly towards my tent. I went out to meet him. It was Tony, but a completely different Tony from the buoyant, optimistic youth I'd met a week before at the halfway tent. He was coughing continu-ously, wasted and depressed. He actually croaked, 'I'm feeling bad, Andy.' A superfit youth, he'd never known illness and exhaustion and he was shocked. His body had failed him. He'd come down with bronchitis and was full of Urs' pills, and had been sent to Base with instructions to stay seven days. He slumped in the Mess Tent, trying to breathe between coughing bouts, and brought us up to date on events on the hill.

He and Sandy had made it to CB's on the 26th and settled in there for the night. His earlier cough was becoming continuous, he had no idea what the matter was. Nick and Terry had carried an O$_2$ cylinder each – a particularly impressive effort on Terry's part, given his late arrival – to CB's, and then they set off down. There was a lot of fresh snow on the traverse across the couloir below the snow cave, a foot-hold crumpled and Terry found himself sliding downhill ... to be jerked to a stop 50 feet down by his jumar clamped on the fixed rope. One of the snow-stakes had pulled; the others held. Heart pounding, he got to his feet and carried on, very carefully. Thank God for those fixed ropes, Bonington had certainly been right about them. They made it back to ABC through steady snowfall without further mishap. Nick was still feeling terrible. Amoebic dysentery is debilitating at the best of times, but on Everest . . .

Urs and Andy arrived at ABC. Urs examined Bob and was slightly mystified not to find the symptoms of mountain sickness. It could be some unidentified and unresolved chest infection. Or a blood infection. Or even some kind of psychological effect. If his condition persisted, Bob might have to go back to Llasa for a chest X-ray.

Next morning at CB's Tony was in need of some commiseration, after having a dreadful night coughing and struggling to breathe. After 45 minutes of continual coughing he finally managed to spit out some phlegm. 'Did you have a bad night, then?' Sandy asked.

Tony restrained himself with difficulty, and merely grunted.

'Do you want to go down?'

'I'll go on as far as I can.'

The chances of them fixing the 2nd Buttress already looked slim. A lot of fresh snow made it hard work to use the fixed ropes. Progress was exhausting and downright dangerous once they left the ropes behind above 7090. Sandy finally arrived at the foot of the 1st Buttress, dumped his load and sat amid plumes of spindrift waiting for Tony, who was labouring one hour behind. To keep warm, Sandy tried to dig a snow cave, but soon hit ice.

Tony finally appeared through the snow, gasping and staggering. He'd been trying to catch Sandy up to tell him he had to go down. He told him now, unpacked his load and set off. After a moment's hesitation, Sandy followed, knowing he couldn't do much good alone up here, and also he was worried about Tony, who was clearly on his last legs. With fresh snow building up continuously it would be very easy to slip and one slip could take him all the way.

They made it safely to CB's. There they met Rick and Jon on their way up to C2 to sleep the night and try in their turn to push the route further. They persuaded Sandy to stay on the hill and help them, while Tony slumped into the corner in his own world of despair.

Tony Sandy stayed up and I made a harrowing descent, slipping and sliding down the fixed ropes. I've never felt this bad, never. It was a white-out crossing the glacier and I couldn't even tell the slope of the ground beneath my feet, so kept falling over, quite lost at times between wands. Very upset too as I thought I'd blown any chance of going higher – cried with relief and fear when I eventually reached ABC. Bob had to help me off the glacier. Urs told me I *only* had high-altitude bronchitis. Seven days at BC should see me back yet.

So Tony had come down next morning. All he could tell us was that the lads were planning a mass assault on the hill for that day – a team of ten in all. It was the largest number we'd yet put on the mountain. 'Sounds like the Ypres offensive.' We hoped it would be more successful than that.

Mal was more concerned about the daily snowfall than he had been about the wind – we could have done with that wind now to blast the snow off the hill, but the days had become eerily, obstinately still. 'It makes the hill about ten times more dangerous and much harder work.' There was increased likelihood of avalanche or serac collapse (either of which could wipe out the fixed ropes and anyone on them), and poor footing everywhere on the unfixed sections above 7090. It was a measure of our lack of progress that no one had been on the fixed rope up the 1st Buttress since Andy Nisbet had fixed it nine days before. And from Tony's account, the lads' morale had also taken a battering. They'd done well to shift some loads in such conditions, but that's not the same as moving forward and up. 'I just hope they don't beat themselves into a frazzle, or get avalanched or something,' Mal said. Like Chris before him, Tony emphasized there was no point in us going up to ABC, which was already overcrowded, so all we could do was wait for news of the 'Big Push'.

Bob The ropes are obviously going to be busy today, so I got away early with Terry, and first on to the ropes with an O_2 cylinder. It's hard work breaking trail in the new snow, but steady progress is made and I don't feel to be going too badly. However, after a bite to eat at the top of the ice-bulge it turns out that snow conditions above are dreadful and it is a real struggle to reach the rock outcrop. The traverse is insecure and a couple of chutes show where Sandy or Jon took a slide while descending and the rope-length above is a nightmare of soft snow. At last I crawl into CB's cave . . .

Jon Perhaps we've been too long up here. Rick's remarkable Joe Tasker impersonation. Massive determination, whispy beard poking out of a yellow down suit, head leaning into the slope . . . Not so good at getting up in the morning.

Sandy Left CB's with two cylinders in my sack. Eight inches of fresh snow, blue fixed ropes springing up leaving a trail in the soft white snow as I thrutched with my axe, searching for the lines of safety . . . Panting from my lungs, drips of sweat wash the Factor 15 protection cream into my eyes. It's going to be a hard day. I come to the second snow stake supporting the fixed line, exhausted I leave one O_2 cylinder hanging from a red sling, move on, step here, step there, pant, pant, pant. Sit down, almost there. Kidding myself. Come to C2 three hours later (usually this takes one hour.) 'Hullo, Jon, what's going on?'
    'Oh, ran out of puff, had to come down. Rick's gone on.'
    'Take care, see you later.' So Jon descended the fixed blue, I went on to

C2, watched the black dots from ABC make their way along the glacier. They're wasting their time, the weather's too bad.

Rick Across the flat bit above 7090 with tent, rope, stove and radio. Jon packs it in, exhausted, and goes down. I go on to the foot of the 1st Buttress, snow starts to fall again and I retreat . . .

Bob Rick arrived at CB's from above and together we descended into a maelstrom of snow, and a scene of some confusion. A knot of people wait helplessly at the start of the traverse and Danny hangs from the traverse rope, tired and incapable, watched by Kurt and Julie from below. I sense a bottleneck, so Rick and I sort Danny out then continue down the ropes to the glacier . . . nine inches or so of new snow have been dumped so further progress for a few days seems unlikely.

After Danny had been rescued from his 'bicycling windowcleaner' act (picture the motions made by someone hanging helplessly from fixed ropes and seeking to get a grip on loose snow!), a general decision was made by 'the bottleneck' to descend. And so ended the Big Push, not blown off this time, but ground to a standstill in soft snow. 'The retreat from Moscow,' Rick noted. Very little had been achieved, no new ground gained and everyone was exhausted.

Allen That evening all at ABC, so very crowded and most folk pissed off. We've only a month or so and a hell of a long way to go. We need a wind to clear the Ridge of fresh snow. A bad day, when the Expedition went into reverse.

Jon stomps doggedly into BC the next afternoon, his blond hair matted and blasted. He accepts his first brew. 'What's it like up there, Jon?' He shakes his head, 'It's just shit.'
    Then Rick and Terry, both staggering slightly. Panda eyes, heightened cheekbones, speaking in hoarse whispers, coughing. Terry ill with bronchitis, Rick is thinner-faced than ever, his cockerel coxcomb of ginger hair now plastered across a burned forehead. The deterioration is painful to look at, distressing as lying listening to Tony and Chris and Jon all night coughing their throats to shreds.
    Outside it starts snowing again, which does nothing to improve the team mood of frustration and stagnation. We have lost another week's progress, and this sustained bad weather is beginning to seriously prejudice our chances. Jon and Rick repeat that there is little point in our going up to ABC. With only four weeks to go we have only a foothold on the 1st Rock Buttress, and there is an unspoken awareness that we might have to alter our plans.

Mal Spent today calculating oxygen requirements in case we have to cut and run at some stage. [i.e. Make an Alpine-style attempt on the Pinnacles and the Summit.] Certainly expected to get bogged down at some stage – but it looks as if some direction is required at the front. Pretty much stalemate at the moment. Decisions when I get to ABC but until then low profile as usual.

Jon and Rick debated whether, with hindsight, they should have pushed the route when the weather was still good, and just concentrated on carrying loads when it turned bad. But as they said, that's just hindsight. There would be a lot more 'Should we have . . .?' and 'If we had . . .' in the next few weeks. It is as hard to abandon such speculation as it is to stop scratching an itch.

Sandy But now another variable creeps into my head, like a long time ago in Morocco when we, a few of my (now dead) friends and some Berbers were all sleeping under a canvas below a tree, and about 3.0 am one of the dancing girls of the night before crept in to join her Berber boyfriend Ali. My thoughts come like that . . . friendly, slipping away from religiously strict parents . . . Meanwhile the asses stirred and munched on golden stalks of the old harvest.
  . . . Dismantled ideas: we came here to climb a hill, only this one's higher than all the other plate collisions which make up our tiny world. Trying to remember we're climbing with colleagues/associates – is that the same as friends? Or have we all been too busy, too into the game to be friends? A confusion of bread mixes: yes, we make the dough, we've got the yeast – and nobody is rising.
  So what . . . so what are we all learning from being here, are we becoming any better, stepping on and out of our previous selves, or are we just stepping into more colour photos and frames? . . .

The next day at ABC Allen was sick, so it was Bob, Nick and Sandy, who set off to carry loads up the hill. Sandy was worn out, and vomited going across the glacier. He forced himself some distance up the fixed ropes, then accepted the inevitable and turned back, despondent about his own failure but impressed by Bob and Nick's determination to push on through yet more fresh snow, despite them both feeling well below their best.

Bob It's hard physical graft breaking trail up the first couple of ropes, not helped by the jumars slipping on the icy ropes. But then Nick takes over and I have the luxury of good steps to move in. When I reach the rocky shoulder he's pressing strongly ahead, but I become increasingly concerned about the dangerous snow conditions – a slab about nine inches thick is breaking away very easily – and I shout a warning to Nick, who seems just about to start on the most dangerous part of the traverse before CB's cave. His reply is non-commital and most of it tattered by the wind . . . I shout to explain that I'm going back, câche my load and swoop down the ropes, feeling a lot more relaxed when Nick has recrossed the basin.

It's been a good day's work and we feel that we've made the point that we can work on the mountain in unpromising weather.

Nick noted more briefly in his energetic, rapid scrawl:

Snow deep and difficult – danger of avalanche on traverse below C1. The heat returning across the glacier was terrible – burned my tongue a little! Felt a lot better despite difficult conditions.

That night Sandy made his 'usual calm sort of static friction but frictionless entrance' into the BC Mess Tent. He was in an edgy mood, kept asking questions, launched into an attack on the four hens that had been bought at, I think, Kurt's suggestion. 'Typical stupid British fuck-up, not thinking at all.' His objection was not on health grounds but because of the bad karma that would result in killing anything above the Rongbuk monastery (which no one intended doing). He was furious and jittery about this. 'If anything's killed on this trip, that's it, I'm leaving straightaway.'

But it turned into an exceptionally good evening as Terry and I began writing 'The Ballad of the North-East Ridge' with everyone throwing in suggestions. Because Mal wanted to tape it for BBC radio, I changed the melody from one based on 'Lily Rosemary and the Jack of Hearts' to a new folk/rock one, which revitalized the entire song. It revitalized us too, and the evening became hilarious as we blew away our boredom and anxieties with whisky and laughter, gasping for air as we whooped. Whisky, laughter and companionship, with the reticent Rick chuckling away, and Chris and Tony looking happy for the first time in ages. The evening drew us all together. We felt like a team, a close company of friends as we bawled out the chorus, laughing ourselves into the ground at the absurdity of ourselves and our entire venture.

As we finally left the Mess Tent at 1.0 am into the pitch dark and light snow tickling our faces, Sandy said casually, 'I'm glad now I came down.'

Sandy Really good jest which developed into an ACE time. Hits a fellow from ABC like a brick wall. Obviously a good place to recover. Tony Brindle cough, cough, cough, but everyone well mentally here. Too tired to write, my head active but *not* in control. *Impressed* by the people here, wish I was as confident and prudent about climbing Everest as A.G. is on guitar . . .

Tony A great evening's entertainment – my mind has been in North Wales all day, and the music and song bring me back to this trip and stop the old homesick pangs . . .

The 1st of May was a perfect morning. Everest clear for the first time in ages, little wind. Smiles all round as we slowly filtered into the Mess Tent for breakfast. Perhaps this month would be better to us. Surely the settled pre-monsoon weather had arrived.

By noon it had clouded over again, and snow fell in a desultory manner. General disappointment. We put our thermal layers back on and returned to our sleeping bags or sat and shivered in the Mess. As always, speculation as to what was doing on the hill. In fact, nothing was doing on the hill, as Allen recovered from his diarrhoea, Bob and Nick lay in a dull torpor after their efforts of the day before, and Andy and Urs waited for optimum weather before making their next attempt on the 2nd Buttress.

An aspect Himalayan climbing shares with making a film: a lot of time spent hanging about in suspended animation. I wondered why people with such an appetite for hard technical climbing, for verticality, risk and action, should bother with Himalayan climbing. After all, there was little pure climbing to be done here, mostly endless hard graft with little adrenalin. In three months, the lead climbers would be lucky to each get a couple of days technical leading. As yet, only Andy Nisbet had actually taken out his second ice-axe, signalling hard climbing.

The lads understood my question. They'd had plenty of time to wonder about such things themselves. Rick said he'd always been drawn to mountains anyway, he loved them for themselves, not just for hard-won thrills. He'd moved naturally from winter climbing in Britain to the Alps, and finally to the Himalayas. 'I like big hills,' he said simply, 'when I'm too old for hard climbing I'll still go into the mountains.'

Jon and Sandy agreed, and freely admitted that one of the pluses of altitude climbing was the interesting parts of the world one went through – Peru, Nepal, Baltistan, and now Tibet.

'It's a holiday, a change,' Jon said. 'You can get bored with Scotland or the Alps.' They all enjoyed the dossing life-style of a long expedition, its freedom from the stresses and distractions of life at home; they liked the new company and climbing partners, the companionship and sometimes close friendship. 'Imagine having no telephone, no TV, no news and no transport for two months! And no money . . .'

'And no beer, no London girls, no reggae concerts,' Jon added wistfully.

Rick was fortunate in also greatly enjoying his job as an engineer with Texaco; if he could get away climbing at weekends and fit in one big trip a year, his life balanced out perfectly. For Sandy and Jon – and increasingly myself – it was harder; having no strong home ties, they came to feel at home only when climbing or on expeditions. 'It's the only time I feel real,' Sandy confessed. 'That's not right, is it? . . .' Regret and perplexity in his voice. He stared into his brew, scratched his head as if he could scratch away his thoughts like dandruff. ' . . . But it's Ace. Really!'

We are all here for the entirety of the experience. Personal summits, a day's technical climbing, the chance of breaking new ground on the Pinnacles – these are the targets we have to aim at, but they are not what supports the arrow's flight, the spaces in between do that.

The climbers see Himalayan mountaineering as a different kind of challenge, requiring different qualities from hard climbing in Britain or the Alps. It is challenge to which they are addicted. Thus the pull of the 8,000 metres mystique – an arbitrary height, yet there is the articulation of the challenge. As Jon pointed out, you don't necessarily have to be much of a *climber* to go to 8,000 metres, but you do need uncommon endurance, persistence, judgement and nerve. And luck. It's a test of character as much as of the body, mere physical fitness seems to have little to do with it.

8,000 metres, the foot of the 1st Pinnacle . . . 'Not so much a test of courage as of stupidity!' Jon laughed gleefully.

Danny sits sketching in the corner of the Mess Tent, once in a while shambling over to check on his latest batch of bread. Huge hands and feet, wearing most of his personal possessions round his neck – sunglasses, face-cream, cutlery, keys, Swiss Army knife, pens – he clanks around our camp like the ghost of Jacob Marley in Dickens's *A Christmas Carol*, but grinning happily all day long. To be a 19-year-old rock climber about to go to Art College, and find yourself climbing on Everest getting lessons in high-altitude filming straight from Uncle Kurt – no surprise he's pleased with life.

He lets me look through dozens of his sketches. Most of them are done very fast, notes rather than complete statements. A few are portraits, but the majority are near-abstracts as he struggles to formalize the mountains. 'It's the lines of force,' he explains about one particularly obscure sheet of clashing charcoal. 'I'm trying to get the way the slopes along the valley crash into the flat moraine, and the whole thing then funnels up to Everest, which smashes it all back again . . . It's so violent, yet harmonized. Competing lines of force . . . It's the *scale* I can't get on one sheet of paper.'

Next morning Mal could wait no longer and decided to set off for ABC with Liz. They intended to stay overnight at the halfway tent and celebrate Mal's 32nd birthday (Liz labouring up the moraine carrying wine, cake and presents in her sack), while Chris went straight to ABC. 'Whispering Wattie' still looked as bad as he sounded, yet always seemed to be able to press on.

'A very dark horse' Mal thought, watching Chris, who looked more than ever like a raddled Rolling Stone. 'Much less obviously in a hurry than a Boy Racer, always affable and tolerant – prime Himalayan virtues – keeping his suffering and physical condition to himself. Precise, uncomplaining, level-headed – the ideal partner. How far will Wattie go? But then, how far will I go?'

Mal was revving that morning to be back on the hill. Because of timing, weather and his abscess he'd done little so far, making two carries to C1, and one to 7090. To make up for that, he'd resolved to stay at ABC till the Expedition was over one way or another. Liz was uneasy about that – the whole policy of returning regularly to BC was based on the realization that real recovery was impossible at ABC. Would he not just wear himself out? Could staying up for some three weeks affect his judgement as well as his health?

Mal was aware of these risks, but felt he had no alternative. The weather had set us back considerably, both in time and climbers' energy. 'But in theory we only need one week of good weather from the foot of the Pinnacles. What we have to do now is get ourselves and our loads there. Carrying loads over the Buttresses to nearly 8,000 metres . . . that's when you can expect the wastage to get serious.'

So he set off with Liz around noon in ideal weather, his hopes, plans and worries as firmly strapped down as the bright green Karrimat on top of his sack. 'I'm not coming down till we win or lose . . .' I sat in silence with Sandy below Joe and Pete's cairn, wondering.

Meanwhile purposeful moves were being made on the hill. Still hampered by unconsolidated snow, Bob and Allen moved up to C1 for the night, Urs and Andy to C2 in preparation for finally fixing the 2nd Buttress. Nick carried a load to C2 and went down. His performance seemed to be steadily improving. And Sarah, climbing for the first time at altitude, took a load to the top of the ice-bulge – a fine effort that gave her much personal satisfaction. Now she and Nick prepared to go down to the comparative paradise of BC.

Sarah The last day we were up here I actually managed to get to the fixed ropes. I got above the ice-bulge and owing to the lateness decided to descend. Weather not good, wasn't really keen to go any higher.

I don't really like the fixed line.

I have never been so tired in my life, going up the ropes took a lot of effort and deciding to go down really did me in – I didn't trust the friction brake over the ice-bulge! It took half an hour to fix it up – the rope is so tight. If I'd had the confidence to run down I would probably have got on a lot better.

Back across the glacier was horrendous . . . felt almost dead at ABC. I don't think there's anything quite so demoralizing as fixed ropes to feel just how strong you aren't!

Andy G. This is one of the most preposterous places I've ever written from: the halfway tent on the East Rongbuk glacier. It's in a dip in the moraine ridge, near the base of the ice-towers. Everyone who's stayed here spends some time nervously eyeing the distance between tent and tower. If one of these fangs fell straight out . . . A spectacular site, sheltered, five hours from the nearest human, and with an outlook on to the North-East Ridge.

Arrived here late afternoon, five and a half hours from BC. I opened up the tent, found matches and a new gas cylinder, filled the billy from a melt-stream and got the brew on. No hurry, gradually adjusting to the silence and solitude, broken only by gunshot cracks from the ice-fins and a drifting chough. Unroll the bag and Karrimat, set out my toys – notebook, writing paper, Walkman, book, munchies. Now, four brews and a cigarette later (must be acclimatizing, I really enjoyed it), I'm sitting on the convenient sloping rock near the tent, looking at Everest in the last low yellow sun.

You come round the corner on the moraine, and it's a shock every time: the entire North-East Ridge, seven miles away, towering over Changtse. It's like seeing a lover again, feeling the excitement, belief and commitment rising in oneself again after the long and doubt-filled inertia of Base. Snow clouds play 'now you see it, now you don't' as my eyes run up and down the Ridge, gauging, estimating, almost *feeling* this route with my eyes, remembering the flow of it.

It mounts in developing surges or movements, music transposed into stone and ice. The initial pyramid is a decisive opening statement of intent. The steepness of the ridge between 7090 and the Buttresses is a surprise, much more of an incline than I'd remembered. The lads refer to it as a walk, but I can see now just how hard-going it must be, into the jet stream above 7,000 metres. The 2nd Movement, the irregular swells of the Buttresses, also looks much bigger and longer and steeper than I'd remembered. Mixed ground this, a lot of rock showing again as the wind strips the snow away. Can see from here the thin white finger of the gully where Andy Nisbet fixed up the 1st Buttress. He and Urs should be somewhere above that today, trying to fix the route and finally decide on a C3 site. The cloud clears and in a showman's flourish reveals, way above and beyond the Buttresses, the jagged staccato Pinnacles. Mist clings to them, they remind me of the Cuillin ridge, just as black and sinister. The 800-foot build-up of Pinn 1, then the utter mystery of the ground beyond the Pinn 2 – where do you go, what's it like, what took Joe and Pete 14 hours to get to the Col below Pinn 2, *what goes on there?* Wattie's now dreamed three times of approaching and tackling Pinn 2, and Sandy's thoughts are often there. Then an unresolved number of Pinnacles clustered close together, ending in the abrupt vertical bastion of Pinn 3. We know it must be turned on this side, but how we don't know. Nobody alive has been near enough. Joe and Pete may be there somewhere – a thought all the lads push to the back of their minds. After this crescendo, there's almost another mountain altogether, rising steadily from 8,300 metres, to the summit, two-thirds of a mile – but at that height it might as well be 20 to 30 miles. I'm looking at all the near-mythical features of that summit ridge, imprinted on the mind by countless pre-war photos. Spot the point just above the Pinnacles where the North Ridge joins ours, the limestone Yellow Band (hard to imagine that being laid down on the sea-bed), the 1st Rock Step, the 2nd Rock Step 'jutting like the prow of a battle ship', the couloir Colonel Norton reached . . . Is that Japanese ladder still in place on the 2nd Step? 'It would be a bit inconvenient to get up there and find it had gone,' Andy Nisbet observed drily last time I saw him. Beyond that, the final steepening, God that must hit you hard, the final kick in the teeth, and the *wind* . . . Then the slope relents, the last 100 or so feet and there you are on the highest and final note, transfixed in the sky, and the spindrift banner streaming miles back from your feet . . .

God it's so BIG and we're only one-third of the way up it.

Sitting here in the late, almost mellow, afternoon sunshine, a rare hour of feeling at ease and fully awake. My inner camera has already clicked and this hour will always stay with me. The showdown is approaching. On the hill fate is being worked at.

That day brought fresh snow, and high winds that on the Ridge blew plates of snow-crust high into the air. But by now the lads were adjusting to working on the hill in wild weather. The two Glenmore Cowboys did an invaluable day of shuttling loads between Camps 1 and 2, each going up and down *twice*. By that evening most of the C1 loads had been shifted up to C2. The time had definitely come for pushing the route out.

Which was what Andy and Urs were trying to do. They'd started brewing at 6.0 am, and set off at 8.0 into the teeth of the gale; feet, face and hands were soon numb. Urs in particular grew uneasy, staggering on along this sloping ridge-pole in the sky. When they finally reached the bottom of the 1st Buttress, the fixed rope was buried under two feet of snow. Each length had to be dug out with an axe, feet repeatedly giving way to leave them waist-deep in powder. Spindrift simultaneously poured down on them from above and came swirling up from below. 'I found it exhilarating,' Andy told us later, though he confessed it was also very tiring. 'Urs thought the weather was awful. I thought it was a poor day.' Poor day it must have been; just wading up the initial snowfield and into the gully took two hours.

Then Urs pulled on an old Bonington peg. It came away and he fell ten feet on to his back. That completed his demoralization. He decided to go down, leaving Andy to continue. This splitting of a partnership was dangerous; the North-East Ridge is not a sensible place to be alone on in bad weather. It also rendered the remaining climber ineffective, for there's little one person can accomplish alone. It had happened already with Jon and Rick, and was to happen more frequently as extreme altitude drove its wedge between a pair, ruthlessly separating the weaker from the stronger.

Still, Andy accomplished all that was open to him. He went on to the 2nd Buttress. He looked for a suitable bank for a snow hole, but nothing obvious there. The wind had shaved the Ridge of excess snow, so he pushed on up the 2nd Buttress, finding most of the ground acceptable. He came across sections of the last expedition's fixed rope, much of it still usable. He checked and replaced the anchor points, jumared up, made a traverse and forced himself up the final ramp. He sat there coiling rope and taking stock while snow and ice particles howled by him. About 7,600 metres, he guessed. He exulted in the knowledge that he was capable of going further. 'Maybe I'll go on to 7,850' (the height of a proposed camp near the 1st Pinnacle) he thought, for the ground looked straightforward enough. He got up and went on 20 metres; suddenly feeling weary and acutely aware of his isolated position, he turned back. Then turned again to go up. 'Maybe I'd better not,' he finally decided. No useful purpose would be served by his going on. So instead he made some additions to Bonington's fixed rope, checked the remainder and set off on the long solo stumble down the canted Ridge towards 7090 and ABC.

Allen met them at C2, and noted that Urs was 'very tired and disheartened', all his customary buoyant optimism knocked out of him, shocked by the ferocity of the wind and needling spindrift.

Eventually Andy turned up. The pair of them set off down the fixed ropes to ABC. Bob and Allen descended to C1, while Kurt and Julie came up the fixed ropes for the first time and settled down in C2 for a couple of days' filming from 7090.

Mal Strolled into ABC – made a mistake with Bizet – back to the Thompson Twins for the long final section. The place was abandoned – everybody on the hill except Wattie hunched over a stove.

Andy, Urs and then Danny eventually arrived at 8.0 pm pretty done-in. Fixed 2nd Buttress – token progress, but at least re-established the route in very heavy snow conditions. Plan definite to establish a couple of our tents between Buttresses 1 and 2: I could hear Bob on the radio but not vice versa, they are going to try for a snowhole below Butt 1 – so am extremely frustrated.

That evening at ABC another setback developed. Andy Nisbet was becoming snow-blind. The day had been overcast and he had been quite unaware that he had taken off his goggles. Such is the vagueness induced by altitude that Urs hadn't noticed either. And now he was suffering for it, waking up in the night blind and in great pain. 'A beginner's mistake,' he cursed himself, and yet one made by the most hardened Himalayan veterans; both Messner and Kurt had gone through that agony.

Urs injected painkillers, bandaged one eye over and numbed the other one so that Andy could fractionally open it. Andy stood trembling with pain and eventually was moved to say, 'Urs, that bandage is beginning to hurt.' For him, this was a massive statement of distress. His voice quavered as he added, 'Urs, it would really help if you loosened that bandage.' And later, 'Urs, I think I'm going to pass out.'

I met them next morning shortly below ABC, stumbling slowly down the rocky moraine. Andy said next to nothing but gave off waves of pain while Urs explained. With about ten per cent vision and no depth of field, he was going to have a harrowing time getting to BC. He was expected to recover in a few days, but their early departure was a blow to the Expedition.

Later in the day, reinforcements in the form of Jon and Rick arrived at ABC. They did not look greatly refreshed after four days at Base, but they felt they had to get back into action. Rick wearily slung his sack in a corner of the Mess Tent and announced, 'I wish to resign my membership of the Boy Racers . . . Can I be an Old Fart, please?'

Bob and Allen were the only ones working on the hill, shuttling the remaining C1 loads up to the 2nd snow cave, and intending to find a site for the elusive C3. But once again a pairing was split by the divergence of climbers' performance when load-carrying above 7,000 metres.

Bob Feet completely numb by 7090 so I have some food and take a Ronicol before continuing. My energies seem sadly depleted for some reason, and after a few hundred yards I grind to a halt, panting and dizzy. I sit for a while but to no avail, so I shout to Allen and with a heavy heart turn and carefully pick my way back down the Ridge, feeling the huge masses of Everest and Makalu mocking my puny efforts.

Allen Took an hour to 7090, then along the Ridge for the first time – two hours to the foot of the 1st Buttress then up fixed rope. First ones are OK but the upper couloir full of slabby powder, which is very hard work and really cold. Blasted the last 20 feet and lay gasping and panting in the snow at the top. Bob was nowhere in sight and weather had clouded in. Then went to foot of 2nd Buttress and probed the snow for a snow-hole site but max. depth was only about four feet. Going OK at about 7,600 metres, but I'd forgotten my hill-food and finished my water. Tempted to go higher but weather still cloudy and snowing.

About 3.0 pm made my way slowly down after leaving some lengths of fixing rope. Very slow on the Ridge – visibility v. poor, difficult to see old steps and now very conscious of the size of the Kangshung Face cornices having seen them from above. Had a bout of dry retching on the way to C1, but saw one possible tent site and one possible snow-hole below the 1st Buttress . . . Actually felt quite good and pleased, Bob though is really down.

The 5th of May brought little action. Allen and Bob came down from C1. The latter took his first brew and promptly staggered outside to throw-up. Blue at the lips, he somehow managed to joke, 'I knew I shouldn't have had all those beers last night.'

The Basque team passed through on their way to their ABC further up the moraine. This time they intended to go for the Summit from their camp above the North Col. We wished them luck, slightly doubtful of their success and safety, for there was still a lot of fresh snow on the sloping slabs below the crest of the summit ridge.

Sandy arrived from Base Camp, in good spirits but looking tired. By now no one looked fresh on returning to the fray.

Rick was in a talkative mood, psyching himself up for the critical period ahead. The weather had to give us a break; we had to establish a Camp 3 and Camp 4 in the next few days. He too was concerned about the way the pairings, which had worked lower on the hill, were now beginning to fall apart. 'There's a big difference between climbing once a 7,000 metre peak, and sleeping and carrying loads repeatedly above 7,000 metres. That's where people's performance diverge.' He could see us having to postpone our exit and climb into June, if the weather permitted.

And the lads spoke increasingly of having to partly abandon the original limited oxygen plan, for the O_2 loads were becoming a monstrous logistical problem due to lack of time and manpower. Instead, Rick suggested, we needed 'a pair who are willing to put their necks on the block and go for the Pinnacles without oxygen. I'd try it – it's the only way to find out.' I noticed Allen Fyffe listening attentively, and Sandy nodding agreement. Jon was silent. Bob sat in a trance of fatigue and depression.

Only Mal and Chris were on the hill, having set off through snow flurries that morning with Mal determined that the time had come – long overdue – to set up a Camp 3, probably before the 1st Buttress. That was much closer to C2 than he'd wanted, but from Allen's report there seemed little alternative.

Mal In CB's cave. Chris's turn for the cooking so an opportunity to read and write, snug as a bug but tired. Whole of fixed ropes needed cleaning, and soft snow. Going well despite this, however. Chris swearing because he's just made a meal of cheesy milk powder instead of potato! Met Kurt and Julie on their way down, surprisingly both said it was colder than they'd ever known on the hill (and Kurt's had 27 expeditions!). Radio fucked – I'm really destined to be out of contact – I transmitted in the hope that ABC could hear. Hope message got through as some important points: need food bags, Jon to come up, Liz and Andy *not* to attempt the traverse yet.

Jon and Rick are talking in the Mess Tent next morning, Rick is concerned about the current weather (more snow and high winds, will we never get a break?), the shortage of time and progress. Jon, 'You're just too impatient, mate, that's your trouble. The one thing that controls everything is the weather, and there's nothing we can do about that. So just relax and do what we can each day and see what happens.'

Rick laughs, 'I guess you're right. But there's no way we're going to get all the loads up there that were planned.'

'I could have told you that three months ago, mate!' Laughter.

They plod off across the glacier. If all goes well and Mal and Chris finally establish Camp 3 today, Jon and Rick hope to sleep there and go on through the Buttresses tomorrow and try to dig a snow cave within an hour of the 1st Pinnacle. If they succeed we've made a big leap forward. If, if . . . Sandy wonders if Jon will be able to stay with Rick – he was coughing even as he set out and looked drawn though still game.

Bob, Allen and Danny set off down to BC for a much-needed break.

Meanwhile Mal and Chris have appeared at 7090 and we can sit and watch them slowly dragging their suffering bodies up the gradient towards the foot of the 1st Buttress. A ringside seat for the Sultans of Pain Show. We urge them on across the mile of thin air between us. They arrive there two hours later, find the site Allen had identified, and start digging a platform out of the slope for the tent they'd carried up. This as always is exhausting work and takes much longer than expected. After two hours the platform is nearly finished when they hit the inevitable ice; they pitch the tiny two-man tent anyway with one corner of it hanging over nothing then lash it down. At last: Camp 3. The news, relayed by radio down to ABC, brings smiles all round and a perceptible lifting of spirits. We're finally moving forward again; we are still in the game.

May 7. I lie listening to the snow swishing on my tent overnight and as usual think part, 'Oh, no!' and part 'maybe I won't have to climb tomorrow'. Up at 8.0 into an exhilarating morning – blue, very cold, white, our tents half-buried. Brews with Sandy and Liz, mentally rehearsing the day. Wish this was second nature to me as it is to the lads. I have to concentrate so hard, and not let up till I get back here tonight. This time I've got to make CB's. Load some hill-food bags and a shovel in my sack; feel alert, excited, geared up, fully engaged with myself and the world around me. This is much better than lying around waiting and wondering. This is the hour when the adrenalin kicks.

Impatient to be off, Sandy breaks trail alone across the glacier – a bit dodgy because the crevasses have been opening up and are now covered in snow. Only a few inches of it, but enough to make a big difference with every step. The initial pyramid looks smaller every time I return to it. I know I can do this if my commitment and weather conditions hold. Let's put it to the touch. . . .

Clip in jumar, add safety krab, peel off the top of my windsuit and start jugging up. Not thinking much, just counting steps up to 100, checking on Sandy above and Liz below. The loose snow becomes a problem, my feet and the iced-up jumar are slipping and sliding. Slow down, adjust to it. Easy, easy. . . . Aim for the first snow-stake, then the next.

Maybe one and a half hours later the ice-bulge looms, making the heart beat a little faster and sharpening concentration. Out with the axe and do it slowly, methodically. Either I'm more at ease, or simply too tired to make a big deal out of it. Still, nice to clip my krab into the anchor at the top. And now into new ground, working across and then up the far side of the rock rib. The snow is loose and awkward here, beginning to swirl back into my face.

Finally reach the beginning of the traverse, clip in and look around. Back down to ABC, across to the Karma valley, way over towards Kangchenjunga and Jannu. Feel HIGH in every sense. Look at the traverse up and across the couloir before me: this is my moment of truth. I've seen this section months before in Bonington's *Unclimbed Ridge* and worried about it ever since: awkward traverse, steep enough, exposed, avalanche-prone snow underfoot and big seracs poised overhead. They're the real danger, but nothing can be done about that.

Sandy's waving and shouting from the far end of the traverse. Fragments reach me, 'Okay . . . be very careful. . . . Weather . . . if you feel strong enough. . . .' His concern heartens me. Snow falling now and the birling spindrift reminds me of Scotland and my very first day's climbing with Malcolm in Glencoe. Only 16 months ago and here I am. . . .

So I set off into new territory, stepping carefully into old footholes or making my own where they're broken away. Very aware that four of the lads have taken falls here, so do it by the book at each snow-anchor: clip the safety sling to the stake, un-clip jumar, re-fit above the anchor, then add the safety sling then move on. It's a slow fumble with gloves on, skin sticking to the krab when I take them off. *Concentrate.* Feel exposed. I'll never like heights. Only concentration drives out this mental and bodily unease that is as all-embracing as sea-sickness. Snow's slabby in bits – a couple of sections break off at my feet and slither down into the white – powdery in others. End of the traverse. The line steepens up the bank out of the couloir. Everyone says this section is much longer and more exhausting than it appears. They're right. Down to ten steps at a time now, something part grin and part snarl on my lips because I'm suffering and I know I'm going to make it. I don't encourage this thought but feel rising exhilaration. Come round a corner, see a big sling round a rock outcrop, lots of gear and stuff-sacks clipped in, a profusion of rope: CB's.

Last few steps, clip in, for Sandy warned me this is a place to be careful, the slope drops down steeply from the lip of the cave. Sack off, clip it, slump at ease at the mouth of the cave. There's no one here – Sandy must have gone on. The solitude is wonderful, my pleasure is all my own. 6,850 metres, a new height, a contribution however small to the Expedition, and a personal goal. I simply sit awhile, a solitary dot in the Himalayan vastness.

Back to business. Finish my flask and munchies, dump my load in the cave. It looks neat and spacious. Very secure-feeling in here, watching snow swirl by the door. . . . Weather's clagging in fast, better get going. No one to keep an eye on me, it's only the second time I've been alone on a mountain. Anxiety is there, but also the pleasure of self-responsibility. Get to my feet, suddenly I'm wobbly and a little light-headed. Find it hard to care to go to the bother of setting up a friction-brake on the fixed rope, but do so, ordered by some objective and critical little observer sitting at the monitors in the back of my head. He's about one inch high, looks like Malcolm and speaks like Sandy. . . . Light-headed, yes.

One hand on axe, other holding the friction-brake, I step carefully into the remains of my old footsteps. Round the shoulder, into the couloir. See Liz motionless across the traverse, wave through the driving snow, go for it. . . .

Make it across in quick dream-time. Liz kindly congratulates me through her own disappointment – she's too tired to go on today, and the visibility's very poor now. We both know that our own goals are nothing compared to the lads', but that they are emotion-ally significant to us.

So we set off down, myself with increasing confidence and speed. Now I'm not always clipping in at the anchor-points: a black mark. She's a slow descender. At the bottom we rope together and set off across the glacier for ABC, both suddenly near our limits, stumbling, veering through the other-worldly world. We end up counting steps on the flat, feeling sick, and dry-retch a few times. Halfway across Liz stops and looks at me. One of us is swaying slightly. 'What am I doing here?' she asks in honest bewilderment. There's no answer to that, so we plug on again. A vacant clarity now, nothing remains but the effort and crunch of the next footstep, snow tickling as it melts on the face, and the bitter taste of altitude. Half-dead yet so directly alive; no barrier now between self and world. We're too exhausted to divide experience into 'me' and 'not-me'. On the endless final upslope to ABC Mal and Chris come up behind us through the gloom; they're done in too but pleased with life, as well they might be. They'd gone back up to C3 with hill-food bags, gas and oxygen cylinders and left them with Rick and Jon, who were now ensconced in the tiny tent.

Finally off the glacier, take three rests getting up the 20-foot moraine bank, sick again. Liz and I sit in the Mess Tent like the grey dead, scarcely able to speak and certainly not up to smiling, the slightest movement is too much effort. A brew and slowly the greyness lifts, leaving only a weariness and peace. And some satisfaction too. One of the Sultans of Pain for a day. I'm more astonished and impressed than ever at the lads; it's humbling to realize they keep doing this over and over. They must surely feel as bad as I do – yet continue. This impresses me more than any nail-biting vertical derring-do. The lads are so used to this that it scarcely enters their conversation or diaries. But I'll put it in the book, just to say: This is how it feels, this hurts.

We mumble through soup and some other inedible substance. Mal's in good form, pleased to have set up Camp 3 and finally coming into his own. 'I'm going a lot better now than I was. At the moment most of it depends on the weather. I'm beginning to think we'll have to adjust the oxygen situation. . . .' Liz, part amused and part affectionate, says wryly, 'You're beginning to rev, aren't you?' 'Yeah, I suffer from low-altitude paranoia – I'm no good below 6,000 metres Every day and every load counts now.'

With Sandy sleeping at C2, and Jon and Rick in the dubious comfort of C3, it feels like we're moving forward. We are. But the arithmetic is becoming cruel. Mal points out several of the lads are well below their best, time's running short, and we've some 20 loads to go to C3, which in turn need to go on to a C4 before we can really hit the Pinnacles. That means several severe altitude carries for everyone who's capable, and then we need a couple of still-strong pairs to fix the Pinnacles, then probably another pair to go for the summit after that. . . .

Bed early. I fall asleep or unconscious, wake up middle of the night with my head-torch still on. Switch it off, see a huge white moon glow through my tent. Asleep again. . . .

May 8. Once or twice in a lifetime you may witness something for which there is no explanation. Or rather, there are explanations, but they are too disturbing to contemplate for long. Today we saw a man who wasn't there.

I was sitting outside my tent after a late, leisurely breakfast. It was a fine morning, the best since we first set up ABC, blue and still. Visibility was perfect and I watched with casual interest a figure moving up the ridge between 7090 and Camp 3. He was clearly silhouetted against the snow, arms, legs and everything, and was going very well. It would be Sandy, on his way from Camp 2, where he'd slept the night before, carrying a load to C3. Mal and Liz sat outside their tent, checking on his progress with binoculars . . . a red windsuit, must be Sandy.

We watched the figure on and off for an hour, looking really for Rick and Jon going over the Buttresses on their way to find a Camp 4, but there was no sign of them. We went into the Mess Tent for more brews – then Sandy turned up.

'What are you doing here?'

Sandy seemed taken aback. 'Well, I kept being sick during the night and this morning, so I came back down.'

'You mean you didn't go along the Ridge to Camp 3?'

'No, I told you, I was sick. I didn't even go up to 7090, just came straight down. What's the fuss about?'

We told him about the climber we'd watched on the Ridge, went back outside to look but no sign of him. We looked at each other. Jon and Rick had slept at C3 and gone on, so it could not have been either of them. And no one else was on the hill.

Liz and Mal thought instantly of the red windsuit, Pete Boardman's windsuit that we'd found in CB's cave and now hanging in a corner of the Mess Tent. I was too dumbfounded to think coherently at all. If anything I thought not so much of ghosts as of a kind of visual echo or recording; I felt we'd been watching for an hour an event that had happened three years ago and was still somehow imprinted on the Ridge itself. Sandy remembered cases of previous such sightings, like F. S. Smythe's in 1933, or Doug Scott's, Alex MacIntyre's, Nick Escourt's. . . .

'Well,' Mal said at last, trying to be jocular about it, 'I don't care who he is as long as he carries a load!'

It's something we still think about, once in a while. Mal, Liz and I were rested and well; perfect visibility; binoculars and the naked eye. . . . And for an hour we saw a man who wasn't there.

Sandy Me, I'm from the Highlands and I believe in such 'imaginings'. What happens to people's souls and spirits? Where's Haston, Boardman, Tasker, Pete Thexton, Brian Sprunt, Rob Bruce, all the lads – where are they?

Don't fully comprehend why I am here. I have a feeling that I ought to be, that it was intended for me to come to Everest, by some authority. I never imagined being here, the idea of actually lying in a tent at ABC still takes me by surprise.

For some godforsaken reason we (I) front-point as good as some other people, for some reason I can jam my ice-axe in, torqued to the max, in cracks that other people have failed to, and so my body heaves exhausted over some rock or ice-bulge and hence a First Ascent. . . . And God or whatever – me, I'll go for God – set the sun a-shining just before I got frostbite, or slowed the winds down just before we got hypothermia, or set the correct abseil position in the rock just when we needed it, or opened a little window so we could see the direction when we were totally lost. Some people call it luck, me – luck and unknown but most welcome INTERVENTION.

Here, we're here, I'm here, hoping that my own ability and the rest of the lads' ability and the gods will see us OK. We're gamblers, we've got no cash; we have lives, we love them, that's the stake. The reward for me is to continue this life, on this planet, driving down the roads I know and walking through the door of my friends' houses ... and between that, *Inshallah*, a summit or two.

Jon Camp 3 is loosely inspired by a large rock Allen discovered near the foot of the 1st Buttress. There's a hole behind it which has been excavated to form a gear stash. Then there's a platform for one of the Wild Country special Mountain Gemini tents, skewered to the ground with an assortment of stakes and ice-axes. The tent is very light but very small, with the floor space of two Karrimats and barely enough room to sit up inside. Lots of hoar-frost in the morning. I didn't catch much sleep at all that night but never mind, it's our big day tomorrow, when we push out the route up to the site of Bonington's 3rd snow cave at 7,850.

The Camp 3 tents were to continue to be a problem. We'd had them specially made smaller to reduce weight, but they ended up too small. Also plates of ice formed inside, and the Velcro-fastened door (to save weight) wouldn't close properly and let spindrift blow in. With that and the wind's hammering away at the exposed position all night, no one had anything like a good night's sleep or rest there, which severely damaged their effectiveness the next morning.

Jon Away by 10 am after Rick, who's some way ahead (the tent only allows one person to move at a time) and will remain so all day. The worst part is the 1st Buttress, split by a horrible collapsing couloir. Not very steep, Andy climbed it on shafts, but it must have been a struggle. Bits of Bonington's orange climbing rope contrast with our bright blue polyprop. A small gear stash, then soloing again up alternating snow-covered gravel and firm, easy-angled nevé. The 2nd Buttress is much smaller than expected- .Then an easy ramp protected by CB's rope – anchored to God knows what. Easy rock climbing in crampons. Then off and up soloing again. ...

Put the legs into automatic and let the brain monitor the body – am I hyperventilating? Are my lungs filling up with fluid? (Pulmonary oedema). Have I a headache? (Cerebral oedema). The landscape drifts past, some false summits then I turn on to a broad plateau. First view of the Pinnacles – they look technical and forbidding, can't wait to get stuck into them. But not today – my breathing tells me it's the first time my body's been this high, my right foot is very cold, can't feel any toes, must get down. Rick's digging a snow cave – no sign of Bonington's – and will come down later. A man with the discipline to achieve desired objectives. He always seems surprised and disappointed when the mountain tells him otherwise. Perhaps he likes mountains because he can be beaten occasionally – though not often as he's one of life's winners and calculators. Leavened with his faith, he's a great human . . . I shuffle down, very tired, having to sit down now and then.

Meanwhile we sat in the almost-warm sun at ABC, scanning the Buttresses with binoculars. Finally we spotted a figure high on the 2nd Buttress, then another some distance behind. Rick, then Jon. They were going slowly, but steadily getting there. The perfect weather brought some much-needed relaxation and optimism.

'I don't know if faith moves mountains, but it certainly helps you climb them!' Mal remarked. At the same time, he had to be realistic. 'At the moment I'd say we were poised between success and failure,' he said as we sat on our barrels looking up at the Ridge. 'If Jon and Rick can find Bonington's 3rd snow cave near the Pinns, or dig one out themselves, we've a real chance, if the weather stays like this. But I'm beginning to think we'll have to adjust the oxygen situation. Maybe use part of a bottle to carry two others to the foot of the Pinns. . . . Time's getting tight and people are getting seriously wasted.' He passed me a cigarette; I lit up and watched it burn fitfully, like ourselves up here, not enough oxygen for real combustion. 'Yes', he continued, tugging at a beard as wild as mine, 'it's time to bring up the sick and the lame, women, children and convalescents . . . and bumblies. Think you can do another carry?' His eyes were hidden behind mirror shades; I regarded myself in miniature in them. I looked rough: wasted youth. 'Terry and I are planning to carry to CB's day after tomorrow,' I said. 'If we can, we'll go on to 7090 the next day. Wattie reckons that'll be all the loads up there that we need.'

'Thanks. That'll help. Liz wants to try for CB's, she can go with you.'

I nodded, feeling nervousness and anticipation chase each other round my body at the prospect of 7090. Over 23,000 feet, high enough for any bumbly!

Rick Past Andy and Urs' high point and on over mixed ground to another nevé slope, slight false summit, finally we are at 7,850 on a flat plateau. Jon has dropped behind. Almost windless. Jon belays me over the rim of the Kangshung Face down on to the top of 'Fantasy Ridge'. I probe about but cannot find Bonington's snow cave. Jon's feet are cold and he starts to descend immediately. I dig into the slope for two to three hours. . . . Only now do I realize how tired I am. Descend slowly.

One of the best days I've ever had in the mountains. Maybe we're getting somewhere.

We waited for news from them on the 7.0 pm radio call. Tony arrived, looking unshaven and ragged, as if he'd just come off the hill rather than being on his way to it. He said his bronchitis had cleared up, but he was still coughing regularly. He also brought good news from BC – Andy was recovering quickly from his snow blindness, finding lying in his tent for two days with bandages over his eyes to be 'very boring', and he'd be up with Urs in a couple of days. Mal was heartened by this sense of urgency; we needed all the manpower we could get.

Then Rick came in on the radio, clipped and laconic as ever.'Well, we've a very small snow-hole at Camp 4.' A silent cheer, smiles all round. Mal asked, 'Well how big is a small hole?' 'Very small. Tony-sized! But it could be bigger. I'll go back to work on it tomorrow if I'm feeling strong.' Pause, a fresh explosion from static on the radio. 'Right now I'm not feeling very strong.'

Evaluation: quite good. We've a Camp 4 site, and good névé snow bank to enlarge it in. It would have been better if we'd found CB's old cave. Jon's probably approaching his limit and is coming down. Rick's obviously capable of going to 8,000 metres and beyond; Mal hopes he isn't going to burn himself out going back up there tomorrow – and alone. What Rick was doing is roughly like climbing two major Himalayan peaks in consecutive days. Once again, it is a situation brought on by unequal partnerships.

Terry Today was the day of the exploding kippers! As all tins are frozen, we normally put them in the kettle to defrost. Andy G. put two tins of kipper fillets in the kettle at lunchtime and then forgot about them. We were both sitting outside watching the action on the two ridges (Basques on the North Col as well). All of a sudden there was a dull explosion from the Mess Tent and when we went in the place was absolutely plastered in bits of kippers. . . .

Another day of stable weather. We sat in the crisp morning air watching two black dots emerge from C3 and separate, one toiling up, the other coming down fast. Eventually Jon arrived at ABC to 'a Warhol-like 15 minutes – Kurt's camera, Julie on sound, Terry, Liz, etc., on professional Walkmen. 'It's a white hell up there.' Hoarse-throated, lip-salve smeared, skin peeling – 'I'll never do a good Boy George impression. As tired as I've been for a few years.'

As Sandy and Chris patiently submitted to several takes of their setting out for C2, made the necessary comments on how desperate the Pinnacles looked, one more time, etc., we sat and watched Rick moving screamingly slowly up the Buttresses. His suffering communicated itself across the mile of blue. He stopped, sat down, went on again. Jon shook his head, 'Rick has this single-minded desire to burn himself out as quickly as possible on this trip. He's fucking phenomenal. . . .'

'Pretty awesome,' Mal agreed, but he worried about the safety of a solo climber going to near-as-damn-it, 8,000 metres for a second day running, with no one near him on the hill. And we couldn't afford to have Rick burn himself out entirely on this push: he'd said to Jon at C4 that the Pinnacles terrified him just looking at them, but he had every intention of getting into them. Rick *believed* in a massive way. If he and Jon had been able to work together to complete digging out a C4 snow-hole the day before. . . . If. . . .

Still the yellow dot stumbled on. At the foot of the 2nd Buttress he stopped, and remained motionless, for five minutes. Then he turned to look down the way he'd come, then the distance ahead, utterly alone in the moment of truth. Then he slowly leaned forward into the slope and took the next five steps.

Rick I take a bale of fixed rope and move oh so slowly to the foot of the 1st Buttress. Must make use of these good conditions. At the top of the 1st Buttress I pick up two sections of gash fixed rope and a snow saw and move on even more slowly. By the top of the 2nd Buttress it had become an exercise in will-power (almost no sleep again last night). Finally make 7,850 in about five hours. . . .'

The fixing rope intended for use on the Pinnacles was an interesting demonstration of Rick's priorities – carrying it to 7,850 meant he was too exhausted to enlarge the snow cave greatly before heading back down. That was not Rick's fault, but it was disappointing, for setting up a Camp 4 had been the whole point of Jon and Rick's push. We were now firmly in the pattern of accomplishing a crucial bit less than planned and hoped for.

So Sandy and Chris slept at C2 that night, while Mal dossed alone ('sleep entirely undisturbed by ghosts') at CB's. Their aim was to carry some loads to C3, and on to 4 if possible. The carries to C4 would be the most crucial of all, and the hardest.

'Expedition on a very fine line,' Mal wrote as he lay in his sleeping bag sipping the day's final brew. 'We need ten days' climbable weather.'

Himalayan Thuggery

IOTH – I8TH MAY

'Puts our necks on the chopper, doesn't it?'

Kit for tomorrow: sleeping bag, down boots, Karrimat; spare gloves, socks, balaclava, sweater. Lip-salve and suncream, pee bottle, loo-roll, head-torch, lighter, drugs (sleepers, codeine), water bottle. Munchies, drinking chocolate, ½ book, notebook, pen. Cigarettes, cup, spoon. Camera, radio battery. Pick up O$_2$ gear.
Wear: thermal underwear, salopettes, down jacket, pile jacket, wind-suit, gloves, balaclava. Koflachs with Alveolite inners; cramps, harness, jumar, 3 slings, 3 krabs. Prayer-scarf. Lucky stone.
Bottle up and go.

Fresh snow in the night but a beautiful morning. Alpen, brews, shortbread, oatcakes and more brews. As usual the stoves work poorly, take hours to melt the ice and we end up not drinking enough. Tony, Terry and I kit up methodically, saying little, concentrating. Share out food for tonight, hill-bags and the O$_2$ gear Mal requested. Last look round my tent, then zip it shut. Terry and I rope together, nod, okay youth? I lead off towards the Raphu La.

A wondrous arena as always, this shallow, shining crucible. Only the crunch of our feet and the deep pant of my breath. I'm becoming addicted to emptiness and silence. Terry and I have quite different paces – I like to trudge slow and steady, stopping as seldom as possible, while Terry goes fast in long energetic strides and stops at most of the wands across the glacier. He says climbing and its shuffling-dosser life-style is his necessary counterbalance to the money and comfort-saturated world of advertising. 'A sort of appeasement,' he says. But he goes at both activities in the same forceful, buoyant way.

At the bottom of the fixed ropes we look up and see Liz nearing the ice-bulge – she slept in Kurt and Julie's tent on the Raphu La last night, to give her an early start today. She's set on finally making CB's this time. Tony's on the next rope section below, on his way to C2. The hill's getting so busy we've had to book CB's in advance for tonight's doss.

On to the ropes. Seems natural now – clip in jumar, add safety krab, deep breath and go. Short steps help, looking for a sustainable rhythm of legs and arms. Start counting steps, almost like a mantra, slowly emptying the mind. Soon only the slabby snow underfoot exists, that and my slipping jumar. It's this simplicity I come here for. All problems are immediate; they're either up to me (like making myself carry on) or completely out of my hands (like the seracs above the couloir traverse).

Liz is on the ice-bulge now. She's so slow but so determined. The slower you go and the more often you have to stop, the more determination it must take to push on again. Terry below is still rushing short sections then leaning, gasping, over his axe.

Enjoy the ice-bulge – how large it loomed in my mind a few weeks ago! Over the top and quite confidently traverse to the rock rib. This one-time high point is now just a half-way mark. Soft, deep snow behind the rock rib, I'm feeling oddly assured and have to remind myself to clip in properly and not be too casual.

A wait at the start of the traverse: Tony's sitting half-way across, waiting for Liz to finish and get on to the next rope section. He waves, at ease and in no hurry. I wave affectionately back. Off with the sack, clip it, cut a snow ledge and settle down to wait. Five minutes of pure ease and happiness in this elevated openness, looking across the Himalayas to Kangchenjunga, to nearby Makalu, to Changtse, to the North Col, where we saw the Basques go up yesterday. I'm climbing on Everest and just being alive is being in love.

Liz finally struggles over the far rim of the couloir – she'll definitely make CB's now – Tony gets up and follows very carefully in her footsteps. The crest above him is wildly corniced, we glimpse the sheer flutings of the upper Kangshung Face, and the seracs that castellate the skyline. Hope they don't collapse today, they've got to sometime with all the new snow we've had. Tony gets across, I gather myself and set off after him under the deep blue altitude sky – then inside two minutes conditions change completely. First spindrift swirling up in my face, then snow whirling out of the grey. Tony's disappeared somewhere in the murk. Not so much alarmed – bad weather curiously exhilarates me and I'm quite happy not to see the drop below! – but peeved because I'd wanted Terry to take a picture of me on this traverse to match the one in CB's book. Still, as Sandy says, that's just COSMETIC SHIT! I'm here and that's what matters.

Tony's steps are already filled in, so I carefully stomp my own. A six-inch slab breaks off regularly and slides into oblivion; I'm too inexperienced to know if this is a bad sign or par for the course. Move on faster, axe in left hand, sinking the shaft deep into the slope, pushing the jumar ahead with the right. Adrenalin and concentration drive out anxiety. The half-way stake. Clip in, relax, look up at the shadow of the looming serac and decide to move on. Now the rope curves uphill into the purgatory section – steep, footsteps collapsing, one false crest after another. Down to ten steps now.

Over the top, see the tangle of ropes and gear outside CB's. A warmth like whisky in my brain. Clip in to the stake, clip my sack and crawl inside. There's Tony and a tired but beaming Liz, radiant with unspoken satisfaction. I congratulate her and she hands me a brew in exchange. We sit there feeling pleased with ourselves; I'm tired, but much more clear-headed than last time I was up here.

Tony moves on after some chat. He's buoyant and optimistic again, but his cough sounds bad. The cave darkens as Terry's bulk slithers through the doorway, covered in snow but grinning broadly.

As snow melts on the stove, we arrange ourselves carefully in the cave. It's small for three plus our gear, and we can only move one at a time. The chamber is kneeling-high at the far end, but only crouching at mine. A mild claustrophobic anxiety at the back of my mind, especially when we fix the Karrimat across the entrance to keep out spindrift. But the blue light filtering through is soothing, and this cave is much more peaceful than a tent.

Liz is unhappy at the prospect of descending alone through the gloom and the freshly covered slopes. Terry suggests she stay the night. Three in this cave? Well ... We look around, find Chris's double bivvi bag and Allen's down boots and gloves – and a one-piece down suit. Up to you, Liz. She decides to stay, so one by one we slowly take off our crampons, boots and damp socks, lay out our mats; Terry and I slither into our sleeping bags. Liz tries on the down suit and finds it warm, then gets into Chris's bivvi-bag. Lying between us, she reckons she'll be warm enough. So we settle in for the evening. I make the mistake of lying next to the snow-filled bag, so continually have to twist over to fill billies from it, which I pass to Liz who passes them to Terry and the precariously balanced stove beside him. Terry also believes he is in the worst position and Liz probably does too. All our movements are slow and cautious in this overcrowded cave. So easy to knock over a stove, or knock snow off the walls on to ourselves. Patience and restraint needed all round. The heat of the stove makes water drip down on to us.

Eventually we have our stew and eat it with little appetite.

Rummage in a hill-food bag and find two pepperoni sticks, which we share – after all, we're climbers now so we can use what we find. As the dessert treat, Terry produces some hoarded Bovril cubes, which seem like the last word in luxury. As we lie silently drinking in the dim light, it occurs to me we're not really masochists at all, but enlightened hedonists. Only scarcity and discomfort can yield such intense pleasure in simple things, transforming a luke-warm mug of Bovril into the elixir of life, and two pepperoni into an experience of near-mystical intensity!

Sunset. Liz holds my ankles as I squirm out to the entrance. It's stopped snowing and the sky is glowing over Kellas's peak and the darkening valley below. I take pictures for us all, come inside and re-fix the Karrimat. Mal comes on the radio from Camp 2 above us, and is surprised to find Liz still with us. She assures him the situation, though cramped, is under control; he asks us to bring the oxygen regulators and masks up first thing tomorrow so he can take them on to C3 in the morning. C2 is full up too, with Mal, Sandy, Chris and Tony all dossing there. Apparently Sandy and Chris put in a really good day's work at C3, enlarged the first snow platform, re-sited the tent, then dug another platform and put up a second tent. Camp 3 is as good as it will ever be. Good wishes for tomorrow, see you, youth . . .

I take a sleeper and get through the last brew and settling-down for the night in something of a daze, only vaguely aware of Liz crawling over me towards the entrance.

An uncomfortable night of elbows and knees and bodies competing for comfortable space. We doze on and off, Liz and I making an insomniac's brew at 2.0 am to relieve sore throats and pass the time.

8.0 am Terry's alarm goes off, dragging me out of muzzy-headed sleep. Odd how here we are tied to sleeping pills and clocks, the symbols of high-pressure urban living. Terry volunteers to take up the most urgently required oxygen gear, so gets up first while we lie letting him clamber over us. He scrapes out more snow from round the entrance, and starts melting for the first brew. I've always wondered why it takes climbers two hours to get going in the morning – now I know. Just getting dressed when you can't sit up, when every movement could knock over a stove, or bring down snow from the walls, is a slow, precise activity when you feel like one of the living dead.

A brew, we force down a half-defrosted Xmas pudding each, then Terry leaves with a 'see you up there' and a farewell thumbs-up. More room now; I retrieve socks, gloves and inner boots from inside my bag, pull on the layers, breathing steadily. Put on harness and crampons while kneeling at the entrance – a relief to be able to clip in. Quite a lot of soft deep powder snow overnight, the hill-food bags are buried, and visibility is very limited through the mesmeric snow. Still – I've come here for 7090 and Mal's waiting for my gear. Liz says she'll see if she will follow on or not; she'd initially intended just CB's, but now she's more than halfway to 7090 . . .

Terry The route up to C2 was not very long, you could see most of it from C1, but a very steep traverse with a fixed vertical section over the ice, and then a 30-yard section actually into the snow-hole at about 50°. Trouble was the whole of the route had been plastered in new soft deep powder snow during the night. So I struggled. All the way – it was absolute purgatory, worth it though . . .

Wake up, Andrew. You're mid-route and this is serious. Put my fist through the axe's wrist-loop, clip in jumar, safety krab; sack on, unclip safety sling, and slowly, stiffly, set off up into new territory, wiping snow off my goggles.

Proper hard this is, like the last section up to CB's, but ten times longer. Loose snow on ice – so kick in firmly, test the step, sink in the axe, push the jumar along, pull, another step. Push the mountain down and it pushes me up.

One long rising traverse, roughly parallel to the crest of the Ridge I can see dimly up on my left. On my own in this grey-white world, absorbed in care and effort and the ground under my feet. It comes to me that this is what I've always sought – an experience that would absorb me entirely. Then even that thought slips away. Now I'm vacant, counting steps, feeling the strain, head cleaned out like a billy-can scoured with snow.

Jumar is slipping again, icing up. Unpleasant, have to use it only as a safety line, which means more leg effort. Steps are insecure, sending slabs off down the hill. A steep section, soft with it. I finally reach and clip to a stake, knock the ice off the jumar, continue . . . Round a corner, if I'm where I think I am, I'm glad I can't see down, it's a long drop. Then I see Terry up above, wave. 'Hey Terry, how much further?' But it's Mal, who shouts back, 'In there!' and points to his right. I come on another 20 yards and realize I'm practically there: the usual tangle of gear, and a deep slot into the slope. 'Well done, youth,' he says, asks after Liz.

'Push the route.'

'I intend to,' he grins, and stomps up the fixed line to 7090.

I crawl into the cave. Terry and I grin at each other, Sandy gives me a brew, a quick pat on the back, and sets off after Malcolm. Terry and I lounge back in the spacious cave, beaming like idiots. I light up a celebratory cigarette; it tastes just fine. After a brew Terry says, 'Might as well go up to 7090 while we're here.' I nod, so we stiffly plod through the thickening snow – no sign of Liz – and clip into the short length of fixed rope up the steepish last 100 feet, on to the crest of the Ridge. So this is my summit, typical, can't see anything. No Buttresses, no Pinnacles, just 80 yards of whirling snow. 'Could be on Rannoch Moor,' I joke to Terry. He's quietly selecting a few loose stones, I pick up a couple. Nothing special about them, just little splintered rocks, but they took a bit of getting. We take a few photos; nothing will come out, of course, but it doesn't matter. We know we've been here.

A last look around. Well, that's it. Time to go home. Beam me down to Scottie, please.[1]

We descend back to C2. Terry starts brewing, but it's snowing heavily now and oddly mild. Even I know that could add up to trouble. No reason to hang around. I give myself the usual Get It Together pep-talk (climbing would be a lot easier if it was second nature to me as it is to the lads, but then it possibly wouldn't mean so much) and set off resolved to do this dodgy descent as fast as possible. Side-hill, down-hill, ploughing deep footsteps which crumble and slip. It's far too warm. At the first snow-stake – Hey, Liz! – bent over her axe, gasping, she straightens up looking very tired and pissed off and relieved to see someone. 'How far is it?' 'No distance, you're almost there' . . . 'Really!' I add, seeing her sceptical look. She says she's having trouble with the jumar slipping all the time, having to test it; I suggest she doesn't pull on it and just uses it as a safety line – much faster. I can see exasperation on her face, she obviously thinks it's a silly suggestion. But it's up to her, she'll make it now anyway, however slowly and cautiously she moves.

I congratulate her in advance and slither off into the white world and crawl 30 minutes later into CB's, where I'm writing this waiting for the brew to boil. This is like home. Liz has tidied it up really well. God this drinking chocolate is the business. Better start another brew for Terry and Liz coming down. Feel satisfied. Not ecstatic, just satisfied. Summits are only something to aim at, like the horizon, a helpful illusion.

[1]Terry's daughter, Amy Everest, was born on the other side of the world precisely during the ten minutes he spent on his summit.

. . . So here's Terry blocking out the light. 'Hi, Andy!' 'Don't tell me, it's a white hell out there.' He nods, plastered in snow from head to toe, grinning with pleasure. I can see he's tired though, as I pass him a mug. Then 'Hey, Sandy!' It's our puzzled Highlander. It feels good to be in control and be able to casually present him with a brew. His eyes flick over me, assessing my condition in a moment. 'Yes, the youth's fine,' I can practically see the thought. When I'm concentrating I can usually read Sandy's reactions to anything these days, so we must be getting closer. And he knows I can, finds it almost embarrassing, grins at me sheepishly and looks away. He's had a busy day – he took another oxygen cylinder and some climbing gear to C3 to add to his and Chris's double carry of the day before (that's a major advance, surely), left the gear some-where near the C3 tents and set off down, worried about finding his way in the near white-out, very aware of the Kangshung Face cornices somewhere on his right, peering for disappearing footprints. 'Not too nice, eh? Pity you two didn't get a view.'

'Well, it's just consumer durables, Sandy,' I say, and see him start slightly as I use his phrase. He'd called in on Liz at C2, seen her safely on her way, overtook her on the way down here. Now he was keen to move on – I am too. Sandy said the descent could be wild, and we should keep in sight of each other. So Terry agreed to wait for Liz and come down with her. 'See you at ABC,' then off.

I notice how careful Sandy is transferring himself from the cave to the fixed line, do the same. Soon I'm standing above the couloir; it looks wild. Sandy is going across very carefully, setting off small avalanches, kicking steps which slip away as he moves into them. He's even facing into the slope and front-pointing at times. I glance up at the looming seracs above, they're what I'm worried about. It's much too mild, too much fresh snow. Sandy's past the mid-traverse snow-anchor. My spontaneous prayer is as always in two parts: *please let me get off with this; but if I don't, that's alright.* Here goes . . .

The rock rib, can't remember a thing about that traverse, it must have been too demanding to stand back and observe – hey, concen-trate, you're okay but don't ease up now, double friction-brake for the ice-bulge and over we go, in the mountains there you feel free, and I'm suddenly beneath the bad weather in dazzling sunshine of a still and perfect afternoon, there's Sandy way below glissading towards the bottom waving his arms and having a whale of a time, but I'll just walk down leisurely for there's no hurry now and I don't want this moment to end, tramping down the fixed narrative ropes of the North-East Ridge on a sunny afternoon . . .

We sit in companionable silence at the bottom, feeling mellow as the sun and hushed by the majestic tranquillity of our surroundings.

'Well, that's me done,' I said finally. 'Now I'll just watch you guys.' A lingering regret almost – with all the necessary loads now up to 7090, this will be my last snow/ice climbing till Scotland next winter.

'I envy you,' Sandy says. Eh? 'I wish it was like that for me – just one target, you do it and enjoy it and that's enough. Me, even if, *Inshallah*, I make this summit, I'll not be satisfied, I'll go on needing another then another. It just keeps on renewing itself, like this snow, you know . . .' and his thoughts wander underground out of sight and sound.

Ambling back across the glacier like two middle-aged gentlemen rambling down the 18th fairway towards the golf clubhouse, exclaiming about the clouds and suchlike. Sheets of white clouds rising vertically above the North Col, the Basques must be struggling above there today, hope they're alright; rapid clouds boiling up the Kangshung Face; spindrift hissing horizontally across the blue; stately galleon clouds fully rigged drifting overhead . . . A fall knee-deep into a small crevasse reminds me to keep my eyes firmly on the ground. We plod on together, the umbilical intimacy of the rope between us.

'That's it, thanks for the company,' Sandy says as we unrope then stumble up the moraine bank to the Mess Tent, where Sarah has the life-saving, consciousness-raising brews waiting.

Terry and Liz turned up four hours later, at dusk. They'd struggled on the way back, wading through ever-deepening fresh snow. We say 'Hi' in hoarse whispers, can scarcely speak for burned lips and constricted throats, the product of two days of gasping and coughing freezing, very dry air. The sweetness is there, but sunk to the bottom below our fatigue, like cherries in a cake.

Terry Liz and I congratulated each other when we got down to the little lake and took our gear off. Even though we were both knackered, we agreed that it was the most exhilarating day we had ever spent climbing. We both felt on top of the world for reaching our own personal height records of 7090 . . .

Wonderful, wonderful Sarah had stayed up to cook for us. As we walked up the path from the lake to the Mess Tent everyone was putting their heads out of their tents congratulating us. A lovely warm glow to finish off the day.

As we catch up with the news it's clear there's been some real progress in the last couple of days, with crucial carries of O_2, food and climbing gear being made up to C3. Tonight Mal and Chris are sleeping at C3, intending to carry on to C4 tomorrow. If they can get loads up there and enlarge the miniature snow cave we're right in there. He said on the radio that it was wild, he and Chris being shaken around in their separate tiny tents. But he was in excellent humour, openly pleased with the bumblies' carry, and congratulated Liz – unusual for him. Tony's on his lonesome up at C2 tonight after carrying to C3. It was planned that Nick would go up to join him today, but he'd turned back at the Raphu La when the snow came on heavily. Mal's obviously bothered by this news. There's so many people on the go now, all out of sync with each other: Sandy with no one in particular, Tony ditto, Allen, now Nick. Seeing today's weather, Rick followed Jon down to BC for a short rest, but there are doubts as to how long they'll stay together. The general feeling is we're not using our now limited energies as well as possible, but nobody quite knows what to do about it: making up suitable pairs again would mean people having to hang about to get in sync, and we feel there isn't time for that. We're waiting for Mal to re-deploy our forces – but he's on the hill now, working very hard, frequently out of contact with ABC, and of course completely out of contact with BC. So it looks like the 'rolling maul' method will continue a little longer.

Urs and Andy are up again, ultra-keen, like greyhounds kept in the traps too long. Urs is emphatic that he wants to do the Pinnacles without O_2, and Andy is optimistic that it can be done. Unvoiced doubts in the air – Urs has been super-confident before, but seems a changed person in bad weather above 7090. After a rest-day they will be ready to go to C3 and then, *Inshallah*, a start on the 1st Pinnacle. All the necessary gear will be there for fixing it. We're so near to achieving something.

Jon: 'It's now going to get very, very naughty.'

Chris slumped forward in his arms dangling resting position, croaked his story through a mangled larynx at ABC next evening: 'I cooked the most fantastic meal, was really chuffed, drifted off to sleep . . . Getting on for 1.0 am I woke up, thought "God, I feel *awful*." So I went outside, decided it wasn't that, went back inside – and immediately had to rush for the cooking pot . . . [long pause] Filled it in one. [Laughter] I spent bloody ages filling it with snow, washing it out . . .'

Andy Nisbet: 'That was very noble.'

Chris: 'It wasn't very noble . . . I had another meal after that!'
[Delighted laughter].

Mal 12th May. Bad during the night, chaotic when I spilt a pan of precious
water down my sleeping bag. Chris is in one tent, myself in the other –
strong wind and a lot of rime ice. Up at 6.30 – Chris sick so he opted to
descend. Took one O_2 bottle as load and set off. Very windy with high
spindrift. Deep snow in couloir on Butt 1, eventually got up to 7,850, felt
great and moving well. Fantastic views, now well above Changtse and
almost level with Cho Oyu. Could manage 8,000 metres easy even with a
load, which is a confident feeling. Descended to ABC in the late afternoon,
Raphu La awful with deep snow. Chris fucked and off to BC; Urs, Andy
and Sandy off to Pinn 1 tomorrow. Progress under way, but Expedition
on a very fine line.

A lot is going on in this brief entry. There's the joy and confidence
that everyone who made 7,850 felt, knowing now for sure that they
could go to the magic 8,000 metre mark without oxygen, thus
adding the world's 14 highest mountains to their future options.
Chris's illness. Urs diagnosed bronchitis, like Tony's, so he would
be out of things for a while. Another partnership split. As with many
other events, we did not realize how crucial this was to be. If Chris
had been able to carry with Mal to 7,850 they might have had the
energy and security to put in a couple of hours work enlarging the
C4 snow-hole. And that could have made all the difference when
Andy and Urs arrived there two days later . . .
    But unknown to us at the time, something far more serious had
happened on the North Col route. Kurt and Julie were camped on
the Col, filming. In the afternoon, Kurt was working outside the
tent. He spotted four figures descending, in pairs, the top of the long
snow slope that runs down to the Col. Relieved to see them again,
he called to tell Julie, who was inside the tent, the good news. But
minutes later the figure second from the front seemed to stumble,
then slide, an accelerating slide down past his partner in front, who
was in turn jerked off his feet. The two of them tumbled over and
over gathering momentum as Kurt and Julie watched helplessly.
Finally they crashed into a rock outcrop and lay still.
    Mari, the Basque leader, emphasized later that Kurt and Julie's
level-headed help made all the difference, and possibly saved a life.
But when Kurt reached the Basques it was too late to save one man:
Juan Jose Navarro, the climber who had stumbled first, had been
killed by the impact with the rocks. The remaining Basques were
still profoundly shocked, almost helpless. Kurt had been through
this before, all too often. He examined the injured Basque, Antxon.

Some concussion, shock of course, something wrong with his hip or leg, and possibly a broken arm. It was imperative to get him back down to the Col. They had already covered the dead man with stones; Kurt rallied the shocked climbers and helped Antxon to the tent on the North Col. All the Basques were in a bad way, passive and shocked, and had to be given brew after brew as the leader, Mari, explained what had happened.

They'd gone up to their tent at 7,500 metres, then the weather turned bad – a lot of fresh snow and a full Everest gale. Worst of all, they couldn't get their lighter to work in the draught and so ended up spending three days up there, trapped, without a single brew. So when the storm abated and they began to descend, they were all in very bad shape, weak, seriously dehydrated. The slope they were on was easy, 20° Kurt estimated, but one stumble by an exhausted man and that was it.

All for the want of a reliable lighter.

Meanwhile our Expedition carried on on the neighbouring ridge, just a mile or two away. Tony made his second consecutive carry to C3 and returned to ABC, coughing badly and not very happy. Nick went to C2 and slept the night there, the only person on the entire route. After de-briefing Urs and Andy that morning, I decided to head down to BC. Important things should be happening soon with our first attempt on Pinn 1, but I was done-in, and had to write my penultimate newspaper piece for Terry to take out with him. Then I should be fit enough to come back up and stay for however long it took us to finish this mountain or for it to finish us.

I enjoyed the ramble down to Base, feeling brain and body slowly come alive again as oxygen seeped back into my system. I met Allen looking fit and Bob looking exhausted on their way up. I hurried through Rock Alley, where the stonefall was becoming regular, skirted the melting ice-lake, down to the rock shelters of the pre-war Camp 1. The world took on faint smells of life – moss, rabbit droppings, deer. It became very warm, I felt my skin crisping like bacon.

Good old BC. Walked wearily across the flat stone-field, as always savouring this moment. Slung my rucksuck down by my tent. I'm done now. All I have to do is listen, watch and write. Step inside the Mess – Jon, Rick, Danny, a warm welcome and the usual flood of questions. Fresh bread, cheese, coffee. Talking with difficulty through a parched and tattered throat. 'Get it down your neck,' Jon grinned, 'This place is the business!'

Sandy Mal came down to ABC, not too exhausted, Oh was Liz pleased to see him, their affection real real obvious. When one sees such open and contented sharing caring, one can't help but wonder what one is missing . . . Or when Nicko radioed in at 6.0 sounding ace and content and Sarah came in late – the disappointed look on her face . . . When I realize that I see such things I ask myself, 'Allan, are you getting lonely, kid?' Old farts develop thataway, Tinker may say.

But still shut such thoughts off! Got to, unless it was easy to pray, 'Beam me out of here, Scotty,' and end up wrapped in the warmth of D.'s eiderdown and arm . . .

Monday 13th May, ABC
'Aye, okay, give me a second.'

Sighing in his head, Sandy squirmed out of his bag. Another day on the hill. He seemed to have been doing this most of his life. Well, he had been, his choice made when he was 25 and finally left the distilling industry for this dosser existence. Still . . . pull on fibre pile, then his blue Gore-tex windsuit (never red, he'd had a premonition he would die on the hill wearing red), then his Berghaus jacket with the Pilkington logo. Pulling up the leg-zips he remembered his mum sewing them on and thought momentarily of parents, home, the daffodils would be fully out there . . . He pulled on the Koflach boots, picked up his harness and stomped over to the Mess Tent.

Breakfast of tea and oatcakes and Alpen while Andy scoffed his favourite 'Ready Brek', which Sandy personally would not feed to a porky pig. Then finally away, aiming to make C3 in a single day. Andy took on the extra work of breaking trail across the glacier and set off up the fixed rope, then Urs who felt he was going well, and Sandy in the rear.

'One more time,' he thought – Kurt's catch-phrase. Only this is the real thing, not for cameras. Another windy spindrift morning, jugging up the ropes with sacks bulging with dossing gear and technical climbing equipment for the Pinnacles. All the familiar landmarks reached and left behind – the ice-bulge, CB's, then straight on to C2, where they found Nick in good form after his lonely vigil and ready to make his carry up to C3. It heartened Sandy to see the way these selfless and crucial high carries were being made at last.

Then on to the Ridge above 7090. Windy as always and deathly cold, but the sky clear for the time being as Sandy broke trail along the ridge-pole of the world. They finally arrived after 6.0 pm at the two tiny tents of C3. Nick left his load and set off down; Urs and Sandy shared one tent, Andy had the other. They brewed and waited for the 7.0 pm radio call. Mal came in on the dot and said immediately 'We need to speak to Urs.' His voice sounded taut and urgent. Sandy immediately thought: who's hurt? It was that kind of voice.

'The Basques have had an accident, one dead and one injured.'

Mal and Julie explained briefly what had happened. The Basques had been helped down to their ABC; Bob and Mal had gone up there to look at the injured Basque, who seemed to have got off lucky with bad bruises, a broken wrist, and severe shock. Urs wasn't needed as yet, so he could go on to the Pinnacles, but they'd keep in touch. . . .

Sandy We both felt very sick inside, water on my eyes. Said to Urs it was the Factor 15 suncream running off my forehead, but he knew and felt the same. We were wondering who was dead and who was injured, what Kurt and Julie went through as they helped the rescue. We saw black dots today on the North Col but did not consider it further. Urs appeared most shaken. He said, 'Looks like God does not want me to get to 8,000 metres,' but I felt more – a lot more – than that in his speech.

We brewed, Andy came over from his tent and the three of us squatted on the tiny floor area, steam from our lips and noses, and talked over the bad bad sad and almost anticipated news. Andy departed, I asked him to take great care in going to his tent, only a few yards but a good place for an accident . . . as is anywhere on this hill. 'Okay, I'm back!' he shouted.

Sleeping tablet took over. . . . Thoughts in my head of the value of Alpine-style climbing, its high death-rate, my future Gangapurna trip. Should we forget the idea? Haston dead in an avalanche, Alex MacIntyre, so many others. And now another Basque killed on the so-called 'piece of piss' North Col route. . . . Is it worth it? There's daffodils, new lambs, disco action and easy hills to climb back home, beaches to lie on, good books to read, films to see . . . and of course . . . other mountains to climb!

With such turmoil I tried to sleep and did so intermittently.

Half-awake at 7,300 metres . . . stove, pan, some snow, where's the lighter, warm it in hands inside the sleeping bag then light the stove, blue flame and condensation spitting from the billie on to the stove, hands cold, back under armpits. . . . Careful not to move in case the stove gets knocked over, spindrift and hoar frost falling on to one's face and sleeping bag. . . . 'Hi, Urs, how did you sleep?'

'Awfully. . . .'

Another morning in Sandy's world, but today there's a cloud hanging over it, something he doesn't want to think about too much yet. It hangs between the three of them, unmentioned, as they gear up to go to C4.

The Plan. Urs and Andy to go to C4, complete the snow-hole started by Rick, spend the night there, and start on the 1st Pinnacle next day. Sandy to carry food, gas, an O_2 cylinder and regulator to C4, and then return to C3.
Actual. Andy Nisbet broke trail up the snow-choked gully on the 1st Buttress, on to the 2nd and up the mixed ground there. At the top of the 2nd Buttress Sandy conferred with Andy as they waited for Urs to catch up. Sandy was tired and low, thinking of the Basques, of the black clouds looming over the North Col; he was worried about finding his way back to C3, and so they decided he should dump his load and go back now. This was a repetition of 11th May, when Sandy had to leave his load short of C3 in poor visibility. Then again he had been the odd person out in a threesome, with the other two planning to sleep overnight at their destination.

So Sandy set off down, and the plan had gone adrift already. Not crucially, for Urs and Andy still had everything they needed for the 1st Pinnacle; more prophetic were Sandy's reasons for turning back, which he admitted were as much psychological as physical.

Andy had had a 'really dreadful night' (strong words for him) at C3, unable to sleep at all, all kinds of thoughts whirling through his throbbing head. In the morning he felt downright ill and it took him one and a half hours to have a brew without throwing up. The weather was deteriorating now, the spindrift blinding at times; he wasn't enjoying himself but he kept on going.

Urs was shaken by the violence of the weather. He hadn't really believed it when Mal had spoken of crawling on the Ridge, putting it down to un-British exaggeration, 'guide stories'. Now he believed as he struggled to keep his footing, and his morale leaked away with his energy. Climbing was only part of his life; the rest of it was in a remote valley in Switzerland with his wife Madeleine, their joint medical practice and their children. The Basque death played on his mind. How easily that could happen to him as it had to so many. . . . Over 7,500 metres was well into the 'Death Zone', he knew the figures. . . . Why should he risk losing the pleasures of home for this? What was he doing here at all? His ABC dreams of climbing the Pinnacles, of going without oxygen above 8,000 metres, had vanished with the hill below him. He went on, hating it. Terrible! Terrible!. . . .

They found the C4 'rabbit hole' round 3.0 that afternoon. They'd expected to find it small for 2, but this was ridiculous. So they worked on and off for four hours to enlarge it. At the end of scraping around, kneeling and doubled over in hard nevé at nearly 8,000 metres, they were exhausted and had a hole that just might sleep both of them. They also discovered there was no food or brewing materials there. Another high-altitude mix-up, as typical as it was crucial. Rick insisted that he'd told them twice there was nothing at C4, and Andy had a clear impression he'd been told there was food, etc., there. Of course Sandy had been carrying hill-food, but his load was back at the top of the 2nd Buttress.

They drank warm water and lay in their bags in the now coffin-sized snow hole. Urs looked at the ceiling just above his head, felt himself starting to hyperventilate, his head whirling with the Basques, thoughts of Pete Thexton's death on Broad Peak – was that hyperventilation? – home, the prospect of another night up here, a terrible claustrophobic attack he'd had on K2 in a cave bigger than this, growing tension making his breathing faster and faster, hyperventilation –

– 'Andrew, I must go down!'

No time for discussion. He was in a panic, knew only that he couldn't spend the night here, had to get down the hill before the light failed entirely. He crawled out of the coffin, laced up his boots, took his sack and gasping wildly set off along the gloomy Ridge. . . .

Leaving Andy wondering what had happened, uncertain whether to follow or stay. Which was safer for him, which was safer for Urs? He felt too shagged out to go down. But the North-East Ridge was a dangerous place for an exhausted and panicky doctor/climber to descend in the half-dark. 'A little worried' he lay down again and hoped sleep would come to ease his head. It took all his self-discipline to close his eyes and empty his mind of fear for the night ahead.

'Sandy!'

'What the hell?' Sandy thought, glanced at his watch: 9.30 pm. He hastily unzipped his tent and to his astonishment saw Urs, beard and face encrustedwith ice, swaying slightly. 'What's happened?,' fearing the worst.

'Oh it's hell up there. Awfully! I come down, Andy stay, he is tired but OK in snow-hole.'

'Here, have a brew.'

'No, I go down to Camp 2.'

After a few more words, Urs went on; getting to the haven of C2 was the only thought in his fear-filled mind – that and the possibility of wandering over the Kangshung Face. He was now on his last legs, beginning to stumble. He sat down for a rest, woke up to find himself sliding into a hollow 20 feet further down the Ridge. By now it was fully dark, he made his way by the pale light off the snow, searching in vain for the footprints of the morning. . . .

He made it after the most nightmarish hours of his life and stumbled into the C2 snow cave, where Bob and Allen had settled down to sleep. They fed him brews as he told his story. Like Nick and Sandy they were perturbed by his precipitate departure, which went right against climbing ethics. Now Andy was up alone at Camp 4 and no one knew what condition he was in. 'Tired but OK,' Urs said, but then Urs was in no state to judge and Andy was notoriously reticent about his condition. Few enough people had slept at nearly 8,000 metres without oxygen, let alone one with a record of altitude sickness. And of course now there was no chance of him doing anything on the 1st Pinnacle. Allen Fyffe put it tersely; 'This is a balls-up due to lack of real communication and again little has been achieved. Now concerned about Andy's safety. . . .'

Meanwhile the object of everyone's concern was having a long and sleepless night in the tiny C4 snow-hole while the wind howled by outside. His head was bad, he was weak with hunger and dehydration; his throat was torn by coughing and by dawn he had coughed up blood.

'But considering it was at 7,850 I thought it was quite a good night.'

Next morning he found he couldn't sit up. It took him nearly an hour to put on his boots, then he started on a brew, i.e. hot water. Feeling a bit better, he thought he'd better do some work, and spent four hours scraping away at the hole on and off until he felt it was habitable for two. By early afternoon he knew it was time to go down. As soon as he stood up to walk, he found his legs wouldn't hold steady. He set off lurching towards the Buttresses with only the last threads of will-power and his axe keeping him upright. He came to an awkward, steep section coming down the 3rd Buttress. One slip and he'd go all the way. He began down-climbing, his feet dropped away and he was left hanging by one axe, on the very brink of disaster. 'Gripped? I was *mummified*.' He re-applied himself to the slope and waited two minutes to regather his frayed nerves and energy and let his breathing return to normal before continuing. At the bottom, he staggered, and remembering the Basque tragedy, held his axe in braking position all the way.

Meanwhile Sandy and Nick had woken in the C3 tents, covered in spindrift as usual. Another wind-blasted morning. As Sandy had expected, Nick was too tired to go on up to C4 as originally planned, so they both descended to C2, Sandy looking back constantly for a black dot coming over the Buttresses.

It took only half an hour, downhill and with the wind behind them. There they found Allen Fyffe looking fit and alert; he told them Bob was in desperate shape again, coughing and headachy and blue at the lips, so he'd gone down. Another disappointment for Bob and the Expedition. Urs was about to depart, looking wasted but in a better state of mind. From somewhere Sandy and Nick found the commitment to make another carry with Allen back up to C3, which virtually completed the shifting of loads up to that point, though they primarily went back to look for Andy. Though things were going wrong at the front, the hard graft of the back-up work was still on target, in the teeth of sustained bad weather. That was why Sandy felt sure we were still in with a reasonable chance. The next stage would be the ten or so crucial carries over the Buttresses to C4, while another pair put it to the touch on Pinn 1.

He thought it over as he forced himself forward through the wind towards C3. Yes, Malcolm's 'wastage' was happening, that was to be expected, but we can still do it. Andy and Urs should probably have been split up earlier, all the signs had been there . . . and there was that long looked-for dot crawling over the top of the 2nd Buttress, that's a relief. . . .

'Great to see you, man, do you want a brew?'

'Yes please,' whispered the frozen face that hid Andy Nisbet. He flopped down in the C3 tent, too exhausted to take off his crampons. Nick and Allen set off down, while Sandy cooked and brewed, concerned for his friend's condition. Andy lay down for a while, then said he was as ready to go down as he would ever be, so they set off.

Sandy had never seen him like this, so slow and weary, constantly having to stop. He seemed to be shrinking visibly, as if the flesh were melting off his bones (by the time he had got back to BC he'd lost a stone in three days). Down to 7090, to C2, to CB's, Sandy shepherding him down the fixed ropes, Andy now moving like a marionette whose strings were loose, flopping about with every step. 'A bit spaced out, my body had stopped doing what my head told it.' On to the glacier and across it, all in a very slow dream, stopping over and over. . . .

Finally up the moraine back into the Mess Tent, to relieved welcomes from Mal, Tony, a slightly guilty looking Urs, Sarah, Jon, Rick, Nick. Mal had been concerned enough about Andy that he'd begun packing gear to go with Tony back up the hill to find him and help him down – so they were doubly relieved! Urs and Andy would obviously be out of it for several days (and no one was going to rely on Urs above C3 again); bit of a fiasco really was the general consensus. Urs and Andy had been nursing themselves for this push and it had achieved virtually nothing. But, like Sandy, Mal wasn't over-downhearted; he and Tony were going up the next day for the second attempt on the 1st Pinnacle, which was still enough to make the heart beat faster. . . .

I have in front of me two photos: one of ABC buried and forlorn under fresh snow, with two figures in full gear leaning towards each other as they rope together for the plod across the fixed ropes; the other is of Rick, dapper and smiling in the sunlight in front of the Mess Tent at BC, leisurely sipping a brew and squinting up the valley towards Everest. A guitar is leaning in the background against the tent; above it, scrawled 'NO MORE HEROES ANY MORE'.

A tale of two kingdoms. The difference in outlook in both senses – what you see and mental attitude – between BC and the hill was absolute. As was the lack of communication between them, the delay involved. Together they are crucial to an assessment of what was to happen.

Meanwhile we waited in the now warm weather at BC for news of Andy and Urs' Pinnacle attempt. Looking at the hill and trying to guess the conditions there, I thought it was like looking at the stars: by the time the light-news gets to you, its source could be long snuffed out. They could have fixed the entire 1st Pinnacle, they could be dead, and we simply wouldn't know.

Terry was packing up to go out on the jeep. For weeks he'd been wrestling with the decision whether to be here for the climax of the trip, or try to get back in time for the birth of his first child. Now he'd his personal summit under his belt, he knew where his priorities lay, though leaving at this point was hard for him. Liz had trimmed his beard, and at this moment he was shaving, preparing for his re-entry into the world.

I retyped my penultimate piece to go out with Terry, and added the final update: the weather was getting worse, not better, and so were we; nevertheless we were poised for the Pinnacles and still very much in the game.

That was Rick's assessment as we chatted across my typewriter. He was becoming more open and humorous as the trip went on, seemed to be pacing himself well. 'We're up on manpower', he said in his quietly emphatic, dry voice, 'and there's a lot of motivation up there – I'm beginning to think we're back up to 50/50.' Jon rolled his eyes. 'You're appalling, Allen, you know that?' Jon was much less optimistic and openly admitted he was still feeling quite wasted; though he was ready to go back on the hill, he did not share the vision of going through the Pinnacles without oxygen.

But Rick felt that was the only option. Food, brewing materials and technical climbing gear were the essentials for C4; we simply didn't have the manpower to carry oxygen as well. 'Anyone carrying oxygen now is wasting his time.'

Rick had timed things well. From the middle of the trip, he'd been calculating a final rest at BC before going for the Pinnacles; there'd only be one chance for each climber, and he wanted to be in good shape. So when the heavy snowfall had come two days before, with fresh climbers on the way up, he'd decided this was the chance for him to get in a few days' break before going up for the last time. He described the set-up at C4, how he'd dug this 'rat hole' into a snow bank in the Kangshung Face. From 7,850 the Ridge was a completely flat, broad plateau, then started rising and became the foot of the 1st Pinnacle. From C4 to there was perhaps one-third to three-quarters of a mile, 650 vertical feet, a two-hour plod. Pinn 1 looked 'pretty formidable, but the snow arête on the left is the obvious line.' He'd finally finished *Les Trois Mousequetaires*, he was ready to go.

The jeep that was to take Terry out brought mail-manna. We were astonished to hear that Chris Bonington and the Norwegians had made the Summit by the South Col route, way back in April, one of the earliest ascents on record. They'd made very good progress, and got to the top before the bad weather really started. Jon dived with glad cries into the latest climbing magazines that had arrived. Rick quietly read through letters from parents and his girlfriend. The Clachaig Inn in Glencoe had sent us the *Oban Times*, plus the *Beano* and the *Dandy*, which showed a realistic assessment of our mental capabilities at this stage in the game. I had letters reminding me of the decisions awaiting when I got back home. That seemed distant and unreal; the Pinnacles dominated our imagination.

An evening of guitars and hot toddies. 'Bunch of old hippies,' Jon muttered amiably as we cut a swathe through the mid-'60s by the irregular glow of the petrol lamps. We finished with 'Base Camp Blues' and 'The Ballad of the North-East Ridge', then stumbled through the dark to our tents, wondering as always what was doing on the hill.

There is nothing romantic, spiritual or profound about the explosive shits, even in the high Rongbuk valley; stars circling Everest and the pre-dawn wind. I'd been lying awake wondering about the *meaning* of this trip. What is really happening behind the plethora of physical events? But there is no meaning, or so it seemed to me, hanging over the shit-pit (a fraught experience now that the Rongbuk nuns had quietly removed our security rope!). There is only the experience itself passing through you, intensely and often scarcely digested, like these goddam shits. This is happening now, this, this, this. That is the most truthful thing one can say about it all; stars and shits and the pre-dawn wind.

The 14th dawned blue and cold. A lot of spindrift was ripping off the Ridge, where Urs and Andy were on their way to C4, so it was obviously wild up there. When will it let up and give us the optimum weather expected before the monsoon? Two groups of trekkers turned up in trucks. You'd think after our isolation we'd be over-joyed to see new company, but their questions, cameras and excla-mations detroyed the austere beauty around us. We felt this hill was for us, for us and the Basques alone; we didn't want anyone else coming and diluting our experience.

Kurt and Julie turned up in the evening, looking sombre and tired. They broke the news to us about the Basque accident. Shocked silence, guitars quietly put down. Then the questions. Who? How? When? The big, bearded one, the smiling and tired one who'd made that crème caramel for Urs' birthday just a couple of weeks ago. Juan-Jo.

'Well, it puts our necks on the chopper, doesn't it?' Jon said quietly.

I kept think of how we didn't even know Juan Jo's second name yet had shared brews, jokes, whisky and hill-information with him, shared being here. And how casually we'd waved the Basques good-bye and wished them luck as they set off for their summit bid in what we privately thought were unlikely conditions.

My first hill-death. I realized that all the lead climbers here had been through that before, and at much closer quarters. What had that done to them? What was it doing to me? This tragic and oh-so-simple accident was a savage reminder to us all of the reality of climbing on Everest. Malcolm would feel it most, I thought; he'd be reminded of his responsibility in bringing these lads here, even though he knew it was their choice.

Now they're laughing in the Mess Tent and a man we knew is dead on the mountain, gathering snow. I sit at the entrance to my tent with the sleeping bag up to my throat, smoking a last cigarette.

I'm chilled to the bone, and my imagination is very dark tonight – dark as the starless sky. Bad weather for tomorrow. But at least I can see it is dark. The man on the North Col cannot see even darkness. I borrowed Jack's Bible sometime back, and keep turning to the sceptical 'Ecclesiastes' for its sustained rhetoric on the vanity of human endeavour. Now I come on this: *Who knoweth the spirit of men that goeth upwards, there is nothing better than that a man should rejoice in his own works, for that is his portion.*

The obscure joy of the living in still being alive. Maybe that is why they are laughing.

Rick It brings home how close to the edge we walk. As I wrote to Roy, 'I want to be bold but I want to live and love also.'

Next day I talked with Rick before he set off for ABC, resolved to go for the Pinnacles, not knowing what the situation would be when he arrived. This was Pinnacle Day for Urs and Andy; a lot of spindrift, and evil-looking cloud in the afternoon. He agreed it would soon be time for re-forming climbing partnerships; he had hopes of linking up with Allen, but he had already been load-carrying up there for a few days and they would be out of phase with each other. Rick looked weathered, fit and relaxed, but he had clearly been seriously taking stock of what lay ahead.

'If I knew I could do it, I wouldn't be going up. . . . I'd be on my way to Lhasa!' He picked up his sack and ski-pole, but lingered a minute to add, carefully choosing his words, 'I would not like to think that if I fell off or something, and we had the summit in our grasp, that the Expedition would just pack up and go home.'

Then he grinned, said 'See you later,' and set off nimbly for the glacier snout. I watched him till he disappeared round the corner, feeling a vague anxiety shifting in my chest. This was three years to the day since Boardman and Tasker set off from ABC to climb the Pinnacles and never came back. And also the anniversary of Marty Hoey falling to her death down Central Gully.

Rick Met the three Basques on the long moraine. Shook hands and briefly embraced Mari. What more can you do or say except shake your head and walk on? God help them, and us.

A party-party developed that evening, for Danny's 20th birthday, the bumblies' 7,000 metres, and Terry's departure next morning. We'd suddenly realized we had too much whisky left, so got stuck into that, with pâté and even caviare for starters, then a vast spaghetti bolognese, wine and cake. Danny became extravagant in his gestures, knocking over cups, falling off his chair in fits of giggles. It was a night of laughter and singing and banishing our anxieties. Kurt played French, Italian and German songs, even one from Greenland. Chris: 'Where did you learn that, Kurt?' Kurt: 'In Greenland, of course.'

I fell asleep round 2.0 am to the sound of laughter, shouting and thumping, as Danny was assisted to his tent. 'Look, look at the stars!' He pointed up dramatically, tottered and fell flat on his back, giggling helplessly.

Meanwhile Tony lay in his iced-up tent at ABC, re-reading for the *n*th time his newly delivered letters from Kathy, feeling very happy. He was even looking forward to setting out for C4 tomorrow with Mal – like Sandy, Tony had been unattached most of the time, and Mal had been his partner on the Mustagh Tower. Liz reckoned that he knew this was his last chance to do something big on this trip, and prove he was capable of operating at extreme altitude. He fell asleep thinking of 8,000 metres.

Terry and Mari, the leader of the Basque team, left next afternoon, the 6th. Mari was going as far as Lhasa to phone his news to Juan Jose's family. Little wonder he was silent and drawn. And resilient; he and the other two lads intended to go back up and try again for the summit.

Their jeep lurched into the distance, bearing away our news reports and precious mail, Terry still not knowing how things had gone in the Pinnacles push.

We were astonished to see Urs picking his way towards us. He was supposed to be at C4! We crowded round for news. It was clearly bad; this was a very different Urs from the one I'd last seen at ABC. All the bounce had gone out of him. It was all 'Terrible, terrible!' The weather on the Ridge was terrible, they could hardly stand up in the wind, the spindrift was blinding and the cold extreme. Camp 3 was terrible, the tents tiny and letting in spindrift all night. Camp 4 was far too small for two people, even after they'd worked at enlarging it.

We waited for Andy to arrive and give his version. But when he stumbled in, gaunt and hollow-eyed, almost shocked, what he had to say was not much more encouraging.

'When I went up I felt really well, in very good condition, and now in three days I'm a physical wreck.'

'Is true,' said Urs, feeling his bony shoulders, 'you feel like a boiled chicken!'

He told us of his night at C4, the time spent enlarging C4 the next day, his harrowing descent. 'Now I'm more exhausted than I've ever been in my life . . . and I've been quite tired before.'

There wasn't much time to think of the implications of this latest setback, for a boisterous group of Austrian climbers had turned up, on their way home after a successful ascent of Shishipangma. They'd had good weather, caught a perfect day and went to the summit from a camp at 7,000 metres . . . It pointed up the difference between their route and ours – imagine if we'd been able to go for our summit from 7090! We'd already had five climbers up to 7,850 and we were only just starting on the major problems of the route.

Still, the North-East Ridge had appealed to the lads precisely because it was unclimbed and super-hard, and we settled down to celebrate the Austrian success.

The Austrians' joviality was made all the more poignant by the presence of the two remaining Basques. Quite untypically, I went over and embraced them, and was glad I had, despite the tears in their eyes at the warmth of our welcome. They had come over from their Base Camp to be taken out of themselves, to help get over their friend's death and their own shock. We gave them distraction in an evening of communal singing in many languages: Austrian (boisterous drinking-and-climbing songs), Scottish folk-music and American rock 'n' roll, Urs drunk and beaming as he sang in Fench and German, Wattie and Danny simply drunk (Wattie playing a mean second guitar in Terry's absence), Kurt sitting yodelling on a film barrel with 'THE HIGH-ALTITUDE BLUES' scrawled above his head . . . The Tibetan cook sang a song, Antxon and José Manuel finally did the same and lost that distant, distracted look for a while, Luo wrote a poem on the friendship of many nationalities which Jack translated . . . A good night of warmth, laughter and closeness in the midst of triumph and tragedy, and for a while we could forget that we were still pushing up the narrow ridge between the two.

No warmth and laughter for Allen Fyffe, lying cramped and alone in one of the tiny C3 tents. The wind howled across the Ridge and battered at the tent; he wondered how firmly it had been anchored. The noise made sleep near-impossible, and he would have taken his first sleeper of the trip, only he remembered that he had none with him. Still, working at Glenmore Lodge in all seasons is a good training in stoicism. He burrowed deeper into his bag and prepared for a long, insomniac night.

Rick Bob and Nick at ABC. Bob still not strong. Jon and I to follow Mal and Tony; if they succeed on 1st Pinnacle, we are to push on through to the 2nd. Joy. General air of pessimism over dinner.

While down at C1, Mal and Tony were happily falling asleep in the comparative comfort of CB's. Mal had finally made his decision about oxygen use; good to have that off his mind . . .
    Allen begins 17th May by taking the battery out of his radio at 7.0 am and putting it down his longjohns to warm some life into it. It may stir the battery, but it does little to lift his lethargic high-altitude feeling. At 8.0 he makes the radio call to ABC to say he's feeling rough and will put off the decision whether to try to carry to 7,850 today – a new altitude for him. He looks out on a clear blue sky, and the wind is finally easing. He collects ice and starts to brew, huddled in one corner of the tent to make room for the stove . . . The first drink makes him feel marginally more alive than dead, so he decides to make the carry.
    He picks up food-bags and gas. The first three fixed ropes up the 1st Buttress are on perfect névé, the fourth is awful. Fresh snow has collected in the gully here and it collapses beneath his feet, leaving him hanging gasping on the rope, praying that the anchors are good. It's very cold in the shadow and his hand pushing the jumar soon loses feeling from grasping the cold metal. He stops to re-warm it, having no intention of losing the fingers that are part of his living.
    He makes it to the top of the 1st Buttress, continues on past his previous high point, over the 2nd Buttress and on to the 3rd. Gradually it steepens and narrows; rocks on the right and a cornice of unknown size on the left define the line, and he soon begins to feel uneasy in his solitary state. (This is where Andy Nisbet had his 'mummifying' experience while descending from C4.) Allen decides those who came this way before him were either a lot braver or a lot less imaginative than himself; he cuts a line of deep steps – a rare enough procedure these days, but standard in Allen's early climbing days in the '60s, before the advent of front-pointed crampons and inclined picks on ice-axes.
    He carries on over several false summits and comes finally to a flat plateau and spots some gear and an unlikely rope trailing off down the Kangshung Face – he climbs down it, finds the C4 snow hole and crawls inside. 'A real rat hole' he decides, but notes that the snow is good névé and could be dug out to make a decent refuge for four or more. Back up the rope, takes a good look at the Pinnacle. Pretty impressive . . . but not outrageous, not the visible parts anyway. He debates carrying some gear on to the foot of the 1st Pinn, but the weather is closing in and anyway he'll be on the

Pinnacles next time up. He'll leave it till then to make their acquaint-
ance. There is no doubt in his mind that he'll be back; he's carried
a load to 7,850, is tired but fully in control.

So he sets off down, taking the time to fix an abseil rope down
the unpleasant section of the 3rd Buttress – typical Allen, paying
attention to small safety details. Like Bob, he's a family man who
plans to live and climb for as long as possible. Some of the Boy
Racers' casual ways astonish them both.

He finds Tony at C3 and gladly accepts a brew from him. Further
down he meets Mal plugging on up through the mist, and is amazed
and delighted to be handed his mail – a thoughtful touch that pleases
him. Mal is having a bad day, tired from the start, feeling the strain
of his second carry to C4. But he's determined that this time he and
Tony would improve C4 into a viable doss, and finally mix with the
Pinnacles. Given climbable weather and everyone performing to their
maximum, the Expedition was still in with a chance of doing the
Pinnacles at least, thus completing the unknown part of the route
to the summit.

'He looks tired,' Allen thinks, but as always, keeps it to himself.
Mal's been at ABC or on the hill for a fortnight now, far longer
than anyone else, and the strain is beginning to show. They chat
briefly then move off on their separate courses.

At C2 Allen finds Jon and Rick who plan to go on to C3 the next
day, then C4, then take on the Pinnacles where Mal and Tony leave
off. There's no saying just how far they will go, but Rick's sights
are set on going right through the Pinnacles if possible. That's one
of the reasons why they're carrying an extra lightweight tent between
them, for an overnight bivvy. In fact, they're so laden down with
gear that Allen offers to help them with the carry tomorrow. He sits
and brews and eats and chats with them in the spacious C2 cave,
writes up his diary for the day till he feels tired and besides he finds
writing basically boring: he'd rather sleep.

Meanwhile Sandy has arrived at Base Camp, optimism on two
legs despite the latest setbacks on the hill. A heated divergence of
opinion develops between him and the much more pessimistic Urs
and Andy. Andy now believes that with the continuing bad weather
and the wasted condition of half our party and the demands of the
route itself, we will not climb this hill. Not only will we not make
the summit, he thinks it unlikely we'll succeed in doing anything on
the Pinnacles. 'We've just not enough strong climbers.'

Liz is angered with his 'defeatism'. 'It's not defeatism,' Andy
replies in his quiet, stubborn way, his eyes lowered, 'it's just realism.'
Neither Liz nor Sandy can accept that. Believing it can't be done is

surely a self-fulfilling prophecy; he has to believe. 'If you didn't believe we could do it, you shouldn't be here,' Sandy argues, and Liz adds, 'At least keep your pessimism to yourself, otherwise it'll affect everyone else.' She is angry, protective almost, protective of Mal's expedition; she knows how much was at stake for him here. For us all, but the pressure is inevitably greatest on the leader; it's the leader who is the hero or the whipping boy in the public eye.

'When I came out here,' Andy says, beginning to be agitated, 'I believed we had a 70 per cent chance of doing the Pinnacles, maybe 20 per cent of the Summit. Now I've revised that down to two per cent for either.' He goes on to list the factors against us: weather, time and logistics. Originally ten lead climbers once seemed like a lot, but now there are never more than seven fit at one time, and nearly half of those will always be at BC or on the way to or from there. Those on the hill are badly and unequally paired. So often it seems people have gone high, split up, and consistently achieved less than planned and required. And returned wasted.

'That's just defeatism!' Liz breaks in.

'*Realism*,' Andy insists, uneasy as the emotional temperature rises. 'But I'm prepared to go up one more time and give it everything I've got – even if that's not much . . . I seldom think I'm going to climb a route when I get to the bottom of it, but that doesn't stop me getting to the top. That's just the way I work.'

'That's 'cos you're from Aberdeen!' Sandy jokes. 'Maybe that's okay . . . But most of us folk have to believe we can and will do it, even if we're proved wrong.'

'So maybe you could keep your thoughts to yourself,' concludes Liz.

A long, awkward silence. Andy is clearly unconvinced, Liz and Sandy tense, Chris keeping his opinion to himself. Me, I'm worried. For the first time I'm having to consider that the Expedition will have no success at all. We always knew it was odds against, but I'd always unconsciously assumed success, partial or total. I think we all had. Sandy defines success as breaking new ground on the Pinnacles; from then on we're winning. But now Andy, who is level-headed and up to now one of our strong climbers is quite certain we won't even get near that.

Urs breaks the silence between us. 'It is not a question of the man, or the tactics, or the courage . . . We are not heroes, I was very frightened . . .' He waves towards Everest, swathed in cloud once again. 'It is a question of the mountain and weather. The summit is chance . . . What is interesting are the moments while we try to get there.'

And Sandy nods, in harmony with him once again.

Our Base Camp discussions were more than academic. Luo was pressing for confirmation of our 31st May exit date, and it was beginning to look as if we'd need an extension if we were really going to climb this hill. As deputy leader at Base Camp Sandy had to let Luo know soon – his personal opinion was we should extend our time by a week. It would do no harm. It could make all the difference. So Chris left on the morning of the 18th, still gaunt and hoarse but not bronchial now, with a message to Mal suggesting that Sandy extend our time; we had to hear from him by the 20th . . .

18 May. Mal and Tony are on their way to C4. Mal's carrying out his decision to use a medium flow of oxygen in order to carry oxygen to C4 and still be in condition to start on the Pinnacles the next day. Worried by our lack of progress and the ever-increasing possibility of the monsoon, he'd decided to depart from the original plan of not using O_2 at all before the Pinnacles. With our limited number of oxygen cylinders (mostly still at C3), this meant the summit was less likely though still possible: the emphasis had now been switched to the Pinnacles. If we could climb them the Expedition had achieved something significant.

Using O_2 seemed to balance out the extra weight of the cylinder. Mal finally arrived at C4 with half a cylinder left for use on fixing the 1st Pinnacle the next day. That would be the breakthrough that mattered; the team needed the morale-boost of fresh progress on the route.

As the weather clagged in, Tony lost sight of Mal up ahead. A hard physical day for him, coughing a lot and weary. Several times the wind brought him to his knees, and he'd stay there gasping and blinded till the gust abated. Still, he consoled himself, you don't expect to be bright-eyed and bushy-tailed carrying a sack to nearly 8,000 metres for the first time. And he hadn't yet had an acclimatization night of sleeping at C3. But he made it, then he and Mal put in three hours of work enlarging the snow-hole. At the end of that they had the best two-person cave on the route, which would be an important launching-pad for all future attempts from then on up, particularly given the unsatisfactory nature of the C3 tents.

They brewed up and settled in for the night. Tony picked up Base Camp faintly on the radio for the first time, something about extending the departure date . . . Soon they would be approaching line-of-sight from BC, and direct communication would become possible again. That would be a big help in co-ordinating those still strong enough to climb high on the hill.

Allen Spent a fair night at C3 with Jon and Rick. However, had a gripping crap as I had to dash outside in unfastened outer boots . . . It's probably as dangerous as anything on this trip, standing on a snowy ledge with my down suit round my ankles trying not to mess myself or fall down the Kangshung Face – an ignominious end!

Set off before the others and carried a load to C3. Made fair time and met them as I was going down. Wished them luck, collected my gear at C2 and headed down the ropes for a solitary trudge over the glacier. Off down to BC tomorrow . . .

Sarah Didn't sleep at all last night, it was also very cold. Set off not feeling brilliant – legs felt like lead. Once I got on to the fixed ropes didn't feel so bad, but all the way I kept thinking what is the point of this slog. (It's boring just going on the fixed ropes.) I kept warily looking at the clouds, hoping it wouldn't snow.

In fact it was quite easy convincing myself to go back:
– avalanche conditions on the traverse (heavy fresh snow night before)
– no one coming up after me or coming down
– if I go down I don't have to spend another night in the tent on the Raphu La
– I chickened out.

Started snowing heavily and wetly in the afternoon – bad sign. Monsoon?

Sandy Myself getting really annoyed at this gross negativity. Who really cares if we get the summit, the Pinnacles, compared with 'Star Wars', nuclear fall-out, etc.? I discuss all this with A.G.; it's good we do – saves a falling out, a break in friendship. But futility . . . negativity . . . pheasamism – me I cannot even spell the word I have such little regard for it and the persons who accept and live with such backward-looking thoughts. Once you set your hand to the plough, don't look back . . .

But I find myself locked up inside my head, millions of ideas, not for sharing . . .

Meanwhile head says well, when I die (like pronto, kid), I guess somebody will scribble my obituary . . . OK, no fucker will print it . . . big deal.

But soon to go to ABC. There'll be a swap-around of tents, there'll be ideas spread and arguments . . . the end of an expedition or the summit . . . This and more will accumulate into friction . . . but then again friction is what drives trains along their tracks!

Why am I so OUTSIDE? Thoughts turning, like car wheels slipping and spinning in the snow, occasionally gripping and throwing up crazy thoughts. Head sore . . . stress perchance. Folks go to ABC tomorrow – so pleased, time to be by myself. I need that more and more – but I really wish I did not . . . Company I want, sure need . . . to talk . . . but can't here. So little in common, but all these people are my friends, therefore if I cannot relate to them . . . then who can I relate to . . . me at fault? Me different . . . I'm busy today asking why.

When a stone falls from a mountain on to a glacier, sure we can predict that eventually the stone will come out on to the moraine bank someplace . . . but we cannot predict what precise route that stone will take. We're born, we'll die; between that, what?

I sometimes think somebody's already arranged it.

Passing through, kid, that's all . . . A stitch in time. Everest here for years and years, we passing through. What'll we make of it? What will the media make of it? Me sleep now. Soon with luck I'll be on the Pinnacles.

Jon and Rick moved up to C3 and stayed there overnight, ready to follow Mal and Tony on the 'rolling maul' assault on the Pinnacles.

Below them, Nick and Bob had made their way through threatening weather to C2. Bob was cheered to feel much better than he had last time, but both of them were concerned by the black clouds that were gathering, quite unlike anything we'd seen yet, and the air was odd, still and mild. Snow began to fall heavily in the afternoon.

So that evening on Everest all the Bases were loaded, with pairs at each of the top three camps. We were as ready as we'd ever be to go for it. So much depended on what the weather would pitch at us tomorrow.

Mal Whew, writing diaries at 7,850 metres is weird. Tony not in good shape, very bad with throat, etc., but hanging in there. We are brewing continuously, my turn to cook which is shit. No UFO's yet! Living here is very different from below – still did expect it to be a bit awkward – stoves hardly go – mind you, neither do Tony or myself! A bit damp from digging snow-hole so we are coldish, however should be OK to continue tomorrow . . .

The Last Days

19TH MAY – 3RD JUNE

'The race is not to the swift, nor the battle to the strong . . .
nor yet favour to men of skill; but time and chance
happeneth to them all.'

The 19th of May, Pinnacle Day. Something odd has happened to
the weather. There's a luminous haze in the air, it is almost sultry.
And no wind at all, no spindrift on Everest – which is very white
this morning after overnight snow. Andy Nisbet joins me, his wild
hair and beard looking like an orange Elizabethan ruff.

'What do you reckon, Andy?'

'It could be the monsoon coming early . . . On the other hand, it
could finally be the calm climbing weather we're supposed to get
before the monsoon.'

He's looking a lot better today. 'Pessimistic' he might be, but he's
preparing to go back to ABC tomorrow. However, Urs seems to
have lost all heart in the venture; this worries Andy, who doesn't
want to be left alone on the hill again.

Sandy emerges from the Mess Tent and stands beside us. No need
to tell him what we're discussing: it's Pinnacle Day and something
odd is happening to the weather.

Mal and Tony start their day at 6.30 by scraping snow into the
billy, warming the lighter and setting the stove going. They lie in
their pits as it burns fitfully, stirring only to add more snow to the
sinking mush in the pot. Outside, a few desultory flakes of snow
begin to fall.

When they finally emerge from the snow-hole, heavy black clouds
are massing over the North Col. It is snowing steadily now and the
air feels much less dry than usual. The wind is beginning to gust.
Tony makes a face, Mal shrugs. The former takes a load of climbing
gear – pitons, krabs, slings, nuts – for use on Pinn 1, while Mal
takes on two O_2 cylinders plus a bale of fixing rope. It's a very big
load for a man hoping to climb later in the day, but once again he's
using one of the oxygen cylinders. A nod and they move off along
the gradually steepening incline, which eventually will merge into
the 1st Pinnacle, now invisible.

Bloody typical – Pinnacle Day and now it's started snowing and blowing down here at BC. The hill's disappeared completely. God knows what's happening up there, but it can't be good. The few of us left here sit chatting in the Mess Tent, Urs shows us some stretching exercises, but our minds aren't really on it. We keep looking up the valley where Everest used to be. Even Sandy says, 'Pretty depressing, isn't it?' However, open discussion of our chances is now banned, so we try to keep our thoughts to ourselves. Liz is determinedly bright; in an unspoken, mutual understanding Sandy and I spend a lot of the day talking about anything with her, anything to distract her mind from the knowledge that Mal's somewhere on or about the 1st Pinnacle in dirty weather, and both his safety and the success of this Expedition are very much on the line.

More trekkers have arrived, pointing and exclaiming and asking if we've been to the summit yet. Jack and Luo are playing bridge with Andy and Danny, a pleasant change from listening to Danny learning the guitar. I pack to go up to ABC, wanting to be in on the final denouement whatever it may be – and write a bunch of postcards saying we'll probably be home a week late. We're just waiting, powerless to influence events.

Jon has had a bad night at C3, and watches Rick pull away ahead of him. Over 7,300 metres his body is telling him it's had enough, there are no resources left to call on. As the snow thickens around him, he clips into the fixed ropes on the 1st Buttress and begins to push upward, without much conviction, coughing steadily.

Mal[1] We were numb. Not cold numb, although there was that at times, just battered numb – numb from eight weeks of strain, from scything wind cutting at the flesh, from swirling, pirouetting columns of spindrift driving and dancing around us, from sustained effort and load-carrying, from eating, drinking and living high on the North-East Ridge.

I plodded on, lost in a world of spindrift, casually watching as Tony was again hurled to his knees; everything on automatic, both sides of my brain arguing, bullying and reasoning . . . I'm hurting, but who wouldn't . . . after all I am carrying an enormous load . . . at this sort of altitude I deserve to hurt. Anyway I'm managing 50 paces between rests even though the wind's blowing out Tony's tracks and the bastard snow is falling as it has been for weeks and I'm over 8,000 metres and stunningly tired, it's bound to hurt, what a wimp, ignore it and keep going . . .

Well really am OK but my lungs are heaving and thighs burning but

[1]These passages are derived by kind permission of the *Alpine Journal 1986*, from Mal Duff's article therein.

what the hell this is EVEREST and we're higher than the South Col and life is tough . . . I wish my goggles wouldn't keep steaming up and freezing and I wish I felt better, I'm more tired than ever before and why did I try oxygen to carry an extra load when I was doing great before without?'

What's bothering Tony is visibility and the possibility of avalanche: there's far too little of the first and too much of the second. He's groping along in a restricted world on the way from nowhere to nowhere. Fresh snow is massing in the sloping bays he's trying to cross. It's like wading through glue, only this glue could break away at any time from the hard crust beneath. Classic avalanche conditions. He finds a rock that gives at least the illusion of safety and slumps down. Climbing the 1st Pinnacle is out of the question today, so why go any further? They've still to get back to C4 . . . He looks back and Mal, who's been close behind him all the way, has disappeared. Oh no! He waits. And waits. Would he have heard Mal shout? Then he sees the head emerging from a dip, but something's surely gone wrong because Mal is swaying, scarcely moving forward at all . . .

Mal Tony crouched on a rock 40 yards away, a small spark of life where none should exist. The spindrift swirled and battered, whirling over the Ridge, pluming up 200 feet before hurling itself upon us . . . Reaching the lee of the rock and contacting Tony, another human in this madness, becomes all-important. A shattering pain suddenly erupts in my lower chest – a muscle rip in my diaphragm, can't inflate my lungs! A moment of panic subdued by years of training. No matter what, I must try, try to live, to descend or even to die, but I must try. I must try because this is the big one, the master problem that perhaps I've been seeking for years, unwittingly . . . Think of Pete Thexton on Broad Peak with a collapsed diaphragm, going blind and dying . . . Again I buzz with panic, fight the mental battle for control, the first of many I know before today or I expire . . .

He covers the last few yards to Tony on hands and knees. Something is seriously wrong. He pulls off the oxygen mask and only then realizes that no gas is coming through. They struggle to unscrew the regulator from a thread caked in ice, and then find the valve is totally frozen and blocked. Exactly the same had happened to Dougal Haston when he set off with Doug Scott for the summit on the South-West Face route – the same sense of suddenly feeling he had run into a brick wall, the same delayed recognition of what was happening. Little wonder Mal damaged himself; he'd been carrying 56 lb, getting no oxygen and sucking what little atmosphere there was up here in through the corner of the face mask. How long had he been doing this? And now his lungs feel like wet sponges, his chest has ceased working properly; he knows inside himself that he is maybe going blind and is certainly slowly dying.

'You go on if you want to – I'm going down,' Tony says. He's had enough, there's no chance of the Pinnacles today.

Mal nods. The game is definitely over for him. It's going to take everything he's got to get out of this one. He gets shakily to his feet. His mind is in control, or at least he thinks it is, but his body won't do what it is told. He watches it with dispassionate concern, as though from a great distance, as it tries to perform for him.

Mal We dump our loads, mark the spot and turn downhill. Some of this Ridge is flat and some up and the majority down but it's still an effort and nearly 3,500 feet before I can reach the top of the fixed ropes and slide . . . I can only manage two or three steps at a time and waste tons of energy in concentration so as not to trip or fall because that's bad style and dangerous. It all seems too much effort. Tony goes ahead to C4 to pack his gear and mine because I don't think I can get off this mountain in one day and so having my sleeping bag might be a good idea . . .

I manage three steps downhill or one uphill, with massive rasping pants in between. It makes for slow progress. My name is Malcolm Roy Duff and I live at 14 Hopetown Road . . .

The nasty snowstep above the 2nd Buttress, I am mighty pleased that Allen had fixed it the previous day because it's hard and dangerous. Clip in and slide down . . .

Mixed ground leading to the fixed line down the 2nd Buttress. Tony's clipped in and disappeared into the spindrift. I am confused, miss a wand and end up too low . . . this is easy stuff to fall from and my balance is all wrong and what a bloody awful waste of energy getting back up again.

My name is Malcolm . . . Roy . . . Duff . . . and I live . . .

Rick I meet them at the foot of the 2nd Buttress. They have only made it halfway along to the Pinnacles. Tony is wasted and hands me the medallion for Joe Tasker and a poem to place higher up. Mal is even worse, in a really bad way, asks me if he is between camps 4 and 3 . . .

Jon Mal staggering with fatigue, like a spastic, arms and legs moving of their own free will. Two months is enough for my body and I'm off down as well. Had to lie down on the way back from the Raphu La. That's enough for a while.

Rick Jon has been sitting down for quite a while. When I reach the top of the Buttress I see him turn to descend. I shout down asking if he is going down. He nods. So I am on my own at the front again. Pick up O$_2$ masks and food-bag and continue slowly to C4 . . .

Allen arrives at Base. He seems to be lasting well despite doing a great deal of selfless load-carrying – but next time up he'll be into the Pinnacles; like Rick he's snatching a final rest before going up for the last time with whoever is fit to go. Sandy's talking over waiting on here to team up with him.

Allen is cautiously optimistic and makes a cheering counter to Andy and Urs' view of things. 'If the weather's okay, we'll get through the Pinnacles. Whether we make the top is another matter.' I listen, wondering whose assessment will turn out to be accurate.

Sandy and Allen are deep in earnest conversation. Liz sits at the cooking area waiting for another kettle to boil, her eyes distant.

Bob is having a hard time making his carry to C3 into the teeth of what is developing into a blizzard. Nick has been going well enough, and is there to hand Bob a mug of soup on his arrival. Bob spills most of it, gulps down the rest and heads back down for C2, using a compass bearing to navigate through the whirl.

Mal Tony went first on to the fixed ropes in an effort to establish footsteps because new snow had filled in all the tracks . . . I clipped on to the rope and stumbled and slid, triggering avalanches which thundered down the couloirs. I'm trying not to sag on to the ropes, just in case . . .

Down to the bergschrund. Tied to Tony I'm staggering across the glacier resting endlessly . . .

ABC late in the evening. Over a stone lighter, complete exhaustion. Alive.

Mal had been descending at the very limits of his strength for some nine hours. Like Andy, the physical and mental effort required, hour after hour after hour, had stripped away flesh from the bone. He was finished, something still felt very wrong in his chest. That was the end of our second Pinnacle attempt: the first one hadn't got beyond C4, and this one had pegged out before the foot of the 1st Pinnacle. Now for the first time Mal was beginning to seriously doubt if we'd get much further. Unless the weather changed, he was virtually sure we wouldn't. And even if it did . . .

The other climbers in the ABC Mess Tent that night echoed his mood. Tony said openly he'd had enough, so did Jon. Having recovered from his bronchitis, Chris looked awful but felt well; however, he kept his opinion to himself. In this group, Jon was the most vocal and influential personality. With Sandy feeling oddly out of things on this Expedition, and Mal being frequently withdrawn, it was often Jon who determined the mood of the Expedition, and so it was now. The only people who might have countered that near-resigned mood were either on the hill, like Rick, or at BC, like Sandy and Allen Fyffe.

Somewhere during his harrowing descent and that evening in the Mess Tent, Mal moved from cautious but determined optimism to a sense that the game was up and we were fairly beaten. Yet as he lurched down the Ridge and met one climber after another – Rick, Jon, Nick, Bob – doggedly pushing on up in the teeth of the storm, he'd been deeply moved, almost to tears. He had a sense of all the efforts made over the last weeks, months really, to force ourselves on as far as this; and how we actually were a team though we'd scarcely realized it, all of us driven by the same idea, the same dream as we ebbed and flowed up and down the Ridge.

'I suddenly seemed to see the whole thing quite differently, as if I was watching from high up, us all moving on the mountain. I realized that what we're doing here is only partly physical.'

Nick Felt in a good position, Rick on up at C4, me moving up tomorrow. Regretting the set-back of my shits but getting stronger and this time I feel Rick and I could do great things on the Pinnacles.

'We shouldn't be using words like "success" or "failure",' Sandy asserts at the Base Camp. 'What is success anyway – getting to the top, everybody getting on well, or nobody getting killed?'

'There's only winners and losers in this game,' Allen interjects with his own brand of realism. 'You get to the top or you don't.'

'Oh balls, Allen!'

Fyffey grins, but does not concede the point.

Alone at Camp 4, waiting for his old climbing partner, Nick, to join him the next day, Rick methodically reviewed the options as he saw them.

Rick Thoughts of evening 19th May on the climbing of this mountain. It is beginning to look like I am one of the few team members who can hack 8,000 metres at the moment. Original plan is out the window, we will never get O_2 through the Pinnacles. Much depends on how strong Nicko is and whether in Andy and Urs we have a real summit pair. Only a Pete-and-Joe-type push without O_2 and with all the commitment that entails will succeed now. Without the Pinnacles fixed it is even worse. Will broach the prospect with Nicko but he will see it too clearly. A bad turn in the weather during such an attempt and you are as good as dead.

Assuming all the time that we could go back all the way without O_2 – unlikely. Some helpful factors – rope may be found in good condition. We could always bale out down the North Ridge, but an accident similar to Juan Jose's is so easy when wasted on ground like that. We might be able

to live for several days out of Pete and Joe's sacks if we find them –
macabre, but survival is about shelter, gas and food.

Last resort is going it alone. Save that for a really last resort, even then
I would have to have a companion through the Pinnacles – I don't want
to die that much.

The gap between the outlook of those who were still feeling well on
the hill or Base Camp and those who were knackered at ABC was
rapidly widening.

20th May Sandy woke at Base Camp with a severe pain in his right
calf. When he dragged himself out of his sleeping bag, he found he
could barely walk. What goes on here? He'd had slight twinges the
day before, but this was different. He began rubbing liniment into
his calf while he pondered the decision he had to make today. He'd
had no word from Mal one way or another about the proposed
extension, and Luo was insisting on knowing today, so as Deputy
Leader it was up to Sandy.

He decided to set back our exit day by a week. It would be absurd
to miss a chance of climbing the mountain for the sake of a week.
Perhaps we'd get good weather, perhaps not. Either way, nothing
was lost by an extension.

So Andy and Urs set off early for ABC with the news of his
decision. Some time later, I followed them, then Liz, who expected
to stay in the halfway tent.

For me it was the first time I'd tried to go the ABC in a day. A
long haul, not helped by the snow, which began falling steadily at
noon and quickly covered the moraine. It didn't look encouraging
– black clouds over the North Col, and the snowflakes were big and
moist, quite unlike the usual dry flurries. It was still curiously mild.
Was this the monsoon then, come to ring down the white curtain
on all our endeavours? I thought of *Ecclesiastes*. 'The race is not to
the swift, nor the battle to the strong...' as I pushed on through
thickening snow, wondering what I'd find when I arrived at ABC.

Rick Little sleep, shuffle about and set off late for 1st Pinnacle. Pass one
O_2 bottle, then another with gear and a bale of rope attached. Add bale
to rucksack already containing tent, stove and pan, and continue to foot
of Pinn 1. 8,000 metres at last.

Find Bonington's fixing rope tied off with two tents, two harnesses, a
jumar, figure-of-8 and two ski-poles. Dump tent and rope and stove and
start to follow the fixed rope for a short distance until it emerged on
rocks, totally frayed. We'll need to replace this ... Took the ski-poles and
descended. Nicko arrives pretty tired. Tomorrow: the Pinnacles.

Though no one else knew it yet, we'd finally made contact with the Pinnacles. People were moving into position lower down the hill: Chris went to C2 in good time and joined Bob, who'd tried to carry to C3 but had run out of steam in thick snow and turned back; Nick made the long haul over the Buttresses and arrived at C4, pleased to have reached a new height for him. He felt well and was confident he could go over 8,000 metres on the Pinnacles the next day.

At Base Camp Sandy looks moodily at the mountain obscured by clouds, Danny strums guitar and makes bread, while Kurt and Julie, recently returned from a few days' jaunt across to the Lho La pass, where they could look down into the Western Cwm, cook tea. It is now snowing, and because of that and his pulled calf muscle, Sandy had decided to put off going up to ABC for another day. With an extra week, there is time to wait for the weather to improve. Allen washes his clothes and himself, keeping a low profile and resting before his last return to the hill.

I arrive to find ABC sagging forlornly under steadily falling snow. The atmosphere is strikingly different from that of Base Camp. Jon, Tony, Mal, and now Andy and Urs, each enforcing the others' mood as the hours go by, all inevitably influencing Mal's perspective. At Base the others felt me to be pessimistic because I gave some credence to Urs' and Andy's view that we might be approaching the end; up here I am clearly far too optimistic in anticipating further progress. Such optimism is 'Base Camp bullshit', the prerogative of those who haven't yet been wasted on the hill and are currently enjoying BC life, out of touch with the reality of things up here.

But what about Rick and Nick, the lads currently highest on the hill? On their 6.0 pm radio call they sound very positive. Rick has already been to the foot of the 1st Pinnacle, found sections of fixed rope, and left gear there. He and Nick have discussed their options and decided to stick to the plan of fixing as much as possible of the 1st Pinnacle without oxygen. As far as they are concerned, the game is by no means over. Chris is certain he can carry to C4 in support. Is that high-altitude perspective not realistic? They are after all on the spot.

No one had any real answer to that, preferring to lambast the Base Camp dreamers. 'The idea of staying on received a thumb-down here,' Jon asserts to general agreement. They believe that the monsoon is beginning – what else can this sudden mildness and heavy snow mean? Lightning began to flicker behind Everest. I look round the tired faces; they seem not so much defeatist as resigned.

'I doubt if you can go more than twice to 8,000 metres on this route – and we need much more than that,' Mal says carefully. 'It's up to personal ambition from here on.' The others nod; they are more than tired – they want to be finished with the hill. 'Still,' he continues, 'though I think the game is lost, we'll play it out to the end – that's the tradition, isn't it?'

Tony As I write this at midnight there is a mass of snow outside the tent. Andy and Urs arrived with talk of extending our exit by a further week – but to what point? Very few (like none) of the people coming down from C4 can see any chance in the prevailing weather – we must be realistic at this point rather than crossing the line – this is not pessimism speaking – purely practical observation and knowing one's limits. No one here is capable of the Pinnacles (beyond the 1st) in the current heavy snow. Let's go home!

What is really going on? Are we on the verge of breaking through third time lucky on to the Pinnacles, or have we come to the end of the line, brought to a standstill by the soft but remorseless buffer of snow? Caught between the two worlds of BC and ABC, I don't know what to believe. So I go late at night over to Mal's tent to talk with him.

Three candles light and warm the orange tent as we pass the water bottle back and forwards and exchange cigarettes and points of view. Snow builds up then slides down the sides of the tent. Mal huddles in his sleeping bag, not ill but very far from well; I squat on a Karrimat as we talk. There is a sense of lull, like that of a pendulum at the top of its arc. All of our movement and striving has brought us to this quiet conversation in a warm tent in a world of falling snow. He asks after Liz, concerned for her at the halfway tent and hoping she'll turn round and go back tomorrow if the snow keeps up. He enquires how Sandy and Allen were when I left Base. Well, I say, still keen to go on. He considers that, nods.

'Maybe I've been up here too long. I'm knackered now, and maybe that's affecting the way I see the trip – I am aware of that possibility . . . But I don't think so . . .'

He glances at me with that casual I'm-going-to-lob-a-grenade-your-way look that I've seen twice before – when he asked me if I wanted to come on the Mustagh Tower trip, and again at Mrs Davies's in Rawalpindi when he first dreamed up this expedition:

'I was thinking we could come back here this autumn.'

'What?!'

'Well, I don't like leaving something undone, but I don't think we're going to make it this time. Whoever comes here next has got a hell of an advantage – there's fixed ropes everywhere they're needed all the way to the Pinnacles, three snow caves stocked with food, gas, stoves, and the bloody oxygen that broke us getting it up there in the first place. And they'll gain by everything we've learned. I want the next people here to be us.'

Mal you never change.

But there's sense in what he's saying. Whether it's practicable or not remains to be seen. Count me in if you need me, it's another good dream.

'Anyway, if this is the monsoon the decision's made for us. See what tomorrow brings.'

'Goodnight, Mal.'

'Night, youth.'

I leave him puzzling over a last cigarette and slip and stumble over snow-covered moraine to my tent.

Waking in the night, you put up a hand and feel the tent fabric bulging down under the weight of snow. Give it a push and hear a sshh . . . whoomph . . . as the snow slides down to the ground. A miniature avalanche. Then a thousand tiny wet kisses as fresh flakes whirl on to clean fabric.

Snow settling a crown on your head when you go outside to pee.

Snow, as though the unwritten contract we'd had with Everest was being quietly shredded into a million pieces.

21st May. 'We're going home!'

I look round the smiling faces in the ABC Mess Tent and see relief, as if a heavy burden had finally been shrugged off. Mal nods, 'I told the lads in the 8.0 am radio call to come down and clear the hill. It doesn't matter if we call this the monsoon or not – I only know you can't climb Everest in it.'

I'm scarcely surprised. There was something conclusive about last night's snow, and it's still coming down steadily outside. A white screen at the end of a film, the empty page.

Rick and Nick start brewing at 7.20, and have unaccountable problems with the stove till they discover that powder snow has completely blocked the entrance to the snow cave, sealing off fresh oxygen. 'No wonder we had a rough night!' A snow cave is a little world of its own, and they are quite unaware of conditions outside. So Mal's 8.0 call is a complete surprise, telling them to get off the hill while they still could, and bring everything possible with them. That means we are clearing the hill, that means the end.

Rick When Mal called at 8.0 am and said he thought the monsoon had arrived, I had no knowledge of conditions outside the snow-hole, and both Bob at C2 and I postponed any decision. At 9.0 Bob announced that he and Chris would descend and, having considered Bob's judgement, I was strongly influenced to do the same. I added the proviso that I would still consider going to the base of the 1st Pinnacle. When Nick and I finally emerged from the snowhole at nearly 10.0 into a blizzard, I abruptly decided to descend and Nick agreed.

Rick goes back inside and radios ABC. 'I think you have a point, Mal – we're coming down.'

'Good. Radio in every two hours on the hour. We'll come out and meet you at the bottom of the fixed ropes. And by the way, we're thinking of coming back in autumn.'

'Duff, you're a bloody dreamer – but a good one!'

He and Nick quickly collect their gear and set off down, triggering windslab avalanches every few yards.

Tony descends the now treacherous moraine with a message for Sandy telling him the trip's over and to cancel our extension if possible.

'I don't agree with failure . . . You keep coming back till you've done it,' says Mal, hunched over his brew. He looks less happy than the others. He's just made his only important leadership decision on the Expedition – to call it off. All the climbers at ABC accord with that decision, but what will the others say? And how will it look back home? What's done is done; though he has doubts, it still feels right. He could give many reasons for calling it off – the probable monsoon, the hill now wildly dangerous, lack of time, lack of climbers still capable of going back on the hill – but essentially it's an intuition, an intuitive recognition that the game is up. To ignore such intuitions in the mountains is to court disaster. No one's died on one of his trips yet, and he intends to keep it that way.

So we wait anxiously for the descending pairs to radio in every two hours, knowing that the snow slopes will be wildly out of condition. All that matters now is getting everyone back here safely, then we can have the post-mortems, then we can get excited about coming back in autumn.

Bob Woke just in time for the radio call. To our surprise Mal announces very heavy snow – he suspects it to be the monsoon – and he wants us to evacuate the hill. This seems a bit premature, so we arrange a time to call back and I stagger outside to look at the conditions. There is a steady wind, quite heavy continuous snowfall, and the depth of snow has completely obscured any sign of the fixed ropes. It is also ominously warm so this is either the monsoon or the 'little monsoon' that comes some time before it.

In any case, there is no doubt that we have to evacuate the hill – if it continues to snow the avalanche risk will be extreme (it may already be so), and we'll have the utmost difficulty getting off the hill. If this is the monsoon, we won't be coming back, so we gather together everyone's personal gear before heading down the ropes. We end up with three very heavy sacks; I go first, breaking trail through the deep snow and excavating the ropes, whilst Chris follows, manhandling the third sack.

Above C1 a slab avalanche of about 40 feet width breaks off beneath my feet, and the same thing happens on the traverse across the snow bowl just below C1. These avalanches are not of the full depth of new snow, and I'm terrified that something might release from above the traverse – a distinct possibility since it is now all undercut. If this happens it would be pretty nasty to be stuck on the ropes, though of course in a big slide the snow stake anchors would probably fail . . .

Sandy Enter Allen Fyffe, 'Eh Sandy, you'd better come and listen to what Tony has to say – he's just come down from ABC. Mal's decided to pack it in.' So I dragged myself ever so quickly out of my tent and rushed with a limp over to the Mess Tent.

'OK, Tony, tell me a story,' in my confused head, 'Hi, they tell me Mal's decided to quit. Excuse me I'm totally confused – what the fuck is going on?'

'Well', says Tony, 'all I know is that Mal came and woke me up this morning and told me to say we're clearing the hill and we want the yaks as soon as possible.'

Looking around, Kurt and Julie, Danny, Allen. Thoughts at slow speed . . .

'It's crazy', I said, 'a few days bad weather and we give up. It's not the monsoon, so why?'

'Well, there's three feet of snow at ABC.'

'Aye, well . . .'

Privately, neither Allen nor Sandy could believe in three foot of snow in 24 hours. It seemed a wild exaggeration (as indeed it was, eight inches was more like reality), an exaggeration indicative of the state of mind at ABC.

Allen Kurt and Julie are upset, Sandy confused, and I personally feel it is a bit premature. This bad weather is coming from the wrong way to be the monsoon. If we go home the Expedition will have achieved a great big zero!

Bob It's very strenuous work ploughing through the deep snow, and we take a breather on top of the ice-bulge. I'm worried about the prospect of avalanche on the big open slopes below, but when I'm a few feet down the ice-bulge I realize that the slope has already avalanched in a big way. About halfway down our ropes leave the safe avalanche-scoured zone and head into deep fragile snow, so I elect to leave the ropes and head straight down the edge of the avalanche scar . . .

At the bottom we totter out of range of further snow-slides and wait for the arrival of Urs, Jon and Andy, who help us with the loads. Now the nervous tension is off the trudge across the Raphu La seems even worse than usual, but like all unpleasant things it does eventually end.

Rick Flatten Camp 3 tents, load-up with personal gear and carry on down. Break in the weather briefly as we reach 7090. I collected a few fragments of rock for folks back home (left Tasker medallion clipped into channel-peg at top of 2nd Buttress). Clag descends again as we pass CB's. Fall on the fixed ropes several times in unstable snow. Finally reach Raphu La. Nick is pretty tired. Andy G., and Sarah then Andy N. as well meet us. So this is the end of the 'great game'.

'You know,' said Rick as the five of us waded through snow across the Raphu La for the last time, 'I've never failed before on a Himalayan peak. It might do me good.' And as the last of us steps wearily into the Mess Tent, Jon quips, 'I counted them all out, and I counted them all back in again.'

But Sandy cannot bring himself to accept it. The atmosphere at BC is one of bafflement and frustration: Allen knows this is not the monsoon and he's got at least one more time to 8,000 metres left in him; Liz is trying to adjust from arguing that doubt or pessimism is a form of expedition heresy, to endorsing Mal's decision as the only possible one. Sandy struggles with conflicting impulses and finally comes up with a scheme that will give us another chance.

Sandy We all here think it is crazy to give in. But as Deputy Leader it is my job to carry out commands from Mal. Best thing to do (as I want to give Mal a chance to change his mind) is the jeep shall leave BC (to arrange yaks, flights, etc.) on 23rd May at 1.0 pm. If a message does not arrive from ABC by then the jeep goes out with Luo, ordering yaks for 26th May as per primary plan. This means Kurt and Julie can go to ABC tomorrow and talk with Mal. I cannot go to ABC, calf muscle still sore and I cannot tell which tablets to take because of Swiss names. All I need is a handful of anti-inflammatory pills.

To me it seemed an impulsively made decision . . . a strange one. I understand (I hope) that the lads at 7,000 – 8,000 metres, in snowcaves with three feet of new snow falling probably thought, oh no, the monsoon is here, let's f– off. I would probably have done the same. But my reasons for thinking my own thoughts are (a) It's not the monsoon, this comes from S.E. (Bay of Bengal direction) (b) Yes, bad weather, but we've had bad weather. We're on Everest . . . (c) Yes sure, it's windy in afternoons, often stormy so why not climb in the morning . . . (d) It's Everest, it's hard, we've got to push like on no other hill (e) some oxygen and fixed rope is at foot of 1st Pinn. Therefore if we get a spell of a few days' good weather, what's stopping us going up, using O_2 and fix Pinns 1 and 2. OK, no summit, but at least we may find out about Pete and Joe. Snow caves have food, two guys could do it. I would be willing to be one of those guys.

So that's my reasons, so why not wait the week, only seven days just in case we get good weather, usually before the monsoon we get a settled period of weather. It won't cost us anything more, well . . . a life, maybe two. Sometimes my head agrees with Mal . . . But me I feel disappointed, almost cheated.

2.0 am. I need sleep, it won't come. I want to give this hill another go. The monsoon is *not* here, Mal I think you've been hasty. How I wish we had radio contact. We need to talk.

The snow finally stopped during the night. Next morning the sky was still blue-black over the North Col, but the air was crisper. ABC was camouflaged in snow. We couldn't break camp, nor the yaks get up here, till the snow melted, so I decided to go down. ABC was a depressing place to be now that the call-off drama was over. I packed up my gear, told Mal and set off.

Difficult going for the first two hours, over snow-obscured moraine. Pick my way carefully; I haven't slipped or fallen yet on this trip and won't start now. Look back at the Ridge before turning the corner: the sky has cleared, not a breath of wind. But the Ridge is absolutely white, it would take two or three days without further snow for it to stabilize . . . Just the same, where is this monsoon?

If you've got to fail somewhere – oops, mustn't use that word – this is the place to do it, on this pure, leaping, ball-breaking line. Eight climbers to near-as-damnit 8,000 metres – before we came out here there were only a handful of living, active British mountaineers who had been to that altitude without O_2. That in itself is a major achievement, and yet after all that work and height gain we were nowhere on the Ridge. Maybe halfway along it. Yet so near, only two strong climbers and three clear days away from doing the Pinnacles.

Don't look back, don't think about it. Try not to look forward either, too many problems and question marks at home. Just enjoy this last trek.

I was brewing at the halfway tent when Danny shouted. He was on the way to ABC with a note to Mal from Sandy, asking him to change his mind about not extending. Sandy and Allen and Kurt all say this is not the monsoon – and sitting with Danny in the warm sun amid rapidly melting snow, it certainly doesn't feel like it. Sandy's asked Mal to reconsider his decision in the light of this: he's also pointed out that Allen and himself are still keen to go on, that it costs us nothing to extend, and perhaps Mal's decision is influenced by his own fatigue.

My heart starts beating fast, perhaps we're not finished yet. After a moment's hesitation, I decide to add my ha'penceworth to the scales, as an objective observer, a between-two-camps Himalayan bumbly, and scribble a short private note to Mal. I said that when I'd left them, Sandy and Allen did indeed seem well, that I personally hoped he would extend and so give us a chance of going back on the hill. I felt so caught up with our Expedition that I can't let go even this faint chance of influencing the outcome; I wrote the note to indicate Sandy wasn't alone in his opinion, added a defensive 'but that's just this novice's belief'.

So Danny's now hot-footing it on to ABC, an ungainly Hermes with two notes in his pocket. As I drag on a cigarette and write this beside the glittering ice-fins, it's a beautiful day, mocking us.

Further down, I meet Kurt and Julie on their way up. They too affirm what is now obvious, that this is not the monsoon. They're clearly worried about their film, with their trips to the Lho La and the Karma valley, they've missed nearly all of the action on the hill.

Down at BC at 6.30 pm, very tired. Everyone wants to know the latest news. I try to give as neutral a perspective as possible. Allen and Sandy are clearly restless and frustrated, and this sudden clearing of the weather had done nothing to help. Liz is silent. Tony volunteers to go back up and help carry a load for anyone making a Pinnacle attempt. Sandy's limping badly, but swears it'll clear up with anti-inflammatory tablets.

'I hate leaving things half-done,' he says. 'When you cook bread you don't turn off the oven halfway through. When I'm with a girl . . . ' Sandy grins. 'There are things a fellow needs to complete.'

Bob The prevailing attitude is that the Expedition is over, and most of us are too knackered to seriously question this. If I think things out carefully, I think my attitude is as follows:
i) It will be at least five days before it is safe to go back on the hill
ii) This takes us to the deadline beyond which we'd have to organize an extension of the Expedition
iii) We are still low on the mountain, most people are burned out, and the weather is uncertain

iv) Conclude we should go out on the date planned. The Expedition is finished.

Sandy limps around our camp late at night, singing snatches of songs to try to calm himself, looking up at the fixed, indifferent stars.

Sandy Mal's said STOP. And left me a frustrated man. Knowing full well that I can go high but can't prove it to myself . . . and that leads me to think, do I want to prove it to other people? And then my head tells me – an asshole egotist . . . and I feel insignificant in this world of tall hills.

I could go up to ABC. But all I'd do is argue, lose friends . . . What good is that? And I'm feeling very ALONE anyway these days. Isolated because I've isolated myself, because I know that within me there is this desire to get me high on this mountain and I don't want to dilute this drive with little worries of scandal-talk.

. . . Vibes inside me, telling me to be careful and look out. Will the correct truth be told by anyone? What tales will we all relate? And I wonder as I ask that – am I being defensive? And my answer is Yes! And I'm concerned about my Ego, and I keep telling myself and my girlfriend that is *not* what I think I'm doing here. But right now I'm beginning to think that is in actual fact why we climb, and that leads to 'Well, Sandy, it is time you got out of this way of life?' That's what I'm asking myself so often on this trip.

At 25 years old, I decided to take on this difficult road in life; I wonder if I've seen enough of it now?

23rd May. I wake from a sound and pill-less sleep, stick my head round the tent – not a cloud in the sky, no spindrift on Everest. That 36-hour snowfall was not the monsoon and the hill has made fools of us. We've till 1.0 pm today to change our minds, to extend our time here and go back on the hill if the weather stays fine.

One by one we get up, check out the morning and go to the Mess Tent. Kurt and Julie will be up at ABC by now, having gone up to reinforce Sandy's message and if necessary carry on filming by themselves or with the Basques. They do not regard themselves as bound by Mal's decision, and have already decided to stay on an extra week. They have to finish their film, and are in no hurry to go home. But will Mal change his mind?

We sit outside in the sunlight and sing 'Good Day, Sunshine', 'You Are My Sunshine', 'Sunshine Superman'. Laughter is our only protection against this emptiness.

Noon comes, and still no sign of the longed-for messenger coming round the corner of the glacier snout. Sandy is still limping back and forth between his tent and the Mess. Allen's wondering whether to pack his gear and head up to ABC, just in case. He knows it'll be another couple of years till he can take enough time off to come back to the Himalayas. Other than doing a lot of hard work and proving to himself he can carry above 7,500 metres, this trip has been a 'big fat zero' for him. He stays put, waiting for word from ABC.

1.0 pm. We sense the inevitable. Luo offers to hold back the jeep another 30 minutes. They tick away. Nothing moves on the hill or on the moraine, no clouds in the sky. Only the ice-lake silently and invisibly evaporating. The hens wander as half-heartedly as ourselves, picking at specks.

1.30. 1.40 . . .

'Well, that's it,' Sandy says flatly. Luo climbs into the jeep, the driver guns the engine and they bounce off down the valley to arrange our return.

We don't say much, but go our own separate ways. We need to be alone to adjust. 'There goes my chance of being a 8,000 metre hero,' Allen murmurs drily. Liz announces she's going down to the nunnery. 'It's not as bad as that, Liz!' someone jokes. She gives a wan, strained smile and walks away.

That evening the team returned to BC in dribs and drabs. First Nick and Chris, who was now limping badly after tripping over the extra sack at the end of his last descent. Sandy came with them, having wandered up half-heartedly towards ABC in the afternoon. He'd had a chance to ask the two of them all about Mal's decision, and at least for the time being felt reconciled with it.

They say that Mal's struggling a long way behind. Concerned, Liz sets out to meet him. When she finally does, she's shocked at how tired he looks, how skeletal. She offers to carry his sack, and to her astonishment he accepts the offer. He seems unable to lift his feet properly, keeps stumbling over small rocks.

I watch them walk over the flat moraine towards Base in the brief dusk, hand in hand.

Beer and whisky, songs and laughter in our Mess Tent that night. We did after all have something to celebrate: survival and companionship. With the strain off, we discovered ourselves as a team and as friends. Sandy's last, late entry spoke for everybody: 'We're all happy, all safe . . . Who gives a shit for the rest? . . . Oh well, I do . . . Let's hope for better weather next time!'

Bob Barton returned to Base the following evening to say that Rick had announced his intention to go back on the hill; Jon would be staying at ABC as his 'catcher' in case he got in trouble.

Thunderstruck silence. 'But what's he going back up *for*?'

Bob shrugged. 'He didn't really say. I don't think he's decided. When I left he was intending to go to C2 with Kurt and Julie to help them finish the film. After that . . .'

Mal looked grim. It was hard to see what good could come of this. Rick had broken ranks and gone out on his own. If he was seriously intending to solo high on Everest – just how high did he hope to go? – he was taking the biggest risk in the Expedition so far. If anything went wrong up there, he was in desperate trouble. Just when we were feeling thankful that everyone was safe. And as one or two of the team mentioned obliquely, if by some miracle Rick got somewhere and made new ground on say the 1st Pinnacle, it would only underline that we had abandoned the Expedition prematurely, that the hill was already fit for climbing again, and that we should have extended our time.

It took all of Allen Fyffe's self-control to keep his thoughts to himself. Had he known earlier, he could have been up there with Rick.

'This hill has made us look pretty foolish,' said Andy Nisbet, looking up from his bridge hand. 'Perhaps we are.'

RICK'S STORY

22nd May. The day dawns fine, the heavy snowfall of the previous day did not herald the early arrival of the monsoon as Mal had feared. The mountain is brilliant white, all the rock sections are completely plastered with fresh snow.

Tony had descended yesterday with a message for the yak drivers to arrive as originally planned on 28 May at ABC. That rules out another major push on the mountain, there is no time. We are all feeling weary and must prepare to descend to BC tomorrow.

I know that if I go down I won't come back up, and the prospect of sitting at BC for ten days is appalling. The warm sun starts to clear the snow from the moraines around the tents as gear is sorted and packed.

In the evening Kurt, Julie and Danny arrive, bearing scribbled notes from Andy G. and Sandy, which re-open the debate about clearing the hill. Andy is openly questioning, while Sandy just says that he is not happy but accepts that we are in a better position to judge. We are all a bit defensive about the decision, resenting this second-guessing from BC, especially as it is too late.

My own feelings are mixed. Nick and I did not consider sitting it out at C4, perhaps we should have done. The unstable fresh snow would certainly have dictated at least one perhaps two days inactivity before attempting the 1st Pinnacle. We had food for the first two days and I would then have spent four nights at over 8,000 metres before starting on the difficult climbing. Not a recipe for success. If Mal erred, it was in making the irrevocable decision to call the yaks up before Bob, Chris, Nick and I had got off the mountain. If I had known that I might have been strongly tempted to sit out another night just to keep the Expedition alive. Tant pis.

23rd May. Another depressingly fine day. Those descending today start to dismantle their tents.

Julie does lengthy interviews with Mal and me, discussing the decision to retreat and conditions on the mountain. Kurt, Julie and Danny are staying up here to do some more filming; I decide to stay, so does Jon, and Bob postpones going down.

This is the last chance for many of the promotional photographs of generously donated food and equipment, so we pose, self-consciously, with chocolate bars, radios and rucksacks in front of the big white mountains. Eventually the last figure sets off down the moraine and six of us are left with the big Mess Tent of ABC and our own thoughts.

I am already toying with the idea of going back up the hill. Kurt and Julie want some more footage of the lower slopes, and Jon and I talk about providing the actors.

24th May. Another fine day. Now I am sure I want to go back up the hill. Jon does not feel like climbing but will stay at ABC. Bob decides to descend. I am nervous of being thought a complete lunatic so I hedge my intentions around with talk of 'just seeing what conditions are like'.

Weighing up the contents of my sack is a painstaking task, every ounce will count against me but warm gear is paramount. My precious woollen gloves are wearing thin, darned once already, so I add a second pair of overmitts as insurance. At least all the food and gas is in the snow-holes.

I give Bob the brief message for Base Camp that I am 'going up the hill' and Kurt, Julie, Danny and I set off towards the Raphu La. The snow is still deep and unconsolidated in most places and I am glad to let the film crew break trail. At the foot of the fixed ropes there is much delay as films are changed and Julie does an interview, but there is no great rush, I feel relaxed. Kurt films me setting off and then I wait as he packs up the camera and moves up to break trail for me.

He doesn't falter, plodding steadily up the rope making solid steps for me to follow. The large camera and the small clockwork Bell & Howell together must weigh as much as my own pack. Near the top of the main slope, where it steepens, Kurt stops and passes me the clockwork camera. I film him briefly and pass the camera back. I judge conditions to be good enough to continue although we are shrouded in cloud by now, and tell him I will continue to the 2nd snow-hole. Kurt films me as I move away from him up the slope. I privately wish that he were climbing and not filming, he is impressively strong.

Higher on the knife-edge of the Ridge I emerge from the cloud and can see Julie's tent at the Raphu La. Continuing slowly I reach C2, very tired at about 7.0 pm. At 8.0 pm Jon comes on the radio and we set up a routine for morning and evening calls.

I check the barometer, brew-up and try to get some sleep. I will leave my Gore-tex windsuit here and climb on in the down suit tomorrow.

25th May. Barometer steady. I am still weary this morning, quickly dismissing the idea of trying to make C4 in one push. This leg to C3 is the easiest and shortest section on the hill, but invariably I have felt bad and moved slowly here. Today is no exception. The sky clouds over and snow starts to fall as I wander along the Ridge. I almost turn back but decide to continue to the tents in any event.

I reach the collapsed tents early in the afternoon and spend three hours packing up one and erecting the other. There is still some personal gear here, overboots of Sandy's and Mal's Karrimat.

The evening is clear, giving a fantastic view through the tent door to Kangchenjunga. All is well at ABC. Kurt and Julie are filming through a telephoto lens.

26th May. Barometer still OK, up if anything. It is a glorious day, clear and without a breath of wind. An ideal summit day. The initial gully on the 1st Buttress is choked with unstable snow, and ploughing upwards is laborious. Out of the gully and the going is better, I feel a great sense of elation on this day, progressing well on to the rocks of the 2nd Buttress, and look out at the giants on my left and right, Makalu and Cho Oyu. Alone with my God on this Ridge, I would not be anywhere else.

At the top of the rock section is a bale of lightweight fixing rope. If I can carry anything on the Pinnacles it will be this, since it may prove essential for retreat. It is added to my sack, and I reach C4 in fair shape.

As soon as I am into my sleeping bag I start brewing up, tea followed by soup. This evening it seems more difficult than ever to force the necessary liquid down. Freeze-dried Chicken Marengo, could be worse. All the time I turn the options over and over, tomorrow will be decision time. On the radio I leave it open.

I could leave my gear here and travel light with just a rope for retreat and attempt to get as high as possible in one day, ideally to the top of the 1st Pinnacle to get photographs of the ground ahead, which no one alive has seen.

Alternatively I could take all my gear and push on for a bivvi on the Pinnacle with the aim to go through the Pinnacles and on to the summit. Or through the Pinnacles and on down the North Ridge, where Jon will field me. That really would be pushing the boat out, because what I fear most is a sharp turn in the weather. Retreating down the Pinnacle in a storm without fixed ropes would probably be fatal.

Believe firmly that Pete and Joe were *not* crazy, and that ascent without O₂ is possible.

27th May. A bad night's sleep. In the morning I still keep my options open, telling Jon that I will carry my gear to the foot of the Pinnacles and decide there. He nonchalantly accepts my plans and describes the scene at ABC.

Kurt is now snow-blind from filming through a camera lens without dark glasses. Jon will move to 'field' me retreating down either the Ridge or the North Col. An accident like the Basque's would happen very easily while descending exhausted. We arrange a listening watch every two hours.

Despite my efforts it is 9.30 before I leave C4 and move slowly along the Ridge past Mal's abandoned oxygen set. At the foot of the Pinnacles are the tent, stove and food which I had dumped there on 20th May. Decision time.

Tattered lengths of orange fixed rope extend up the initial slopes of the 1st Pinnacle, but it is obvious that what remains of the fixed ropes run out three years before will not be enough to secure a retreat. It soon becomes painfully apparent that with food and gas for three days, a minimum of technical gear, sleeping bag, tent and a bale of fixing rope, I shall not be capable of climbing the steep ground ahead. There is nothing that I can consider leaving behind if I am to go beyond the 1st Pinnacle, and yet I do not have the strength left to carry it all. Decision made. I shall take just the fixing rope and climb as far as I can by early evening.

Movement is laborious over loose rock and unstable snow to a steepening shallow gully, which leads to a slight notch in the Ridge. I free sections of three-year-old rope and re-fix them in places to assist my descent. At the notch I gamble on finding more fixed rope higher up and abandon the bale I'm carrying, retaining just a water bottle, camera, a couple of slings and my axes.

An almost-empty rucksack is a positive joy, but I need all the freedom of movement on the steepening ground. On the right, rocks slope away into short cliffs, while on the left an icy cornice crest rears up above the precipitous seracs of the Kangshung Face. The snow overlying the slabby rock is soft and breaks away under my feet. The cornice itself is firm névé so I climb as close to it as I dare, seeking firm footsteps. Much of the fixed rope has been frayed away on the rocks; security lies only in the axes in my hands and the crampons on my feet.

At an old peg a faded red day-sack is hanging, its bottom frayed completely away. I am now at over 8,100 metres, and breathing controls my being, every step demanding more from the thin, thin air.

Crossing a snow-covered rock section I am extended to my uttermost, small patches of windslab break away from under my feet and I arrive gasping and spent at a short overhung corner where three tangled skeins of yellow, orange and blue rope are hanging.

I clip in and look at my watch, it is 5.30. To regain the snow-hole at C4 tonight I must turn back, I shall not make the top of the Pinnacle. I start unravelling the yellow, orange and blue knitting to protect the descent and find, hanging from a peg, a clockwork movie camera just like Kurt's. It is Joe's. It is strangely warming to find this new link with the man who inspired my early Himalayan ventures and whose footsteps I have followed to this point.

Eventually I have enough rope to cover the steepest ground below, and take some photos up and down the crest of the Ridge. This is probably about 8,150 metres, the same high point reached by Dick Renshaw on the first attempt on the Pinnacle three years earlier. I turn back, feeding out the yellow rope and securing it at intervals down the Ridge. The demands of the moment are completely absorbing; the time for anguish is later.

At the foot of the Pinnacle I re-pack my sack and stumble off down the easy section of the Ridge. It is getting dark and I make the 8.0 pm radio call a few yards short of C4. Crawling into the familiar confines of the snow-hole brings a tremendous sense of security and relief. Off with crampons, overboots, boots and into the pit. Start brewing. The yaks will arrive at ABC tomorrow evening. I do not believe that I can do anything further, I will go down.

I do not pray but think incoherently in the direction of God and pass into an uneasy torpor.

28th May. I woke in the early hours and put on another brew. In the morning I am even slower than usual, fumbling with overboots and crampons before stumbling out into another cloudless day. Mentally more than physically I have admitted the end and turn downward without hesitation.

Allen Fyffe has arrived at ABC to complete the packing up of the camp and he listens at pre-arranged intervals for my calls. Adding some personal gear and a tent to my sack at C3 leaves me very heavily burdened and I plead with Allen to meet me at the Raphu La.

Descending wearily and warily over the familiar ground I finally reach the glacier and begin to follow the marker wands. At the bottom of the steeper section I can see a figure dancing in the haze above the surface of the snow. It moves forward and meets me.

At Base Camp, perfect day followed perfect day as we waited for the yaks and for news from Rick. We went through a phase of hating the mountain for its mocking indifference, averting our eyes from it like rejected lovers. But while we each struggled to make peace inside ourselves with the outcome, there was time now for relaxation and conversation, for bridge, ma-jong, chess, whisky and laughter. It had not been the most intimate of expeditions, due largely to its size and logistics (only Andy and Urs ever climbed roped together, for everyone else it had been endless slogging up and down the Ridge, in effect alone), yet even in our disappointment and with the strain off now, we were coming out of it genuinely friendly.

Time now to wash, to lie in the sun and feel the grime and fatigue slip away. Liz cuts our hair, we trim or shave off our beards and start to look like regular humans again. Cuts begin to heal, the panda eyes fade and flesh returns to the bone. Whispers become voices. When weather permits, we put on jeans and shirts for the first time in two months and with them feel our street selves again, at once reassuring and restricting. We count off the days till we get home, knowing full well that once there we'll wish we were here again. We day-dream of reunions with family and friends, and at night talk over plans for the next expedition and the one after that. Almost everyone wants to come back to the North-East Ridge, though those with jobs know it will be some time before they can return to the Himalayas.[2] We seldom mention Rick, though he's on our minds. Another non-topic is our individual feelings about the call-off and decision not to extend our time here.

These last few days I lie for hours at a time in the lee of a boulder near Base, looking at the extended, absolute sky as if there were answers there. Sometimes Sandy joins me and we speak our thoughts leisurely as they drift and re-form and disappear like the white clouds overhead. I want more and more silence, the silence of wind over rocks and distant water, the silence of this vast, uncluttered place. I want to go home. I never want to leave here.

'Would you like to come on the Gangapurna trip, Andy? I think we need a singer . . . Could be a good jest – death on a stick, actually! No, it'll be good value . . . This is the only place I feel at home any more . . .'

Silence, the sky dark blue above, modulating through to pale turquoise at the end of the valley where we'll be heading in a couple of days time. By the time we're back in London we'll appear nearly normal, and Everest and the stripped, exhausted beings that forced their way up it with the bitter taste of altitude in their mouths will seem like a dream even to us.

'Maybe there is such a thing as mountain wisdom. A feeling . . . Pity it doesn't survive the journey home.'

'Yeah – hellish, ain't it!' Sandy laughs, at peace for a while. 'That's why we have to keep coming back. To remember it again.'

Sandy The important point of all this Pilkington Everest Expedition exercise is that we learn something, and put this experience into some useful context later, and that any new creases that have formed round our eyes and along our foreheads are creases of experience rather than creases of time spent learning nothing.

[2]The hope of returning that autumn came to nothing, partly because of problems of money and logistics and partly because of the unavailability of most of the team.

As long as we've all moved a pace forward.

May 26. Another clear, calm day. Everest is definitely taking the mickey. We wander down to the Rongbuk nunnery to do some bouldering and lie in the sun. I amble alone in a trance of sky, my shadow moving ahead of me over the stones. The ice-lake has almost gone now, leaving only dry stones. A tiny purple flower astonishes our eyes.

The ruins of the nunnery are scattered among the more ancient ruins of a huge rock-slide. Under rocks there are piles of the clay figures which Urs says contain the ashes of the dead. Personally I doubt it, because there are thousands of them. The *chortens* have all been decapitated and split open by Red Guards during the Cultural Revolution. All the buildings, so organically worked into the rock-slide, have been pulled apart. Rain has turned the clay to mud, which drips down over the faded remains of murals. We find three exquisite Buddhas carved on slate, each deliberately broken across the middle. Beneath a trapdoor we find an underground shrine carved into the rock, with fresh *tsampa* and prayer-scarves laid out in front of an altar. It seems that passing yakkers still make offerings here. In the remains of the largest house a blue Buddha in Paradise smiles tranquilly as his body dribbles down the wall.

It is hard to feel much sorrow or anger amid these ruins, partly because they are in accord with the Buddhist principle of the inevitability of change and decay. Here we are surrounded by retreating and advancing glaciers, avalanches, the moraine rubble that was once the peaks of great mountains, which were themselves on the sea-bed not that long ago. Danny fretfully tries to pin these forces down in his sketches, endlessly dissatisfied.

In this immensity, nothing is tragic. Here we can begin to accept the outcome. The disintegrating blue Buddha smiles. It is, after all, only a stitch in time.

Bouldering at altitude is exhausting. We walk back to BC to finish packing our barrels so we can go home so we can prepare to go somewhere else. We're still Westerners, restless spirits with the next horizon in our eyes. That night in the Mess Tent someone said, 'I think we come here to be humbled as much as to succeed.'

The yaks turned up, and Allen Fyffe nobly volunteered to accompany them to ABC to help pack up the gear there. In truth, scarcely anyone else was capable of walking that far in a day. Mal's decision not to extend may well have been hasty, but it was a brave and responsible one in view of the pressure we all inevitably felt and himself in particular from the media, public awareness and our sponsors. The decision to call a halt is the hardest mountaineering decision, because you'll never really know what would have happened if you'd pressed on. When people are killed through persisting, the decision was wrong; if you quit the mountain and everyone survives, the question will always remain: could we have done more?

Better to have everyone alive. In the end Mal put our safety above an outside chance of success as he saw it. Though the 'If' and 'Should we?' and 'Maybe' persist, no one was seriously going to argue with the *principle* of that decision.

Throughout these last days each of us was trying to digest what the Expedition had meant to us and to adjust to its outcome, in the way that when one reaches the ending of a book or film, one reconsiders everything that went before in the light of it.

In the face of acute disappointment, the necessity is to come to terms with it without self-deception. From the time the Expedition was conceived, only the summit and 'success' mattered – as it must. Getting to the top was the point of everything. But when an Expedition is over, the value is gradually redistributed away from the summit. (If we judged life by its outcome, it would seem a pretty negative affair!)

It was like the end of a long relationship, all the sensations of loss, disappointment, frustration, emptiness, self-questioning, finally easing into an appreciation of all the good things along the way. The bitterness of regret remains and there's no point in denying it, but it is diluted by consideration of the sweetness of the whole. The value of the North-East Ridge for anyone who goes there does not reside exclusively in the Pinnacles or the summit, but is spread along the whole soaring length of it, stretching all the way back through Tibet, China, to the months of planning that went into making the Expedition.

On 29th May, the anniversary of the first ascent of Everest, Rick, Allen and Danny returned to Base with the yaks and the ABC gear (Jon had come down the day before with a précis of Rick's adventure). For the first time Rick seemed truly worn out. He was congratulated in a restrained way, for there were many mixed feelings about his solo climb; his effort of reaching as high as anyone alive on the Ridge underlined how near we might have been to making a breakthrough on the Pinnacles. The main emotion was one of relief that he'd got off with it.

I sit with my sleeping bag up to my shoulders in front of my tent tonight. We'll be leaving here the day after tomorrow. It's midnight, but orange lights still glow in a few of the tents where people lie listening to music, finishing diaries, thinking of home or the events of the least three months. Tonight I don't feel we're separate, just individual: apart yet together. There's laughter from the Mess Tent, where Mal, Liz, Bob and Andy are locked in a bridge session amid strenuous efforts to finish our whisky before we depart. The hills are Danny's darkest charcoal, only Everest glimmers like a ghost of itself. The night is cool and windless; the moon has not yet risen and the stars are like the remains of a vast, smashed chandelier.

The 'Unclimbed Ridge' was the necessary dream. We always knew we might well not climb it, but we came and froze and sweated and had our frights because only that dream can yield those moments of waking we value above everything when experience comes; Experience, intensified, capitalized, absolute.

I throw away the cigarette, watch its red eye briefly light up a stone, then crawl back inside my tent, for the first time truly accepting the outcome. I'm deeply glad to have been here, a dozen tiny kingdoms of warmth and light camped briefly in the dark lap of Chomolungma, Goddess Mother of the World, set free by our own insignificance.

*   *   *

Leaving Lhasa before dawn, our coach moves through the city as we loll back in our seats, vacant, receptive and passive in our half-asleep state. There are bonfires lit at intervals alongside the streets, and a long procession of black figures filing silently past them. The fires flare as each tosses a cupful of yak butter on to the flames, and by the light we can see everyone is carrying bundles of herbs or twigs. Sweet smoke drifts in the coach window. This procession goes on for miles; they're honouring the dead, Jack thinks, honouring memory.

The half-light of dawn filters through as we leave the city. Images of fire, silhouetted stooping figures, smoke drifting over pale water. A three-quarter moon sets behind the draped hills. Then two poplar trees, a single star, a yak-skin raft drifting down the Tsang Po. The dark forms of my huddled companions. The glowing tip of Malcolm's cigarette as he dreams another dream with Liz's head on his shoulder.

Epilogue

During the months spent writing this account, I have read the diaries so often, stared at thousands of slides, and run the events backwards and forwards so many times that it no longer seems to matter in what order they occurred. I see the entirety of our trip as one static whole, just as we could see the entirety of the North-East Ridge from Advance Base Camp. There our eyes could jump from the Pinnacles to 7090 to the summit. In our venture any moment now seems as significant as any other, and what it was all about is as much in the middle as in the curious, hiccuping ending.

That is the fundamental reason why the terms 'success' and 'failure', though deeply felt, are inappropriate.

I put Allen Fyffe's first diary entry *'I'm writing this in Peking but this is how it really started'* alongside Malcolm's last one, *'Desperate weather but Chris and Bob and Nick and Rick safely off with all gear thank God'*. On the wall, the photo of Mal and myself in Rawalpindi is pinned next to the last picture Rick took from his high point on the 1st Pinnacle. If one carried on like this, alternatively working backwards from the end and forwards from the beginning, at what unexpected summit would they meet?

They would meet about midnight on the evening of laughter in the Mess Tent at Base Camp when we first wrote 'The Ballad of the North-East Ridge' while the lamps wavered, the whisky went round, and we finally sang the whole song through from the beginning:

We-e-ll the Mustagh Tower was over,
The ropes had all been sold or coiled away,
We were sitting in Mrs Davies'
While the monsoon rain fell day by day by day by day. . . .

Laughter and harmonious unharmonious voices ring and fade in the Everest night. As good a place to begin or end as any.

The Ballad of the North-East Ridge

(To the tune of 'Lily, Rosemary and the Jack of Hearts')

The Mustagh Tower was over, the ropes had all been sold or coiled
    away,
We were sitting in Mrs Davies' while monsoon rains fell day by day,
We were thinking about bacon, we were dreaming about beans,
We were talking of our women and the things that we had seen,
We were thinking about everything except for the North-East Ridge.

Then Voytek he came over with his intensely European gaze.
We were joined by a Norwegian, seemed like his friends were blown
    away,
They were climbing up on Trango Peak, on the way down
    disappeared,
There was nothing much that we could say but what was really
    weird
Was they still had a permit, for Everest, for the North-East Ridge.

I went away for cigarettes, when I came back Malcolm looked at
    me,
'Want to go to Everest, Andy? You can be my security.'
I knew that he was joking, so I just said 'Why not?
But I didn't think you were interested in Everest such a lot'–
He said 'I'm very interested in the "unclimbed", the North-East
    Ridge.'

On the back of an old envelope we wrote down the makings of a
    team,
The Mustagh Tower 4 again, that was the kind of trip that it had
    been.
There was tiny Tony Brindle, revving from his toes up to his head
He was like a little battery, 90 per cent lead –
He was willing to spark anywhere, even on the North-East Ridge.

There was smiling Sandy Allan, that amiable Hieland honey bear,
A man open to every ploy, he looked for his honey everywhere.
'Climbing isn't dangerous,' he once told me with a grin,
'You open your eyes wide, and then you jump right in.'
But he'd never seen a jest bigger than the North-East Ridge.

We had to have Jon Tinker, that abrasive Cockney Rastaman,
He said 'Duff you walk on water, you're an appalling disgusting
    lucky man.
I'll go with you to 8,000 and then kiss you goodbye,
It'll be a piece of piss, you're all gonna die –
But yes I'm coming with you, to Everest to the North-East Ridge.'

We drove down to see Bonehead on a windy rainy Lakeland day.
We had an hour of his time, you could tell that for more you'd have
    to pay.
He said 'That old North-East Ridge led us a tragic dance,
And the print-out on my computer says you haven't got a chance,
But yes you should go for it, for Everest and the North-East Ridge.'

When it comes to expeditions, everyone around here knows the
    score.
First we needed money, then we needed more and more and more
Liz said 'Terry Dailey is a man who needs a change.
Terry we need a hundred grand, can it be arranged?'
He said 'Liz you leave it with me, 'cos I'm coming to the North-
    East Ridge.'

Meanwhile the terrible twins had just flown in from Nepal,
Nick had lost some more toes, now you only need one hand to
    count them all.
Ricky said to Nicky, 'Hey you know this could be good,
I will be the driving force and you can do the food –
And that should book our passage, with Sarah, to the North-East
    Ridge.'

About this time in Aviemore two cowboys were climbing on the
    range.
Bob said to Allen, 'One more client I go insane!'
But Allen's hair was falling out and there didn't seem much hope.
Then there came a phone call and it threw them a rope
Which pulled them clear of Glenmore Lodge to Everest and the
    North-East Ridge.

In a dirty dive in London town, 'One pint' was chucking up again,
It had been a hard hard day in Alpine Sports, and Sonja was climbing
    on the Ben,
And when some 4 weeks later Wattie finally sobered up
He remembered what he'd promised when he'd been feeling rough,
To beg, borrow, steal our gear for Everest and the North-East Ridge.

Meanwhile back in Aberdeen a red beard is munching marzipan,
When it came to buying hill-food, Andy Nisbet had to be our man.
He was tired of doing new routes and being disbelieved
So he was glad when the invite was finally received
To come and do a new route – Everest, the North-East Ridge.

In a little town in Switzerland, Urs listened to the ticking of his
    clocks.
'If I can't cut up someone soon, I'm going to go out of my box!'
He knew a lot of mountain medicine but it all came down to this,
'If you're feeling bad go down, and always trink and piss' –
He had to be our doctor for Everest, for the North-East Ridge.

For a golden cheque book, we took along a man from Pilkington's.
We got David Bricknell, an upward-mobile company man.
He organized in London, organized in Liverpool,
He gave us cooking rotas and he gave us Base Camp rules –
But he saved our skins in Lhasa, *en route* to the North-East Ridge.

These days it ain't enough to climb it, you've got to get it down in
    celluloid.
When it comes to high-up movies there's just one team you can't
    avoid.
We'd met with Kurt and Julie in Skardu waiting for a plane
And it seemed pretty obvious they'd come along again
To film us at play on Everest, on the North-East Ridge.

To carry gear at altitude you need a special kind of man.
Julie thought of someone . . . then she thought of Desperate Dan.
A noted master baker and quick man with a sketch.
Julie said 'Please carry,' Kurt said simply 'Fetch!
And don't drop ze Arriflex on Everest on the North-East Ridge.'

There's rumours going round that altitude damages your brain,
All I know is since we set out, nothing's been quite the same.
If you want to know the details or take a closer look,

Come on to the lectures or else you buy the book . . .
About the time we had on Everest, on the North-East Ridge.

MEMBERS OF THE 1985 PILKINGTON EVEREST EXPEDITION

Rick Allen Lead climber. b. Middlesex 1955, Senior Operations Engineer with Texaco. Took a degree in chemical engineering at Birmingham University and joined 'The Stoats' mountaineering club. Rock climbing and later winter climbing became increasingly important and after graduating in 1976 he moved to Scotland. Early Alpine seasons led on to Mt. Kenya (West Ridge and Diamond Couloir), then the Scottish Garwhal Himalaya Expeditions (first ascent, solo, of Kisti Stambh, 20,570 ft) 1984, Alpine-style first ascent of South Face Ganesh II with Nick Kekus. Alpine ascents include S.E. face of Pilastro di Roges, N.W. face Gletscherhorn, W. face Blaitiere, N. face Dru, N. face direct Les Droites (winter), N. faces of the Courtes and the Triolet, solo in winter. Member of the Etchachan Club, the Midland Association of Mountaineers, A.C.G.

'I remain firmly convinced that an Alpine-style ascent from below the 1st Pinnacle without oxygen is possible and that within a very few years the approach pioneered by Pete and Joe, which I attempted to follow, will be vindicated on the North-East Ridge of Everest.'

Sandy Allan Expedition Deputy Leader, lead climber. b. Inverness 1955. Worked as lambing shepherd, tractor driver, trainee distillery manager; now climbs, guides and works as a roughneck in North Sea oil exploration. Many new winter routes in Scotland, including early Grade 6 climbs with Andy Nisbet. Alpine routes include N. face of the Dru, face Droites direct (winter), super Couloir Mt. Maudit (winter) 1st British ascent N. face Mt. Gruetta. Expeditions to Nuptse West Ridge '82, Thamaserku West Ridge '82, Mustagh Tower '84. Member of Club Alpine Francais, S.M.C., A.C.G., Eagle Ski Club.

'After Everest thoughts come sometimes, but when it comes to writing it, feels like ego-tripping and really I find I'm totally out of that. . . . After Everest, to Gangapurna on North Face Expedition, learned a lot there. Mainly that I really wanted to be there, in that situation, in control even as our tent got ripped apart and Toni, Paul and I hung on freezing. But me so much in control . . . over the top with control, totally nil emotions at the time . . . just being, with the wind, the gods of destructions, chewing salami, hoping they'd let us off with it . . . Ace! We're all home, all alive, all working together, partying together, climbing together, good friends – how it should be.'

Dave Bricknell Base and Advance Base Camp organizer. b. 1948. Educated at Exeter School and Exeter University (Law). Married with two children. Company Secretary for Pilkington Brothers plc after four years in the City. Fell-walker but with no experience of climbing, no first ascents, no Alpine or Himalayan experience. An armchair adventurer!

'I came back from the trip with an enormous sense of gratitude: to my wife and children who were genuinely excited by my "adventure" despite the worry it must have caused them; to the Directors of Pilkington for having the generosity to give me extended leave; to the rest of the team for accepting me as part of the team and not just a corporate interloper.

'When I first returned to the office I wondered if I'd ever be the same again. It was fun being a "celebrity" – but it didn't last. It was worrying not being able to concentrate on the job and having an appalling memory (had I sustained irretrievable brain damage at altitude?) – but it didn't last. I savoured the delights of a bath, mild English rain and the lush scenery – but it didn't last.

'The trip confirmed my love affair with the mountains, and I have a renewed determination to go back again, but it did not become an all-devouring passion. So many people said "it must have been the experience of a lifetime". Not so. It was *an* experience of a lifetime, a tremendous emotional experience to store and treasure with such memories as watching the birth of my children, signing my first major company deal, finishing my first marathon and passing my Law Finals, but it did not overwhelm them. It was a part of my life but not, I hope, the climax, and has left the feeling of gratitude to Fate that I have been given the opportunity to have those experiences, and a reinforcing of the view that no dream is too remote if you work for it and take the opportunities as they come.

'And I've been bitten by the bug of Scottish winter climbing – perhaps I will never be quite as sane again.'

Bob Barton. Lead climber. b. Barnsley, Yorkshire, 1948. Married with two children. Educated Broadway Grammar school, Fitzwilliam College, Cambridge (BA Natural Sciences), University College of North Wales, Bangor (PGCE Outdoor Education and Physics). Now instructor at Glenmore Lodge Outdoor Training Centre, Aviemore. Began climbing in the Peak District. Numerous first ascents in Scotland and extensive climbing and skiing in Europe. 1972 expedition to Hindu Kush, five first ascents of peaks up to 6,000 metres; '73 Western Alps, first British ascents N. Face Lauterbrunnen Breithorn and N. Face Nesthorn (with Peter Boardman); '74, first winter ascent Quille Couloir. '76, ascent of W. Rib of Mt McKinley; '77, first ascent W. Face Batian Direct Route, Mt. Kenya, first ascent Heim Glacier Direct Route, Kilimanjaro (with D. Morris); '78, first ascent of S. Pillar of Kalanka (with Allen Fyffe); '80, Cordillera Blanca, ascents of Alpamaya, N. Bayacocha (with A. Fyffe); '82, first ascent of S. W. Pillar of Bhaghirathi III (with A. Fyffe). Co-author of 'A Chance in a Million?', a handbook on avalanches in Scotland.

Tony Brindle Lead climber. b. 1959. Qualified as a mechanical fitter, now attending Bangor Normal College for an honours degree in Environmental Studies/Outdoor Education. An enthusiast of free climbing, aid climbing, winter mountaineering and ski-mountain-eering. Extensive rock climbing in Britain, also Yosemite, Eldorado and France. Ten winter seasons in Britain and six Alpine, climbing many of the classic routes and some new ones. Solo ascents of W. face of Mt. Barrille and W. Buttress of Mt. McKinley. Mustagh Tower ascent '84. Member Achille Retty Climbing Club, A.C.G.

'I learnt an awful lot from the trip – and I enjoyed the Expedition – don't enjoy the general assumptions people have of "an Everest man". What's wrong with being an ordinary bumbly anyway? I am not keen on large expeditionary forces, but I did enjoy observing the way such a team operates under stress. I feel the route will be done by a small, competent team supported by high-altitude porters to Camp 4. I would go back as part of such a team, without oxygen, but also without summit ambitions – I don't feel the risk is justified to climb the Pinnacles over two days and then continue, still above 8,000 metres without oxygen – my brain doesn't require much anyway, but it does need a little every now and then!

'One of my best moments was seeing Liz at Camp 2 where she'd carried a load in support of us – quite humbling, really. Another was going off for the Pinnacles from Camp 4 after the effort of enlarging it the previous day. I was finally out front – treading ground where only thoughts had trod since '82. . . .'

Terry Dailey Business manager, co-ordinator, support climber, b. Stockport 1951. Married with one daughter, Amy Everest. Strategic planner with largest advertising agency in UK after graduating as a chemical engineer. Took up climbing seriously in 1975; several Alpine and Scottish seasons, one trip to Himalayas and High Atlas Mountains of Morocco. Two new routes in N. Wales, with Mal Duff. Fairly accomplished busking guitarist, great bass player, terrible singer. Has dabbled in most dangerous sports, particularly hang-gliding and potholing.

Kurt Diemberger Film maker. b. Austria 1932. He has for many years lived by climbing, filming and lecturing. He graduated from hunting for crystals in the mountains to major rock routes, including the N.E. face of the Piz Badile, S. face of the Dent du Géant, the Croz dell Altissimo. His Alpine ascents include early ascents of the Brenva Face of Mont Blanc, the N. face of the Matterhorn, N. face of the Eiger, the Walker Spur, the Peuterey Ridge, first ascent of the Konigswand direttissima. In the course of some 27 expeditions he made the first ascent of Broad Peak in 1957 with Herman Buhl, first ascent of Dhaulagiri; climbed Everest, Makalu and Gasherbrum II, finally a repeat ascent of Broad Peak 27 years after his first one. His classic autobiography, *Summits and Secrets*, is published by George Allen & Unwin.

Mal Duff Expedition leader. b. Nairobi 1953, brought up in Kenya, Surrey, Congo, Solomon Islands, Edinburgh. Married. Full-time guide and mountaineer. Over 100 first ascents on UK rock and ice, including People's Friend, Art of Zen, Point Blank, all Grade 6. Expeditions: Peruvian Andes '79, '80, '82; Nuptse West Ridge '81, '82; Thamaserku '82, Mustagh Tower '84. Member S.M.L., A.C.G.

'Leaving behind one expedition now 9 months old, and flying East into a new adventure. Reflections flit through my mind as we drone on through the towering dark. Everest from China, 11 climbers and 3 months' effort and endeavour all blur into a continuous series of images – BC, ABC, the winds above C2, looking down at the North Col, the Buttresses, 7,850 metres... But most of all I remember the people, my friends and companions who travelled half the world, who struggled boldly, grandly, but most of all who laughed. Expeditions are like that, you remember the good, the bad recedes and thus you're prepared to go back to try again. Of course when that possibility arises you plan and think and reason in an effort to make success more likely. The things that went wrong in 1985 would be changed. That's the important thing, that you learn from an expedition, that you develop as a person, that perhaps you can for a time within a hostile environment be at peace with yourself and your companions ...'

Liz Duff Base and Advance Base assistant, support climber. b. 1947 in Edinburgh. Works in insurance, for Scottish Life Assurance. Has played hockey and table tennis at representative level. Rock and ice climbing, mainly in Scotland with two Alpine seasons, 'mostly seconding plus a very limited amount of leading'. Endless amount of experience as a chalet girl keeping the dossers in line, in Scotland, England, France and Nepal.

Allen Fyffe Lead climber. b. Dundee 1946. Married with two children. Educated Harris Academy, Aberdeen University (B.Sc. in Geography). Climbed extensively in Britain and abroad. In the Alps did the first British ascent of the N. face of the Droites, an early British ascent of the Eiger N. face, and the first winter ascent of the Central Spur of Les Courtes. In 1973, a member of the British Dhaulagiri IV Expedition; 1975, the Everest South-West Face Expedition; 1978, with Bob Barton made the first ascent of the South Flank of Kalanka; 1982, the South-West pillar of Bhagirathi II with Bob Barton. Also climbed in Canada, USA and South America. At present employed as an instructor at Glenmore Lodge Outdoor Training Centre. Qualified guide and member of the A.B.M.G. With Andy Nisbet, co-author of the climbing guide to the Cairngorms.

'Coming back from Everest was for me very like ending a Scottish winter – I was fairly unfit but really keen to rock climb. Something that would give immediate satisfaction and didn't require the carrying of large rucksacks.

'The one positive and heartening aspect of the Expedition for me, besides everyone returning in good shape, was my own performance at altitude. In 1975, on the South-West Face of Everest, I hadn't gone particularly well, but on the North-East Ridge I felt I could have gone some way above the magic 8,000 metres without oxygen. This, however, was balanced to some extent by not having done so because of lack of opportunity at the end.

'I do notice that my short-term memory is definitely worse than before.

'Really our trip fell between two stools – the fast, light and bold or the traditional heavyweight with lots of carriers and oxygen. However, on Everest, and particularly a Ridge as long as ours, the weather is going to be so important that any success will probably need a bit of luck.'

Andrew Greig Writer and support climber. b. Bannockburn 1951. Educated Dollar Academy, Waid Academy, Edinburgh University (M.A. Philosophy). Worked as advertising copywriter, farm labourer, salmon fisherman, now a freelance writer. Introduced to climbing by Mal Duff in 1984 for the Mustagh Tower expedition, chronicled in *Summit Fever*, Hutchinson 1985. Three Scottish winters, one rock route, no Alpine experience. Published four collections of poetry, including *Men On Ice*, Canongate, 1977, and *A Flame in your Heart* (with Kathleen Jamie), Bloodaxe Books, 1986.

Nick Kekus Lead climber. b. Leeds 1957, now living in the Lake District. HND in civil engineering. Started climbing at 15 on the gritstone outcrops of West Yorkshire. Alpine routes include E. face of the Jorasses, Walker Spur, Freney Pillar, Dru Couloir. In recent years has concentrated on expeditions to the greater ranges: Mt. Kenya 1979; an expedition to the Cordillera Blanca, Peru, in 1980, made three first ascents; climbed Kalanka South Face '81; '82 and '83 expeditions to Shivelling and Annapurna III were tragically unsuccessful on unclimbed routes; '84 climbed S. face of Ganesh II Alpine style with Rick Allen. Member of Alpine Club, A.C.G., North London Mountaineering Club.

Danny Lewis Film porter and master baker. b. 1965 in Surrey, studying B.A. Sculpture at St Martin's School of Fine Art in London. Began rock-climbing on sandstone at 14 at Tunbridge Wells; also climbed in North Wales, Derbyshire, Lake District, South Coast, France, Italy, Sardinia. Several new routes on sandstone, including Desperate Dan 6, Republic 6.

'Definitely an anti-climax being back. I lost two stone, hated Chinese food, but gained valuable experience for when I go back to the same route if no one climbs it before then! The higher I got, the nearer I got to my own heaven.

'What next? Eiger North Face or Another Big Expedition!'

Andy Nisbet. Lead climber. b. Aberdeen 1953. Educated Aberdeen Grammar School, Aberdeen University, B.Sc. and Ph.D. in Biochemistry. Research Fellow at Aberdeen University before concentrating fully on climbing. Began hill-walking the Scottish Munros, then moved to rock and winter climbing. Possibly the current leading Scottish winter climber, with some 130 first ascents, including Grade VI. Alpine seasons include N. face Eiger, N. face Matterhorn, first winter ascent of the N. face of the Col du Peigne. Member of Nuptse West Ridge expedition 1981. Member of Etchuchan Club, S.M.C.

Sarah Squibb Assistant at Base and Advance Base. b. London 1963, brought up in Keswick, Lake District. B. Ed. from Bretton Hall College, 1984. Started climbing in 1981. The Everest Expedition was her first, but hopefully not her last. Her personal expedition success was climbing the peak 'Point 6833' on the east side of the East Rongbuk glacier.

Jon Tinker Lead climber. b. Handsworth 1959, educated Highgate School and Exeter University. Politics degree. Works in climbing shop and guides. Climbing eight years. Alpine routes include Walker Spur, Croz Spur, Peuterey Integral, and the N. faces of Ailefroide, Meije (direct), Droites, Dru, Charmoz, Verte (last two in winter). Kenya – Diamond Couloir and new route on West face of Mt Kenya. Peru – sundry 6,000 metre peaks. Attempt on Annapurna III. Ascent of Mustagh Tower 1984. Member Alpine Club.

'Coping with disappointment is an adult skill that climbers can normally avoid; living in a close, private world, there is little need for justification. Coming back from Everest we were all obliged to dissect our experience in public.

'There are two obvious ways to go if we want to go back. One is to try it with a very small team of four or so climbers *à la* Boardman/Tasker. However, at the moment there are very few people in the world with a credible chance of climbing the mountain in this fashion, and only – perhaps – one Brit. None of our team would be up to it. The other option is to go heavier. The necessity would be to employ Sherpas to do load-carrying up to 8,000 metres. It would be a good idea to have a party on the North Col route as well. The debate as to whether we would need oxygen would be interesting, but perhaps having someone else to carry it to 8,000 metres might tip the balance! I'd not wish to use it again, the same view I had on this trip.

'It seems a bit silly to indulge in any post-trip jockeying for position, "If only I hadn't been ill", "If only I'd been at ABC when the trip was called off", etc. Worse, it ends up with Malcolm getting unjustified flak – he's a great bloke who did a hard job very sympathetically. But OK – what if the weather hadn't turned bad? We'd have needed to carry more gear up to the Pinnacles. No one seemed able and willing to use O_2 and carry personal gear in a summit push. Those who were willing to use O_2 – like Sandy and Mal – were knackered; those who weren't so knackered, like Nick and Rick, weren't willing to use O_2. The summit was still the best part of two to three weeks away if we were going to fix the Pinnacles. It seemed improbable that anyone would have the "punch" to go to the top from there. Or to Alpine-style from 7,850? Certainly Rick, who was going strongest at that time, would be the first to say he wasn't as strong and experienced as Joe and Pete . . . So all in all it was probably the best thing for us to get off when we did.

'This year I'm off to Pakistan with Mark Miller, Simon Yates and Dick Renshaw. Just one rucksack each, climbing where we want, something of a change from Everest.'

Julie Tullis Sound recordist. b. 1939. With her husband Terry she ran the Bowles Outdoor Pursuits Centre, then the famous *Fester-haunt* near Tunbridge Wells. Now a full-time climbing instructor and film-maker. Black belt in Karate and Aikido. Extensive rock climbing in Britain and abroad. Expeditions include the Andes in 1978 with Norman Croucher's Peruvian Andes Expedition, Nanga Parbat '82, K2 '83 and '84, Broad Peak '84, where she became the first British woman to climb a 8,000 metres peak. Teamed up with Kurt Diemberger to make films of the Nanga Parbat expedition onwards. Her biography, *Clouds from Both Sides*, is published by Grafton Press, 1986.

Chris Watts Lead climber. b. Norfolk 1957. Married. B.Sc. in Physiology from University of London. Currently manager and buyer for climbing department of Alpine Sports. Began climbing out of curiosity after reading *Everest the Hard Way* and Blackshaw's *Mountaineering*. Has since climbed extensively in UK and the Alps, including Central Pillar of Freney, Frendo Spur and 1st British ascent of the Andreani/Nessi route on the North Face of Lyskamm. 1982 successful ascent of South East pillar of Taulliraju in the Cordillera Blanca with Mick Fowler. 1984 attempt on the South Face of Bojohagur Duan Asir failed after 'a spectacular series of setbacks'.

'All equipment for the Expedition was obtained through Alpine Sports except for those items which were specially designed: Gore-Tex one-piece suits, libond suits, and lightweight rucksacks, all made by *Berghaus*. All other equipment was standard production though occasionally with special modifications e.g. down suits and sleeping bags.

'Companies who must be given special thanks are: *Berghaus* – they gave us a lot of gear at considerably reduced prices, plus they spent a lot of time making equipment when they were very busy. Special thanks to Cornelia and her design team at Berghaus. *Mountain Equipment* – made down suits and sleeping bags at very short notice, and at a discount. *Helly Hansen* – supplied free pile clothing. *Alpine Sports* – allowed use of facilities and sold all equipment at cost price.

'*Retrospective*. At the time when Mal called off the Expedition I felt it was a fair decision; though with hindsight it appeared hasty. It was obvious we had been defeated by the conditions. We were reduced to probably only 4 or 5 people still capable of making a contribution – me, Nick Kekus, Rick Allen on the hill, plus Allen Fyffe and Sandy Allan at Base Camp who were at least 7 days out of phase and therefore effectively out of it. The snowfall during the final night certainly stopped us in the end, but it was only the final straw as we were not by then really capable of anything other than an all or nothing push through the Pinnacles.

'Overall the "failure" was undoubtedly due to the weather, but the lack of communication and the lack of positive leadership probably contributed at least as much. This is not a criticism of Mal, since we all hoped decision would evolve naturally. As it was, his abscess which pulled him down to B.C. at a vital time can probably be pointed to as the single most damaging blow as it showed up the lack of communication and the need for a leader. During that period a lot of effort was being expended and loads were carried, but no one knew exactly why and where this put them in the grand scale of things.

'I feel very confident that the attempt was worthwhile and that the team members were capable of achieving what most outsiders considered the impossible. I would definitely go back, but would expect a more exact plan and role on the mountain. If you go as a team, you must climb as a cog in that team. I wish the next expedition to the Ridge every success; I certainly hope no one is injured, but in the back of my mind I hope they fail as I want just one more try!'

Urs Wiget. Expedition doctor and lead climber. b. Switzerland 1944, now a family practitioner and traumatologist in Vissoie, in the Wallis Alps. Married with 4 children. Began climbing at 16; many summer and winter ascents in the Alps. 1968 member of a scientific survival test winter trip over the ridges of Eiger-Monch-Jungfrau-Ebnefluh (report published by Huber, Bern, 1973). 1979 expedition to the Cordilliera Blanca as climber and doctor. 1981 working, living and climbing for 6 months in Ladakh and Zanskar. 1984 Swiss expedition on K2 and Broad Peak. Active in mountain rescue, also medical teacher of mountain guides and rescue specialists.

These biographical notes and reflections were made in 1985. Since then Julie Tullis died on K2 and Mal Duff on Everest. The rest of us are still pushing out our personal routes and intersect from time to time.

MEDICAL REPORT ON THE 1985 PILKINGTON
EVEREST EXPEDITION

This report covers medical aspects of the Expedition and includes the discussions we had concerning high altitude health. It is not a scientific medical paper.

Given the size of the group, we had very few medical problems. We didn't reach the summit of Mt Everest, but 8 of the 11 climbers reached approximately 8,000 metres without bottled oxygen. All of these climbers came down and returned home in good health. For me this was a much bigger success than the attainment of the summit at the cost of one or more human lives.

This paper is also an expression of my thanks for the invitation and the very good ambiance of the team during the entire Expedition.

The geographic/medical situation:
a) The very high Base Camp (5,010 m) can be reached in 5 days from Beijing. From the medical point of view it was fortunate that a delay in the arrival of equipment imposed a 7 day stay in Lhasa (3,600 m) and a more gradual acclimatization.
b) The mountain is very far away from Base Camp (20 km) and the real operational base is at 6,400 m, at the site of Camp III of the British pre-war expeditions (ABC). This is too high to permit recovery, so the climbers were obliged to descend frequently to Base Camp for rest periods. For the doctor the problem was he could not be in the two places at the same time . . .
c) Evacuation from Base Camp to a hospital in Xigatse or Lhasa would have been possible in 1 or 2 days.

Medical problems.
The only problem which could have become very serious was a cerebral oedema starting the first night at ABC (6,400 m) for one member (Sandy Allan), a very fit climber with previous experience of two expeditions reaching 7,280 without problems. Fortunately I was sharing a tent with him. 4 gr. of Aspirin during the night only partly stopped the headache, and we descended early in the morning to 6,000 m where the symptoms were better. The climber received 3 × 250 mg of Diamox which gave him quite serious paraesthesia in the fingers and toes. We rested all day, drinking 5–6 litres. That night was better, and in the following afternoon we started again up towards ABC. After only 100 m the patient became more and more sick, vomited, again had a headache and was very tired. We

then descended to Base in the same day, where the patient recovered fast and completely. Later on this climber reached 7,650 m without problems and was working normally on the hill.

I think we can find part of the explanation for this cerebral oedema in the very hard work this climber did the day before he reached ABC: in the yak run we had serious problems at about 5,600 m when the yaks shed loads in panic in the middle of the glacier and some of us carried parts of the loads for some distance, only 5 days after our arrival at Base.

Another problem was an acute snow-blindness (Andy Nisbet). We climbed all day between 7,090 and 7,650 m in stormy weather, moving in some haste. Neither of us realized the danger; I was wearing tinted glasses by habit, but not Andy. During the night, pain became acute, the patient couldn't open his eyes. The immediate treatment consisted of a slow-dose anaesthetic eye-salve and an atrophine-antibiotic eye salve. The following day we descended from ABC to BC with some difficulty: to open at least one eye, the patient needed anaesthetic eye drops. We did not risk staying at ABC with this problem; in the event of complications we would have been too remote from specialized help. After 6 days of treatment at BC, the patient's eyes were healed and the climber was again fit to work on the mountain.

The third problem was a mild chronic lung oedema of one of the members, a very fit mountain guide with previous high altitude expierence (Bob Barton). The symptoms started at about 6,000 m on the second yak run. We tried different treatments, the patient descended three times from ABC to BC where he felt no major symptoms, but every time at more than 6,000 m he had dyspnoea and was not fit at all. In the middle of the Expedition he contracted probably a central retina haemorrhage in one eye – my broken opthalmoscope wouldn't permit a certain diagnosis. The eye symptoms disappeared after 4 weeks, without special treatment. Now, at home in Switzerland, I think it would have been better to send this climber down for 1–2 weeks to recover completely, though this would have meant going to Chengdu or Shanghai because the whole Tibetan plateau is too high for such recovery.

All the other problems which arose were of minor importance, such as the very frequent laryngitis and bronchitis. Some tooth fillings fell out and were replaced temporarily. The Expedition leader suffered an abscess under a wisdom tooth, which I treated with an analgesic and a course of antibiotics, and fortunately it subsided. Some diarrhoea and travel sickness occurred, and the beginning of the panaris of a finger. The broken wrist of the injured Basque climber was given a temporary cast.

On systematic examination we found some results of old knee injuries.

What we were laughing about . . .
– Drink and piss to save your life.
– One night without a pee means danger.
– Racing at high altitude means running into trouble.

Conclusion
There is only one failure in the mountains: death.

Dr Urs Wiget

We would like to warmly thank the following for their generously donated products:

Food

W. Jordan (Cereals) Ltd
Mattesons Meats Ltd
Swissco Ltd
J. W. Thornton Ltd
Daniel Quiggin & Son
Farley Health Products Ltd
Ski & Climb International
C.P.C. (UK) Ltd
Sanctuary Mountain Sports Ltd
George Payne & Co Ltd
UB Biscuits Ltd
Weetabix Ltd
Del Monte Foods Ltd
John West Food Ltd
Rowntree Mackintosh plc
Paterson-Jenks plc
James Robertson & Sons
Thomas Tunnock Ltd
Joseph Walker Ltd
Tate & Lyle Ltd
RHM Foods Ltd
Shepherdboy Ltd
John Smith & Sons Ltd
Cadbury-Schweppes Ltd

Cadbury Typhoo Ltd
John J. Lees plc
Fox's Biscuits Ltd
Shaklee (UK) Ltd
Springlow Sales Ltd
Raven Leisure Products Ltd
St Ivel Ltd
Charles Mackinlay & Co Ltd
Brooke Bond Oxo Ltd
Lucy Foods
Derwent Valley Foods Ltd
Halls Brothers (Whitefield) Ltd
Twinings
The London Herb & Spice
   Company
The Rock
Chivers-Hartley
John F. Renshaw & Co Ltd
Romix Foods Ltd
Callard & Bowser Group
The Kenco Coffee Co Ltd
Trebor Ltd
Carshalton Confectionery
W. A. Baxter & Sons Ltd

Gear

Epigas
Firmin Ltd
Life Support Engineering Ltd
The Bristol Wire Rope Co Ltd

Bowater Drums Ltd
Stephens Plastics Ltd
Dale Agency Co
Reed Corrugated Cases Ltd

Index: Kingdoms of Experience